Oryx Sourcebook Series
in Business and Management

Decision Making
An Information Sourcebook

Oryx Sourcebook Series in Business and Management

1. Small Business
2. Government Regulation of Business
3. Doing Business in and with Latin America
4. Decision Making

Oryx Sourcebook Series in Business and Management

Decision Making
An Information Sourcebook

by Sarojini Balachandran
Paul Wasserman, Series Editor

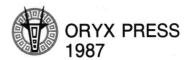
ORYX PRESS
1987

The rare Arabian Oryx is believed to have inspired the myth of the unicorn. This desert antelope became virtually extinct in the early 1960s. At that time several groups of international conservationists arranged to have 9 animals sent to the Phoenix Zoo to be the nucleus of a captive breeding herd. Today the Oryx population is over 400, and herds have been returned to reserves in Israel, Jordan, and Oman.

Library of Congress Cataloging-in-Publication Data

Balachandran, Sarojini.
  Decision making.

  (Oryx sourcebook series in business and management; no. 4)
  Includes indexes.
  1. Decision-making—Bibliography. I. Title.
II. Series.
Z7164.07B263   1987   016.658403   87-7975
[HD30.23]
ISBN 0-89774-270-2

Contents

Introduction

Decision making encompasses various disciplines, such as accounting, economics, finance, business administration and management, computer science, engineering, law, mathematics, political science, sociology, and psychology. It is, therefore, not surprising that the published literature on the subject is vast, which makes it virtually impossible to compile everything in a single-volume publication like this one. What is included in the following pages is a selective annotated bibliography of books, reports, dissertations, and journal articles dealing exclusively with the methodology and applications of managerial decision making.

In the past two decades, managerial decision making has undergone a revolutionary change because of the impact of electronic data processing technologies. A significant amount of literature has been published on decision support systems, which has necessitated a separate chapter on decision aids. An almost parallel development has been the application of mathematical techniques to refine managerial decision-making skills. This development is covered in a separate section on quantitative techniques available to corporate decision makers.

The present volume contains only material published in the English language. Coverage of journal literature is from 1971 to early 1986. Nonjournal materials, such as books, published from 1960 to early 1986 are included. For literature published on the subject prior to 1960, the reader is referred to the excellent bibliography by Dr. Paul Wasserman, entitled *Decision-Making: An Annotated Bibliography* (Cornell Graduate School of Business and Public Administration, 1958) and its *Supplement* (1958–1963). The reader is cautioned that the present bibliography is selective but not extensive. For easy retrieval, a comprehensive subject index has been included, along with author and title indexes.

Methodology

1. Abdel-Halim, Ahmed A. "Employee Participation in Managerial Decision-Making." MS thesis, University of Illinois, Urbana, 1968. 296 p.
   Discusses participatory management and how it affects corporate decision making.

2. Abdel-Halim, Ahmed A. "Power Equalization, Participative Decision-Making, and Individual Differences." *Human Relations* 36 (8) (August 1983): 683–704.
   Three hypotheses relating to power and status difference among individuals and groups at different hierarchical levels within an organizational system are examined. Subordinates' perceptions of participation in decision making are positively related to their perceived and desired power equalization in terms of hierarchical power differentials between subordinates and superiors. Low-level participants' perceptions of the distribution of power within the organizational hierarchy reflect a zero-sum notion of power. Subordinates' desire for participation and ability moderate the relationship between power equalization and participative decision making.

3. Ackoff, Russell Lincoln. *Scientific Method: Optimizing Applied Research Decisions.* New York: Wiley, 1962. 464 p.
   Explains the meaning of "optimal solutions" to problems. Other decision-making techniques discussed include formulating the problem, models, measurement, sampling, estimation, testing hypotheses, experimentation and correlation, deriving solutions from models, experimental optimization, testing, and controlling the model, solution, implementation, and organization of research.

4. Adair, J. *Management Decision Making.* Aldershot, England: Gower, 1985. 177 p.
   Explains some factors that affect managerial decision making. Analyzes the process in terms of knowing one's mind, holistic thinking, thinking in concepts, imaginative thinking, valuing, and evaluating opinions.

5. Adair, J. *The Skills of Leadership.* New York: Nichols Publishing Co., 1984. 282 p.
   Decision making when and where it is needed is a major aspect of successful executive leadership. This book examines how executive decision makers think, analyze, and synthesize before taking action. It analyzes the various steps in decision making, including creative thinking and problem solving.

6. Adizes, Ichak, and Turban, Efraim. "An Innovative Approach to Group Decision Making." *Personnel* 62 (4) (April 1985): 45–49.
Despite the benefits of participative decision making, some managers still resist group decision making and think that it is a waste of time. This article discusses a comprehensive framework for integrated decision making, which increases problem-solving effectiveness and has been used successfully by many organizations. Such a framework views decision-making effectiveness as a function of the quality of decisions and the probability that proposed decision will be implemented.

7. Agnew, Neil Mick, and Brown, John L. "Executive Judgment: The Intuitive/Rational Ratio." *Personnel* 62 (12) (December 1985): 48–45.
The decision-making style of executives covers a range from well-documented rational judgments to intuitive (nonrational) ones. Decision environments also can be scaled from relatively stable to turbulent. Combining these scales results in a four-quadrant matrix, with typical decision styles gravitating around a diagonal axis. Executives and organizations can be seen as operating with an intuitive/rational ratio (I/R) of decision-making strategies that tend to match and shift with the problem domains that must be managed.

8. Agor, Weston H. "How Top Executives Use Their Intuition to Make Important Decisions." *Business Horizons* 29 (1) (January/February 1986): 49–53.
While most U.S. organizations have relied on left-brain analytical techniques to guide decision making, intuition is gaining acceptance as a skill needed by management. The study shows a significant difference between top managers and middle and lower managers in their ability to use intuition on the job. Also, women and those with Asian backgrounds consistently score higher on intuition tests.

9. Agor, Weston H. "Intuition as a Brain Skill in Management." *Public Personnel Management* 14 (1) (Spring 1985): 15–24.
Discusses the growing importance of intuitive skills for managers. Cites a study which reveals that various factors, including management level, level of service, sex, occupational specialty, and ethnic background affect intuition.

10. Agor, Weston H. "Unlocking Your Intuition." *Management World* 14 (5) (May 1985): 8–10.
Discusses how intuitive managers find solutions to most problems and how organizations can create an environment for developing intuitive skills in managers.

11. Aharoni, Yair; Maimon, Zvi; and Segev, Eli. "Performance and Autonomy in Organizations: Determining Dominant Environmental Components." *Management Science* 24 (9) (May 1978): 949–59.
The formulation of a strategy for an organization begins with identifying the opportunities and risks in the environment. Findings indicate that managers do not try to identify all environmental forces. An optimal strategy for a manager seeking to increase autonomy would be to concentrate efforts on dominant environmental components.

12. Akresh, Abraham D. "Management Uses of Statistical Sampling." *Price Waterhouse Review* 23 (1) (1978): 24–31.
Statistical sampling is an important auditing tool, but it is also more than that. Many company executives may not be aware that it can be used in other areas to develop objective information at a reasonable cost. Other uses of statistical sampling include internal auditing, developing management information of tax returns, and strengthening internal control systems.

13. Alexion, John C. "The Decision Maker: Leadership and Responsibility." *Review of Business* 6 (3) (Winter 1984): 1.
Successful decision makers are well aware of the factors of authority and responsibility, but accountability is also essential for good business leadership. Senior corporate decision makers are well rewarded and are promoted on the basis of their decision-making performance, but they also face some risk. Their willingness to assume the challenge of making difficult or unpopular decisions is a true reflection of outstanding leadership.

14. Alexis, Marcus, and Wilson, Charles W. *Organizational Decision Making.* Englewood Cliffs, NJ: Prentice-Hall, 1967. 447 p.
A selection of readings providing a basic framework for decision making. Subjects discussed include closed and open decision models, a behavioral model of rational choice, noneconomic decision making, theories of decision making in economics and behavioral sciences, quantitative decision models, planning and control models, information processing for decision making, and resource allocation within the firm.

15. Algie, Jimmy. *Six Ways of Deciding.* London: British Association of Social Workers, 1976. 104 p.
Deals with six decision methods: intuitions, structuralism, dialectic approach, opportunism, microrationalism, and macrorationalism. Also discusses various techniques for handling the alternatives before a decision choice is made.

16. Algie, Jimmy, and Foster, William. "How to Pick Priorities." *Management Today (UK)* (March 1985): 60–61, 123.
Discusses the Brunel University's Management Decision Programme research called Priority Decision System (PDS), which uses thought processing input with the assistance of a computer for decision making. PDS establishes priorities, policies, and individual and management team views and makes a logical, rational decision. Applications include planning, solving technical problems, setting priorities, and solving difficult problems such as personnel selection.

17. Allais, Maurice, and Hagen, Ole, eds. *Expected Utility Hypotheses and the Allais Paradox: Contemporary Discussions of Decisions under Uncertainty with Allais' Rejoinder.* Dordrecht, Holland; Boston: D. Reidel, 1979. 714 p.
Discusses the foundations for a positive theory of choice involving risk and includes a criticism of the postulates and axioms of the American School by Maurice Allais.

18. Alter, Steven. *Decision Support Systems: Current Practice and Continuing Challenge*. Reading, MA: Addison-Wesley, 1980. 316 p.
Deals with the application of interactive technologies to management decision making through the development of tools that address nonstructured rather than structured tasks. These tools support rather than replace judgment. They focus on effectiveness rather than efficiency in decision process. The book maps the use of computer systems in managerial tasks.

19. American Institute for Decision Sciences. *Proceedings of the Annual Midwest Conference*. Atlanta, GA, 1955–. (Annual)
The American Institute for Decision Sciences (AIDS) is a professional society concerned with decision making in organizations. This interdisciplinary field emphasizes the scientific, quantitative, behavioral, and computational approaches to decision making. Most functional specialties of business are represented among its members. Relevant administrative problems in both private and public sectors are included within the framework of the decision sciences. The goals of AIDS are to enrich the diverse discipline of the decision sciences, to integrate the disciplines into bodies of knowledge that are effectively used for decision making, and to develop theoretical bases for such fundamental processes as implementation planning and design of decision systems. Each of the proceedings contains numerous scholarly papers covering the above areas.

20. Anderson, John C., and Hoffmann, Thomas R. "A Perspective on the Implementation of Management Science." *Academy of Management Review* 3 (3) (July 1978): 563–71.
Expresses the view that to bring about more successful application of operations research/management systems (OR/MS), changes must occur in education, research, and industry. OR/MS can then assist in describing, understanding, and predicting the behavior of the system involved in the management decision process.

21. Andriole, Stephen J. *Handbook of Problem Solving*. New York: Petrocelli Books, 1983. 184 p.
This handbook attempts to solve problems. It is designed to acquaint (and reacquaint) decision makers, managers, and analysts with a whole set of methods and invaluable analytical tools useful to problem solvers of all kinds. The scope of the book is interdisciplinary and is oriented toward bridging the gap between those who develop and test analytical methodology and those who must solve real analytical problems.

22. Aram, John D. *Dilemmas of Administrative Behavior*. Englewood Cliffs, NJ: Prentice-Hall, 1976. 131 p.
Examines dilemmas in management in terms of conflict and choice between individual and organization. Discusses individual and collective interest, organizational control versus individual development and initiative, organizational and personal criteria in administrative decision making, individual preferences and group norms, and leadership requirements for adhering to and changing group norms.

23. Argyris, Chris; Putnam, Robert; and Smith, Diana McLain. *Action Science*. San Francisco, CA: Jossey-Bass, 1986. 480 p.
Action science is an approach to social and organizational inquiry that is designed to generate knowledge that is both theoretically valid and practically useful. Action science can be used to solve problems, enhance

human development and learning, and promote the individual and the organization. The book spells out clearly and in detail the philosophical and scientific principles that form the foundation of action science. It reveals how action science can overcome the limitations of traditional, experimental, correlational, and ethnographic research by addressing the complexity of real life situations and dealing with questions traditional methods overlook.

24. Arnold, John D. *Make up Your Mind.* New York: AMACOM, 1978. 210 p.
Nontechnical book which examines why one needs systematic approach to decision making. The basic procedures are defined as follows: smoke out the issues, state your purpose, set your criteria, establish your priorities, search for solutions, test the alternatives, and troubleshoot your decision. Also examines decision making under pressure and shortcuts to everyday decision making.

25. Aronoff, Craig E., and Baskin, Otis W. "Public Relations—An Integral Part of Your Management Team." *Business* 31 (6) (November/December 1981): 16–22.
Public relations is an important aspect of organizational decision making. This article explains how PR practitioners can make a valuable direct contribution to the decision-making process.

26. Ashmos, Donde P., and McDaniel, Reuben R., Jr. "The Role of Human Service Professionals in Executive Decision Making in Third Party Organizations." *Human Resource Management* 19 (3) (Fall 1980): 16–23.
Explains that it is important for third-party organizations to determine an appropriate role for human service professionals in executive decision making. In developing alternative methods of involving professionals in executive decision making, it is important to incorporate the following theoretical models: Lorsch's notion of differentiation and integration, Terreberry's analysis of environmental flux, Galbraith's thesis of uncertainty and management in an uncertain environment, and the Knight McDaniel's information system theory of organizations.

27. Assad, Michael G. "Management Report Design Considerations." *Information and Management (Netherlands)* 4 (2) (May 1981): 95–104.
Top managers concentrate most heavily on strategic planning. At a lower level, managers formulate more detailed plans and acquire the resources to implement those plans. At a still lower level, managers supervise and control company operations. The decision information required at each level of management is different in terms of level of summarization, accuracy desired, orientation forward or backward in time, frequency of issue, and other areas. Article discusses ways to ensure that managers at each level are properly informed.

28. Barker, Larry Lee. *Groups in Process.* 2d ed. Englewood Cliffs, NJ: Prentice-Hall, 1983. 264 p.
Deals with the impact of individual and group behavior in organizational decision making. Topics include role conflicts, preferences, and expectations.

29. Barnes, James G. "How Will We Manage the Next 20 Years?" *Canadian Banker & ICB Review (Canada)* 88 (2) (April 1981): 48–51.

    Canada has faced a management crisis for the last two decades. To combat this, the author calls for formal training in management skills, planning, decision making, and the development of strategies to meet the challenges of the future.

30. Bass, Bernard M. *Organizational Decision Making.* Homewood, IL: Richard D. Irwin, 1983. 216 p.

    Explains the organizational decision in terms of methods and models, problem discovery and diagnosis, research and design, evaluation and choice, dealing with conflict, constraints on organizational decision process, and decision aids and support systems.

31. Bauer, Raymond Augustine, and Gergen, Kenneth J., eds. *The Study of Policy Formation.* New York: Free Press, 1971. 392 p.

    Collection of papers discussing descriptive decision theory from the administrative viewpoint and the role of information in decision making.

32. Beaumont, Philip B.; Thomson, Andrew W. J.; and Gregory, Mary B. "Bargaining Structure." *Management Decision (UK)* 18 (3) (1980): 103–70.

    Bargaining structure is an important issue. It is essential, therefore, to indicate and analyze different dimensions of bargaining structure and try to furnish some guidelines for management decision. The development, theory, and present framework of bargaining structure in Britain are examined.

33. Becker, Bruce. *Decisions: Getting What You Want.* New York: Grosset & Dunlap, 1978. 220 p.

    Explains the nature of decision making in terms of intuition and logic, obstacles in determining goals, recognizing real problems, determining priorities, developing options, information needs for making a good decision, evaluating information, deliberation and decision, acting on decisions, and appraising the results of decisions.

34. Beer, Stafford. *Decision Control: The Meaning of Operational Research and Management Cybernetics.* New York: Wiley, 1966. 556 p.

    Discusses the role of science in management. Topics include the nature of operational research, the activity of operational research, the relevance of cybernetics, and outcomes.

35. Bell, Robert I., and Coplans, John. *Decisions, Decisions: Game Theory and You.* New York: Norton, 1976. 160 p.

    Deals with decisions where there is time to prepare and think, where there is very little time available, and where it is vital to find the right answer quickly. Also discusses some ways of assessing the value of the information and deciding what bearing it has on the particular problem one is trying to solve.

36. Benshahel, Jane G. "Are You Slow to React?" *International Management (UK)* 29 (2) (February 1974): 22–24.

    It takes time to analyze, weigh, dissect, and probe the deeper meanings of superficial events before reaching conclusions about them. The well-considered reaction is quite often the one that will require the fewest second thoughts. But many executives who are naturally slow to react try to work against their own nature. They try to appear decisive by making snap judgments. They accede to other people's impatience by giving the desired instant yes and no. Too often they stifle their own doubts, both during and after decisive moments. The easier and wiser course is to stifle impulse to talk before ready and to refuse to accede to the pressure of taking a premature stand. They must learn to stall. The best way of doing this is to ask for time to think it over.

37. Benton, John Breen. *Managing the Organizational Decision Process.* Lexington, MA: Lexington Books, 1973. 271 p.
Examines, in both theory and practice, the keys to a successful organizational experience with the newer techniques of planning, analysis, and decision making. Its premise is that perhaps it is time we stopped inventing new labels for our failures and turned our attention to the sources of these disappointments. Its goal is to clarify, for the practitioner and student alike, some of the reasons why systems analysis, long-range planning, program budgeting, and other related techniques have encountered such difficulties in everyday organizational life. The practical guidelines offered will reduce the emphasis placed upon the decision-making process per se and enkindle an appreciation for the actual human and institutional environment in which organizational decision making takes place.

38. Berenbeim, Ronald. *Regulation: Its Impact on Decision Making.* New York: The Conference Board, 1981. 48 p.
Corporate executives have to take into account not only internal factors but also the external environment before arriving at a decision. One such external factor relates to regulatory activity by state, federal, and local governmental agencies. This book discusses how these activities affect corporate decisions.

39. Berger, Florence, and Ferguson, Dennis H. "Teaching the Decision Makers." *Cornell Hotel & Restaurant Administration Quarterly* 24 (2) (August 1983): 40–45, 46.
Analytical and behavioral skills must be integrated in order to teach management decision making. Integration is especially vital in financial management and human-resources management courses. Because of the existing lack of integration, students have not been instructed in the interrelated nature of the decision-making process.

40. Berkowitz, Leonard, ed. *Group Processes: Papers from Advances in Experimental Social Psychology.* New York: Academic Press, 1978. 428 p.
Group decision making, to be effective, must take into account psychological factors such as expectations, preferences, role conflicts, and their behavioral influences. This collection of papers discusses some of these topics.

41. Berlin, Victor N. "Administrative Experimentation: A Methodology for More Rigorous Muddling Through." *Management Science* 24 (8) (April 1978): 789–99.
Administrative experimentation is described as a more rigorous approach to the "muddling through" style of managerial decision making. It includes a class of heuristics for obtaining feedback on management decisions in what may be regarded as a continuous trial and error process. A manager-consultant team or a manager-researcher team can implement these

heuristics in a variety of settings to serve a variety of purposes. A case study describing one application of the approach is offered.

42. Berry, William L.; Christenson, Charles J.; and Hammond, John S. *Management Decision Sciences: Cases and Readings.* Homewood, IL.: Richard D. Irwin, 1980. 582 p.
Contains decision-making cases relating to cost analysis, linear programming, decisions under uncertainty, preference theory, simulation, and models and organizations.

43. Bither, Stewart W. *Personality as a Factor in Management Team Decision Making.* University Park: Center for Research of the College of Business Administration, Pennsylvania State University, 1971. 76 p.
Describes a study of the relationships among personalities in decision groups and the possible effects of these personality relationships on group task performance. This study shows how various theoretical models of group behavior may provide perspective for viewing personality in the group context. It also contains an up-to-date review of researchers' past efforts to look at personality in a group context. It singles out specific personality traits, namely dominance and social adroitness, that seem to be related to group role structure and, less directly, to performance.

44. Blake, Robert Rogers. *Group Dynamics—Key to Decision Making.* Houston, TX: Gulf Publishing Co., 1961. 120 p.
Discusses the concepts of group dynamics in decision making. Explains how power affects human behavior and employee appraisal and how to get better decisions from groups. Also discusses intergroup conflicts, problem solving between groups, and power styles within an organization.

45. Blecke, Curtis J. *Financial Analysis for Decision Making.* Englewood Cliffs, NJ: Prentice-Hall, 1966. 200 p.
This book provides a basic information reporting format, both graphic and tabular, from which almost any company can tailor effective management reporting techniques to fit its special requirements. It will serve as a useful guideline for decision-making executives, as well as financial staff and accountants.

46. Bodily, Samuel E. *Modern Decision Making.* New York: McGraw-Hill, 1985. 300 p.
Employing state-of-the-art modeling languages, such as the interactive financial planning systems (IFPS), this book gives prospective and practicing managers the ability to create models to solve their problems using the most recent computer decision support systems. Modern decision making for managers allows managers to create and run models in time for decision making on the job. It helps them to communicate the model analysis to superiors and use flexible and uncertain components. Also teaches the use of preferences and perceptions in dealing with problems in unstructured situations. Practical experiences are provided throughout the book in exercises and cases. These can be applied to finance, real estate, marketing, nonprofit institution management, planning, small business, and strategy.

47. Boland, Richard J., Jr. "Sense Making of Accounting Data as a Technique of Organizational Diagnosis." *Management Science* 30 (7) (July 1984): 868–82.

According to the rational-analytic approach to planning, decision makers should determine organizational goals. Decision makers interact with their environments through unplanned actions and do not understand their actions until they make sense of the outcomes, after which they can impose order on their actions. This article discusses a study which was conducted to assess the effects of a sense-making exercise in improving managerial planning and goal definition. Managers were presented with accounting reports generated to reflect a number of alternative scenarios of their organizations' future. They were asked to project themselves further into the future and retrospectively analyze how and why their organization had evolved as portrayed in the scenarios. Subjects' reports of their cognitive and emotional experiences throughout the sense-making exercise suggested that it substantially improved their insight into their planning assumptions and goals.

48. Bomblatus, Richard L. "Decision-Making in Middle-Management." *Management Accounting* 56 (2) (August 1974): 22–26.

Several factors essential to effective decision making are described. Suggestions are made as to how the middle-level manager may be trained to make good decisions. The middle-level manager is considered particularly in need of training and practice in decision making and of organizational support to put decisions into effect, since he or she is faced with a relatively large number of decisions.

49. Borch, Karl Henrik. *The Economics of Uncertainty*. Princeton, NJ: Princeton University Press, 1968. 227 p.

While dealing with the economics of uncertainty and economic decisions under uncertainty, this book touches upon concepts such as the Bernoulli principle and its applications for portfolio selection and other topics. Also covers decisions with unknown probabilities, market equilibrium under uncertainty, the two-person zero-sum game, the general two-person game, elements of general game theory, credibility, and subjective probabilities and group decisions.

50. Borch, Karl Henrik, and Massin, Jan, eds. *Risk and Uncertainty: Proceedings of a Conference Held by the International Economic Association*. Conference on Risk and Uncertainty, Smolenice, Czechoslovak Republic, 1966. London; Melbourne, Australia: Macmillan; New York: St. Martin's Press, 1968. 455 p.

Proceedings of a conference held by the International Economic Association in Bratislava, in 1966. Papers present topics such as economic decisions under uncertainty, general decision theory, group decision and market mechanisms, uncertainty and national planning, and sequential decision problems.

51. Boulanger, Robert, and Wayland, Donald. "Ethical Management: A Growing Corporate Responsibility." *CA Magazine (Canada)* 118 (4) (April 1985): 50–53.

Discusses a written code of ethics for managers to be used as a reference tool which provides a standard for evaluating managerial decisions.

52. Boxer, Philip J. "Supporting Reflective Learning: Toward a Reflexive Theory of Form." *Human Relations* 33 (1) (January 1980): 1–22.

Reflective analysis is a technique for analyzing the structure of an organization relative to the manager's experience within it. The technique contains the property of treble articulation, which enables managers to make explicit the paradigmatic organizational structure of which they are a part. Thus, it offers managers a means of consciously deciding how the organization will overdetermine themselves and others. The technique is a primitive application of the potential of fuzzy subset theory, and its effectiveness depends heavily on how much it is used to support the reflective learning process.

53. Brady, F. Neil. "Aesthetic Components of Management Ethics." *Academy of Management Review* 11 (2) (April 1986): 337–44.

Traditionally business ethics practices have been given the task of supplying decision procedures. Ethical theory is an important consideration in business decisions, but the approach is not always agreed upon. A tension exists between utilitarianism approaches and formalist (deontological) approaches to ethics. According to this article, both have their shortcomings.

54. Brady, F. Neil. "A Defense of Utilitarian Policy Processes in Corporate and Public Management." *Journal of Business Ethics (Netherlands)* 4 (1) (February 1985): 23–30.

Utilitarian theory and procedures, which have dominated policymaking processes in both the public and private sectors, are receiving increasing criticism for jeopardizing important social relationships and processes. Difficulties involved in the application of utilitarian procedures have been widely criticized.

55. "Brainstorming Techniques Can Help Solve Your Business Problems." *Effective Manager* 4 (10) (July 1981): 6–7.

Brainstorming is an effective management tool for finding solutions and decision making. Article discusses guidelines set by Geoffrey Rawlinson, author of "Creative Thinking and Brainstorming."

56. Brandstetter, Hermann, ed. *Dynamics of Group Decisions.* Beverly Hills, CA: Sage Publications, 1978. 276 p.

Papers from the fourth symposium held at Ottobeuren, Bavaria, in 1978, cosponsored by the European Association of Experimental Social Psychology and its American counterpart, the Society of Experimental Social Psychologists. Papers deal with small group behavior in organizations and group decision making.

57. Brandstetter, Hermann; Davis, J. H.; and Stocker-Kreichgauer, G. *Group Decision Making.* New York: Academic Press, 1982. 557 p.

This book develops the idea that the prototype for group decision making is a task-oriented collection of individuals who interact and, despite personal preferences and disagreements, reach a consensus. The papers collected here originated from a meeting jointly sponsored by the European Association of Experimental Social Psychology and the Society of Experimental Social Psychologists. All contributions are studies of particular themes in group decision making rather than simply interpretations of data from a few specific case studies.

58. Braverman, Jerome D. *Management Decision Making*. New York: American Management Association, 1980. 241 p.
Explains the structure of managerial decisions and problem-solving techniques, including the payoff table, decision criteria, decision trees, measuring uncertainty, and some tools for intuitive decision makers.

59. Bridges, Francis J., et al. *Management Decisions and Organizational Policy*. 3d ed. Boston: Allyn & Bacon, 1977. 489 p.
The principal activity of a manager day in and day out is problem solving and decision making. To be an effective decision maker, a manager must understand planning, which dominates higher management's time. Planning encompasses goal setting, determination of alternatives, policy formulation, execution of plans, and development of corporate strategy. This book deals with these activities important for a decision maker. It also helps explain the environmental factors affecting decisions, information and communication theory, models and model building, use of quantitative methods, and the social environment in which the decisions are made. The book uses a case study approach.

60. Brim, Orville G., et al. *Personality and Decision Processes: Studies in the Social Psychology of Thinking*. Stanford, CA: Stanford University Press, 1962. 336 p.
Explains the characteristics of the decision process. Also discusses the decision process test and personality tests. Examines the effects of social class and sex upon personality and decision process characteristics and the effects of type of situation on the decision process. Provides a comparison of individual and group decision processes.

61. Brinkers, Henry S., ed. *Decision-Making: Creativity, Judgment and Systems*. Columbus: Ohio State University Press, 1972. 276 p.
Collection of papers presented at Ohio State University, Thomas A. Boyd Interdisciplinary Conference on Decision-Making Aids. Deals with personalistic decision theory and collective decisions. Examines information science as an aid to decision making. Also covers topics such as human creativity and judgment, managing visual information and matching decision aids with intuitive styles.

62. Brion, John M. *Decisions, Organization Planning, and the Marketing Concept*. New York: American Management Association, Marketing Division, 1964. 48 p.
It is well recognized that marketing must be responsible for recommending the very objectives and strategies that must steer the entire business and its efforts. Since marketing is accountable for the knowledge and premises of the marketplace, it can logically be held responsible for translating that knowledge into ends and means goals and strategies as well as marketing plans. This book emphasizes the importance of participation by marketing personnel in the corporate decision process.

63. Bronner, Rolf. *Decision Making under Time Pressure*. Lexington, MA: D. C. Heath, 1982. 165 p.
The book views decision making under time pressure as a problem of overcoming stress. Examines the elements of stress, conditions of time pressure, problem solving under time pressure, and performance efficiency under time pressure. Formulates a psychological theory of decision making.

64. Brown, Arnold. "The Eroding Power of the CEO." *Business Horizons* 23 (2) (April 1980): 7–10.
One of the most important phenomena in business today is the erosion of the authority of the chief executive officer. Erosion is manifested in a shift of power downward in the organization and outward among stockholder groups and government, which renders consent increasingly necessary in the governing of the corporation. As a result there is a decrease in the ability of management to make rapid and effective decisions in response to circumstances. The factors causing this power shift include the growth of bureaucracy within the corporation, the growing and conflicting expectations of the public, and the increasingly important relationship between information and power. Article suggests solutions.

65. Brown, David H. "Where Are the Managers in Government Communication?" *Journal of Organizational Communication* 10 (3) (Second Quarter 1981): 22–23.
Survey reveals that federal employees indicated that their superiors did not consult them on policy decisions. They wanted to become more involved in matters of concern to management. Article reveals ways in which this can be dealt with.

66. Brown, Harold A., and Blakely, Lisa P. "Management Model Increases Planning Flexibility." *Planning Review* 8 (5) (September/October 1980): 22–23, 26–28.
When a firm is faced with strategic decision alternatives which are often varied and can be reasonably quantified, it is likely that a simulation model of the business can become a useful tool in strategic planning. The problem inherent in producing a computerized simulation of a complex management system makes modeling a difficult task. Careful attention to evaluation, specification, and implementation can significantly reduce these difficulties.

67. Brown, Kenneth S. "Management Science—Its Role in the Organization." *Managerial Planning* 21(1) (July/August 1972): 6–10.
Management science is an outgrowth of operations research. It attempts to transform the informality of management experience toward the designed experience. Article analyzes the organization and its decision-making role and the techniques of management science related to them.

68. Brown, Ray E. *Judgment in Administration.* New York: McGraw-Hill, 1966. 225 p.
Administration is an art that it is learnable. This book is an attempt to help the administrator practice the art in a more thoughtful manner.

69. Brown, Rex V. "Do Managers Find Decision Theory Useful?" *Harvard Business Review* 49 (May/June 1970): 78–89.
Discusses a survey sponsored by the Marketing Science Institute on the experiences of such companies as the DuPont Company, the General Electric Company, the Ford Motor Company, the Pillsbury Company, and Inmont Corporation with decision tree analysis. Considers such matters as the impact of decision tree analysis on companies, its benefits, organizational implications, and potential for the future.

70. Brown, Rex V.; Kahr, Andrew S.; and Peterson, Cameron. *Decision Analysis: An Overview.* New York: Holt, Rinehart & Winston, 1974. 86 p.

Companion volume to a larger book by the authors. Contains a detailed case study of decision analysis application, presented as a dialogue between an inexperienced manager and a consultant.

71. Buetow, C. Peter. "Management Analysis and Decision Making." *CA Magazine (Canada)* 111 (8) (August 1978): 90–92.

Article makes a distinction between analysis and decision making. Analysis defines the problem and determines what solutions are available, along with the attributes of each. Decision making compares the alternatives, weighs them based on corporate strategy and philosophy, and determines the risks involved. The decision maker must try to determine if all the alternatives have been considered by the analyst. Exclusion of some alternatives could lead to selection of a predetermined solution. The true decision-making process is selection from alternatives, and it is a managerial process. The process starts with a definition of objectives that will not result in a justification procedure for any activity. Possible bias on the part of the analyst should not be overlooked.

72. Buetow, C. Peter. "What Can Management Consultants Do for You?" *CA Magazine (Canada)* 111 (4) (April 1978): 80, 82–83.

Situations arise within the organization which require outside time and skills. The decision to be made is whether to hire employees or to obtain services from a consulting firm. The major reasons managers buy consulting services are to reduce costs, to increase productivity, to improve the enterprise's performance, to adapt to changes, and to help with the complexity of their social obligations.

73. Burton, Gene E.; Pathak, Dev S; and Burton, David B. "Brainstorming: Turning on the Creative Flow." *Management World* 6 (12) (December 1977): 3–5.

Studies have shown that brainstorming groups generate a greater quantity of ideas than equal number of individuals working alone, and they have been found to be better decision makers than traditional discussion groups. However, any time groups are used, the competitive nature of intergroup relationships may also lead to distortions in perception and judgment due to group loyalty. Group members tend to underrate the activities of other groups and to magnify their own achievements. The manager who uses group decision-making processes may be able to minimize the negative effects of group loyalty by the formation of new groups and rotating participants from one group to another. If a specific group is allowed to maintain its membership over time, the manager must be prepared to evaluate that group's output with an awareness of loyalty's distorting tendencies.

74. Burton, J. T., Jr. "The Subjective Factor in Decision Making." *Supervisor Management* 27 (7) (July 1972): 10–12.

No matter how developed or responsive computer-aided management science techniques become and no matter how many committees are established, the majority of decisions in organizations will still be made by individual managers. A significant number of those decisions will be made subjectively. The idea, regardless of how the decision is made, is to gain time for the most informed consideration of a problem. When pushed to make a yes/no decision with insufficient information or too little time for analysis, the best answer is no. Selective hesitation is a variation of this rule. This allows additional information to be requested, or a committee can be formed to study the problem.

75. Byrnes, W. G., and Chesterton, B. K. *Decision Strategies and New Ventures: Modern Tools for Top Management.* London: Allen & Unwin, 1973. 195 p.
Describes techniques for use in strategic planning, acquisitions, risk management, investment, diversification and new product management, product evaluation, and corporate development with nine case studies.

76. Camacho, A. *Societies and Social Decision Functions.* Boston: D. Reidel, 1982. 145 p.
Provides a comparison of approaches to social choice. Deals with the intensity of preferences and cardinal utility, dissatisfaction with ordinal methods in dealing with problems of social choice, and social decision functions.

77. Carlisle, A. E. "The Golfer." *California Management Review* 22 (1) (Fall 1979): 42–52.
Many managers in today's businesses become unnecessarily involved in minor problems, many of which should be handled by their subordinates. The primary responsibility of the manager is to develop organizational objectives, make decisions on meaningful goals, and effectively communicate these to subordinates. Also, systems must be developed to monitor the progress of the organization and to make necessary adjustments when problems develop. A critical step in developing this approach is to carefully consider all aspects of the organization establishing the goals. A second important step is obtaining the real commitment of subordinates to the attainment of these goals. Part of this process involves understanding the subordinates' opinions and perceptions. Finally, the environment in which the organization operates must be monitored.

78. Carsberg, B. *Economics of Business Decisions.* Harmondsworth, England: Penguin, 1975. 328 p.
Explains the application of the principle of managerial economics to business decision situations. Topics include the estimation of cost-volume relationships, price-volume relationships, optimal price-volume decisions, optimal output, promotion and distribution, optimal use of scarce resources, risk and uncertainty, the portfolio effect, sensitivity analysis, accounting information system, the nature and value of cost accounting, pricing strategy, and the optimal information system.

79. Carter, Charles Frederick, et al. *Uncertainty and Business Decisions: A Symposium on the Logic, Philosophy and Psychology of Business Decision Making under Uncertainty.* 2d ed rev. Liverpool, England: Liverpool University Press, 1957. 158 p.
Discusses methodology and logic of decision making, the mathematical tools, expectations in economics and business, and the impact of uncertainty.

80. Carter, Forrest S. "Decision Structures to Reduce Management-Research Conflicts." *MSU Business Topics* 29 (2) (Spring 1981): 40–46.
Decision structuring models the components of a decision, such as iden-

tifying the problem, alternative courses of action, decision criteria, degrees of risk, and potential results of action. The responsibilities of both management and researchers are detailed for each of the above components. For example, in identifying the problem, management must identify market performance discrepancies and confirm the problem. Researchers must describe the situation and analyze symptoms. Management specifies possible decisions, while researchers suggest probable outcomes. Management designates factors to judge the best decision, and researchers look for relative factors and cause-effect relationships.

81. Cassel, Russell Napoleon. *The Psychology of Decision Making.* North Quincy, MA: Christopher Publishing House, 1971. 322 p.
Deals with psychological concepts applicable to decision making, including organizational climate, accountability, ethnological structures, topological psychology and life space, ego defense and egocentrism, attitudes and values, and ego development. Also covers areas such as the correlates of persuasion, human deliberation and freedom helping relationships, and decision-making competency and leadership decision making.

82. Castles, Francis Geoffrey; Murray, D. J.; and Potter, D. C. *Decisions, Organizations and Society: Selected Readings.* Harmondsworth, England: Penguin for the Open University Press, 1971. 424 p.
Collection of readings on organizational behavior. Decision making is discussed in terms of individuals and groups and their conflicting preferences and goals.

83. Champernowne, David Gawen. *Uncertainty and Estimation in Economics.* San Francisco, CA: Holden Day, 1969. 3 vols.
Deals with statistical decision techniques on handling uncertainty. Also covers risk analysis.

84. Chapman, Myra. *Decision Analysis.* London: Her Majesty's Stationary Office, 1980. 79 p.
This guidebook is a volume in the British Civil Service College Handbook series which is aimed at facilitating managerial decision making at all levels of public administration.

85. Chastain, Clark E. "Toward a Contingency Theory of Management Accounting." *Michigan Business Review* 31 (6) (November 1979): 1–6.
Contingency accounting is an attempt to fit accounting to a particular situation, contingent on situational variables. It is a two-step process which includes evaluating important factors in a given situation and applying an accounting technique in an appropriate manner or making an appropriate accounting recommendation. Article discusses its use in decision making.

86. Chorba, Ronald W., and New, Joan L. "Information Support for Decision Maker Learning in a Competitive Environment: An Experimental Study." *Decision Sciences* 11 (4) (October 1980): 603–15.
An experimental study of decision-maker learning in a competitive environment uses a computer simulation game to make decisions concerning factors such as price and product quality. The object of the study is to identify patterns of information usage exhibited by participants during the learning process under conditions where the cost and availability of in-

formation were controlled. It was demonstrated that decision makers who have the opportunity to select the data reported to them tend to progress more rapidly in identifying a successful strategy than those receiving an externally prescribed report.

87. Churchman, Charles West. *Prediction and Optimal Decision: Philosophical Issue of a Science of Values.* Englewood Cliffs, NJ: Prentice-Hall, 1961. 394 p.

The book deals with concepts, such as costs, utilities, and values, which are important in industrial decision making.

88. Churchman, Charles West; Auerbach, Leonard; and Sadan, Simcha. *Thinking for Decisions: Deductive Quantitative Methods.* Chicago: SRA, 1975. 445 p.

Explains basic decision making concepts like reasoning, deductive systems, ordering, numbers and measures of performance, values over time, probability, random variables and their distributions, measures of performance, conditional probability and the value of information, the use of lines in decision making, linear programming models, and the use of rates of change in decision making.

89. Clampa, Dan. "Managing the Human Side of Change." *Business* 30 (4) (July/August 1980): 9–12.

Many organizations are very effective at managing the logical, mechanical aspects of the change process but less adept at dealing with the effects of change on attitudes, feelings, and opinions of employees—the emotional aspects of change. The handling of a problem of this nature at Devon Laine, a manufacturer of material-handling equipment, is reported.

90. Clegg, Chris W., and Wall, Toby D. "The Lateral Dimension to Employee Participation." *Journal of Management Studies (UK)* 21 (4) (October 1984): 429–42.

The literature on participation has focused almost exclusively on the vertical aspects of decision making to the neglect of lateral factors, in particular, the integration of traditionally separate functional hierarchies. This lateral dimension assumes considerable importance in designing and operating a system of employee participation. Evidence is drawn from case studies and the work of organizational theorists.

91. Clifford, J. *Decision Making in Organizations.* London: Longman, 1976. 273 p.

Basic textbook which explains the concepts and processes of decision making in an organizational context. Includes both individual as well as group decision making.

92. Cochrane, James, and Zeleny, Milan, eds. *Multiple Criteria Decision Making.* Columbia, SC: University of South Carolina Press, 1973. 816 p.

Papers presented at the Capstone House Conference held at University of South Carolina, on October 26–27, 1972. Majority of the topics relate to mathematical models and relationship between formalized decision-making techniques.

93. Cohen, John. *Behavior in Uncertainty and Its Social Implications.* New York: Basic Books, 1965. 207 p.

This book is concerned with diverse types of situations in which decision making occurs. Emphasis is also placed on decision making under stress.

94. Cohen, Stephen L., and Gump, H. Frank. "Using Simulations to Improve Selection Decisions." *Training & Development Journal* 38 (12) (December 1984): 85–88.
Short cost-effective job simulations (exercises reflecting actual job tasks of the position), make interviews more productive. Such simulations give interviewers the opportunity to witness and evaluate applicants' job-related skills and behaviors. Practical research in corporations has proven the value of such simulations.

95. Coleman, James. *The Mathematics of Collective Action.* Chicago: Aldine, 1973. 191 p.
Discusses and develops concepts of human action in terms of causal processes and determinants of behavior and in terms of action based on preference. The latter concept uses classical microeconomic theory, statistical decision theory, and the theory of games. In short, the book presents a mathematical basis for a theory of collective decisions.

96. Collier, Abram T. *Management, Men and Values.* New York: Harper & Row, 1962. 235 p.
Explains how decision-making skills separate leaders from mere managers. Examines what constitutes executive ability.

97. Collins, Barry E., and Guetzkow, Harold. *A Social Psychology of Group Processes for Decision Making.* New York: Wiley, 1964. 254 p.
Explains the process of building a social psychology of group processes for decision making, group and individual performance, group productivity, interpersonal relations, indirect sources of power in decision-making groups, and consequences of small and large amounts of power for the behavior of group members.

98. Conference on the Executive Study, Princeton, NJ, June 1962. *Executive Decision Research; A Report of the Executive Study.* Princeton, NJ: Princeton Educational Testing Service, 1963. 134 p.
Proceedings of two conferences of the Executive Study; June 14 and 15, 1962, Nassau Inn, Princeton, and November 29 and 30, 1962, Palmer Inn, Princeton, NJ. Surveys research relating to corporate decision-making techniques, processes, and practices.

99. Cooke, Steve, and Slack, Nigel. *Making Management Decisions.* Englewood Cliffs, NJ: Prentice-Hall, 1984. 423 p.
Making management decisions combines the techniques of behavioral science and quantitative methods to analyze managerial decision making and to provide practical advice. It includes many examples of real decisions taken from a wide range of organizations. Topics covered include interpretation/diagnosis, formal problem recognition, problem solving, observation monitoring, determining options, evaluation options, selection options, and implementation.

100. Cooper, Joseph David. *The Art of Decision-Making.* Garden City, NY: Doubleday, 1961. 394 p.
Deals with the basics of the process such as collection of information, goal setting, choice, consultation, resource allocation, decision, and implementation.

101. Cornell, Alexander H. *The Decision-Maker's Handbook.* Englewood Cliffs, NJ: Prentice-Hall, 1980. 262 p.
Provides a basic guide to the processes and practices involved in organizational decision making. Covers topics such as goal setting, collecting data, evaluation of alternative choice, uncertainty and risk, making decisions, and implementing them.

102. Cosier, Richard A. "Approaches for the Experimental Examination of the Dialectic." *Strategic Management Journal* 4 (1) (January/March 1983): 79–84.
The dialectical inquiry method of problem solving, which involves making assumptions and counterassumptions about a problem and its possible solutions, has been found to be an effective strategic planning aid in field research. However, this paper finds that laboratory research on the method, using control conditions and comparing it to other problem-solving techniques, has yielded inconclusive results.

103. Cox, Eli P., ed. *Research for Business Decisions.* Austin, TX: University of Texas at Austin, Bureau of Business Research, 1974. 182 p.
This is an interdisciplinary study of qualitative research techniques and their application to marketing problems.

104. Cranston, Douglas C. "If You Choose the Right Fork, Decision Making Can Be Like Eating Cake." *Telephony* 199 (20) (November 17, 1980): 72–74, 78–80.
Discusses the use of decision tree analysis by managers faced with complex decision-making tasks in a complicated business environment. A manager faced with a decision problem must take four steps: sketching a decision tree, developing and assigning probabilities to uncertain outcomes, assigning monetary payoffs to decision tree tips, and using expected value analysis.

105. Cruickshank, David. "Making Management Pay." *Management Today (UK)* (April 1978): 35, 38, 42.
Management efficiency, hindered by incoming information to be processed and committee bottlenecks, is slowed in the decision-making process. During a recent study of productivity in manufacturing and marketing companies, a technique was evolved to measure the input of management resources and the output of decisions, quantitatively and qualitatively. The cost-benefit result was a method of evaluating management resources that opened up new insights into managerial productivity.

106. Cuba, Richard C., and Milbourn, Gene, Jr. "Delegating for Small Business Success." *American Journal of Small Business* 7 (2) (Fall 1982): 33–41.
Examines specific management practices used by the owners of small businesses. Points out the degree of delegation of administrative and technical tasks and how this was a key factor affecting business survival and financial success. Reasons for not delegating were fear of loss of control, lack of management skill, doubt concerning employee skill and judgment, and reluctance to abandon activities the owner really enjoys. Results indicate a high involvement of owners of small enterprises in tasks that are normally performed by nonmanagerial staff in larger companies. The owners that delegated tasks, particularly routine paperwork, achieved significantly higher sales and profits, indicating an obvious need to aban-

don routine tasks and give more attention to goal setting, long-range planning, and decision making.

107. Cyert, Richard M., and March, James G. *A Behavioral Theory of the Firm.* Englewood Cliffs, NJ: Prentice-Hall, 1963. 332 p.
Presents the decision-making process of the business firm. Topics include organization goals, choice, and expectations, price and output models; a model of rational managerial behavior; a model of trust investment behavior; and prediction and explanation in economics.

108. Cyert, Richard M., and Welsch, Lawrence, eds. *Management Decision Making: Selected Readings.* Harmondsworth, England: Penguin, 1970. 359 p.
Illustrates how decision-making processes in the firm have been described. Presents some of the optimum decision rules which have been prescribed for managers. Topics include nonprogrammed decision making, programmed decision making, heuristic models, and algorithmic models.

109. Daniel, Wayne W., and Hubbard, Elbert W. "Decision Analysis: A Method for Making Better Management Decisions." *Journal of Property Management* 44 (4) (July/August 1979): 224–29.
Good decision making is essential to effective administration. The components of decision making, such as past experience, intuition, subjective feelings, and imagination, can be quantified, simulated, and systemized. Methodologies of various decision analyses allow the decision maker to analyze each given situation. The assignment of probability or desirability weights is one of the most difficult aspects of putting decision analysis into practice.

110. Daroca, Frank Peter. "Leadership and Informational Influences on Group Decision Making in a Participative Budgeting Context: A Laboratory Experiment." Ph.D. dissertation, University of Illinois at Urbana-Champaign, 1981. 86 p.
Individual employee goals may conflict with organizational goals. Such a conflict may politicize resource allocation. To ameliorate the situation, participative budgeting has been advanced as a means of eliciting cooperation in goal setting. This study examines the effectiveness of this group process in organizational decision making and its implication for accounting professionals.

111. Davis, Donald L. "Are Some Cognitive Types Better Decision Makers than Others? An Empirical Investigation." *Human Systems Management (Netherlands)* 3 (3) (September 1982): 165–72.
Previously published studies of decision making involving a cognitive style variable and individual differences have not been performance related in the sense of comparing the decision-making performance of one type of manager to that of another. They have only examined attitudes toward some elements of decision making, such as attitude toward risk. This exploratory study uses a computer game to simulate a production environment, with the goal of examining the relative decision-making performance of different cognitive types of decision makers.

112. Davis, Duane. *Business Research for Decision Making.* Belmont, CA: Kent Publishing Co., 1985. 555 p.
Discusses the role of business research in the decision making process. Explains the basics of research, proposal development and evaluation,

research design, foundation of measurement, scaling and instrument design, sampling, model building, analysis of variance and regression, multivariate analysis, and selected statistical packages for business research.

113. Davis, Wayne J., and Whitford, David T. *A Comparative Investigation of Mathematical Models for Resource Allocation in an Organization.* Urbana, IL: College of Commerce and Business Administration, University of Illinois at Urbana-Champaign, 1981. 29 p.

Investigates a set of multiple criteria, decomposition models for hierarchical organizations. To facilitate this investigation the paper has three objectives. First, it presents a generalized decomposition approach to an organizational resource allocation problem. This approach results in a three-level, decision-making hierarchy applicable to a set of decomposition models. Second, it specifies the basic decisions and coordinative mechanisms used by each organizational model within this decision-making hierarchy. Third, it discusses the relationship between these organizational models and pure mathematical decomposition procedures. Finally, an alternative objective function formulation is proposed in order to overcome difficulties with the models.

114. Day, Brian, and Prabhu, Vas. "How to Manage by Number." *Management Today (UK)* (October 1977): 84–87, 162.

Managers should be capable of understanding the basic principles of data gathering and processing and paying attention to assessing the accuracy and validity of all data. The recognition of inadequate information is essential in all decision-making areas. Managers should also have a basic working knowledge of some of the quantitative techniques and their uses and limitations in handling management problems and be able to select the appropriate technique for the solution of any given problem.

115. Dean, Douglas, et al. *Executive ESP.* Englewood Cliffs, NJ: Prentice-Hall, 1974. 290 p.

There are numerous techniques available for use by managers for decision making. Still, there is executive need to understand the psychological aspects of decision making, including intuition and personal experience. The book discusses these aspects.

116. *Decision-Making in a Changing World.* Edited by the editors of *Innovation.* Princeton, NJ: Auerbach, 1971. 189 p.

These are selected essays from the magazine *Innovation.* They are arranged in three sections: the new managerial environment, some tools for decision making, and the framework for decision making.

117. DeCoster, Don T.; Ramanathan, Kavasseri V.; and Sundem, Gary L. *Accounting for Managerial Decision Making.* Los Angeles: Melville Publishing Co. 1974. 462 p.

Deals with accounting analysis for short-run decisions in terms of flexible budgeting, break-even charts versus marginal graphs, learning curve models in profit planning, product pricing models, application of linear programming analysis to determine the profitability of products involving joint cost, multiple product costing by multiple correlation analysis, capacity utilization, decision criteria for investment strategies, capital budgeting, and forecasting techniques for use in the corporate planning process.

118. Delaney, W. A. "The Art of Filtering." *Supervisory Management* 24 (7) (July 1979): 9–12.
In the business world, the word "filter" means the processing of information. A good manager exhibits judgment as to what information one should handle and what to pass along for action. In business filtering, the message should not be altered. Only the extraneous parts need to be removed.

119. Delbecq, Andre L.; Van de Ven, Andrew H.; and Gustafson, David H. *Group Techniques for Program Planning: A Guide to Nominal Group and Delphi Processes.* Glenview, IL.: Scott, Foresman & Co., 1975. 174 p.
Contains an examination of group decision making in modern organizations, profiling small group decision making. Also explains when and how the Delphi technique should be used and when it should not be used.

120. Demski, Joel S. *Information Analysis.* Reading, MA: Addison-Wesley, 1980. 114 p.
Intended as a supplementary text for a course in decision theory. Provides a basis for the study of the economic aspects of information and makes extensive reference to the "cost and value of information." Focuses on information choice questions and on modeling considerations in capacity acquisition, short-run output, and control decisions.

121. "The Devil's Advocate." *Small Business Report* 7 (9) (September 1982): 20–22.
A devil's advocate, by attacking weaknesses and inaccuracies, can be a benefit to a company and its managers. This person plays a key role in the corporate decision-making process, especially within a formal dissent procedure, and can serve as leader in generating ideas.

122. Dickson, D. N., ed. *Using Logical Techniques for Making Better Decisions.* New York: Wiley, 1983. 583 p.
While intuition plays a major role in decision making, most corporate decisions are based on logical reasoning. This book introduces logical techniques and their applications available for managers. Topics covered include collection and analysis of data and deduction.

123. Dinkel, John J., et al. *Management Sciences.* Homewood, IL.: Richard D. Irwin, 1978. 422 p.
Basic textbook dealing with decision theory, decision analysis with additional information, linear programming models, solving linear programs, simplex algorithms, duality and sensitivity analysis, multiple criteria decision making, integer programming, and Markov chains.

124. Dirsmith, Mark W., and Lewis Barry L. "The Effect of External Reporting on Managerial Decision Making: Some Antecedent Conditions." *Accounting Organizations & Society (UK)* 7 (4) (1982): 319–36.
Behavioral research in accounting has ignored the process by which the behavior of the information sender may be affected by the act of communication with recipients. This paper's hypothesis is that the information impact is conditioned by the perceptions of the sender regarding the recipient's degree of reliance on financial accounting information. The importance of the sender's cognitive style is also posted. The findings offer

direction for future research regarding the decision-making process of information senders.

125. Doktor, Robert. "Comparative Advantages in the Management Process: Japan and the U.S." *Training & Development Journal* 37 (10) (October 1983): 56.
The management process in both the U.S. and Japan is composed of problem solving, decision making, and solution implementation. Article compares performance of Japanese and American managers in those phases.

126. Drucker, Peter F. "The Decision Process—No Room for Cobwebs." *Modern Office Procedures* 17 (12) (December 1972): 14–20.
Presents a system that will help classify decisions to help the executive discern between a universal situation and an exception. The author explains when one should make a decision and when one should let the matter take care of itself.

127. Drucker, Peter F. *The Effective Executive.* New York: Harper & Row, 1967. 178 p.
Study of what effective executives do and do not do that makes them so effective. Presents the thesis that effectiveness must be learned. It does not come by itself. It is a practice that must be acquired. This book presents in simple form the elements of this practice. Topics discussed include the elements of decision making and effective decisions.

128. DuBrin, Andrew J. *Casebook of Organizational Behavior.* New York: Pergamon Press, 1977. 326 p.
Contains case studies in backyard gossip, deals with problem situations, such as stresses in managerial and professional life, and discusses political maneuvering in organizations. Examines cases in terms of the puzzle block work teams, leadership styles, subordinate performance, interpersonal communications, and intergroup conflict.

129. Dustin, Kerry C., and Carpe, Richard H. "Business Counseling Services." *Perspective* 11 (2) (1985): 16–20, 25.
Business counselors can be very valuable for companies that cannot afford to have full-time financial advisers on their payrolls. The task of a counselor is to help owners gain more control of their companies' development by ensuring that smaller decisions do not contradict or undermine the total financial picture.

130. Easton, Allan. *Complex Managerial Decisions Involving Multiple Objectives.* New York: Wiley, 1973. 421 p.
Presents a number of decision/evaluation/rating models with variations and suggestions for use. Some of the topics dealt with are decision elements and models, treatment of decision alternatives, and synthesis.

131. Ebert, Ronald J. *Organizational Decision Processes.* New York: Crane Russak & Co., 1973. 331 p.
Presents a unified treatment of the decision-making processes as they occur in organizational settings. Part 1 describes individual decision-making processes and the environmental settings in which they occur. Part 2 analyzes characteristics of the individual and his or her behavior in various activities that comprise decision making. Part 3 shifts to a consideration of additional parameters arising from group interactions within the organizational setting.

132. Eberts, Randall W. "How Unions Affect Management Decisions." *Journal of Labor Research* 4 (3) (Summer 1983): 239–47.
An examination is made of the formal mechanism by which unions can influence management decisions on resource allocation and thus affect productivity.

133. Eccles, A. J., and Wood, D. "How Do Managers Decide?" *Journal of Management Studies (UK)* 9 (3) (October 1972): 291–302.
Decisions are the visible product of the managerial process. Yet we know almost nothing about the real context of managerial decision making. This study attempts to remedy the deficiency by examining decision making under the laboratory conditions permitted by using a business game as a research tool. In particular, the analysis was directed at the way in which decision making can be related to the learning processes, confidence levels, and inherent management behavior of the decision makers. The authors suggest that the most effective managerial performance in a new situation for the corporation would come from a young, previously immobile, management team helped at first by experienced mobile managers who would help them to avoid the worst initial mistakes by drawing up some ground rules to guide in early operations.

134. Eckel, Malcolm W. *The Ethics of Decision-Making.* New York: Morehouse-Barlow, 1968. 111 p.
Deals with the problem of making ethical decisions in our highly complex and competitive industrial society. Focuses mainly on actual problem situations such as price fixing in the electrical industry, especially simulating ethical dilemmas faced by corporate decision makers. It is the result of a survey conducted by a church group. A case studies supplement is also available dealing with actual cases.

135. Eden, Colin, and Harris, John. *Management Decision and Decision Analysis.* New York: Wiley, 1975. 257 p.
Provides an introduction to the nature and quality of decisions, their classification through decision activity and through decision theory, management information systems, model building and operational research, connective information network, information feedback in an industrial setting, and validating a decision model and decision analysis.

136. Edwards, Ward, and Tversky, Amos, eds. *Decision Making: Selected Readings.* Harmondsworth, England; Baltimore, MD: Penguin, 1967. 412 p.
This book brings together a number of papers and excerpts from books addressing the following questions: How do men make judgments of the utility or attractiveness of various things that might happen to them, and how can these utilities be measured? How do men judge the probabilities of events that control what happens to them, and how can these judgments of probability be measured? How are judged probabilities changed by the arrival of new information? How are probabilities and utilities combined to control decisions? How should psychologists account for or think about the fact that the same person put in the same situation twice will often not make the same decision?

137. Eilon, Samuel. *Management Control.* 2d ed. Oxford; New York: Pergamon Press, 1979. 207 p.
Identifies the control function as a central theme in the management process. The essential ingredients of control include the specification of a

goal (or goals), a measurement task feedback information on performance, and a decision to take corrective action. The absence of any of these ingredients can only result in the management of activity becoming ineffectual or even meaningless. A manager may, therefore, be identified as a controller of a system. The book proceeds to explore first the relationships between a controller and his or her system and, second, the interactions between several controllers operating within the same system. The nature of the decision-making process is then analyzed, and various types of decisions are identified, followed by a discussion of problems associated with organizational design.

138. Ekey, David Clifton. *Decision Making.* Washington, DC: University Press of America, 1977. 463 p.
Explains the nature and process of decision making in an organizational context.

139. Elbing, Alvar Oliver. *Behavioral Decisions in Organizations.* 2d ed. Glenview, IL: Scott, Foresman & Co., 1978. 879 p.
Contains case studies providing a framework for various stages of decision-making processes in international corporations. Reflects the different social realms which influence individual managers and on which in turn they exert influence.

140. Emory, William, and Niland, Powell. *Making Management Decisions.* Boston: Houghton Mifflin, 1968. 306 p.
Develops a general model for making decisions, and considers such topics as the decision process, task delineation, and solution finding. Also includes application techniques like linear programming, inventory theory, networks, queueing theory, decision theory, simulation and game theory.

141. Emshoff, James R. "Experience Generalized Decision Making: The Next Generation of Managerial Models." *Interfaces* 8 (4) (August 1978): 40–48.
Article discusses the three phases of the model-building effort: experience-based decision, model-optimized decisions, and interactive decisions. Phase I occured before operations research affected managerial style. The key to good decisions was felt to be experience rather than analytic process. Phase II was the conversion of military operations research to an industrial base. The role of models in decision making was the opposite of Phase I. Phase III was the emergence of online interactive computer terminals. This improvement enabled managers to participate in building the models they would use.

142. Erlandson, David Alan. "An Examination of Decision Rules within Organizational Units as Responses to Governmental Stimuli." Ph.D. dissertation, University of Illinois at Urbana-Champaign, 1969. 111 p.
This dissertation examines the impact of governmental regulatory activities on organizational decision making.

143. Evans, Thomas J. "Systems Decision-Making." *Journal of Systems Management* 26 (8) (August 1975): 20–22.
A model is presented developing a simple framework for understanding the decision-making process with a full system perspective. The assessment process is the key to this presentation. It has two parts—establishment of the importance of a situation and determination of requirements for

action. The ability to know what is important is what separates the consistently good manager from the average performer.

144. Fabrycky, Walter J. *Economic Decision Analysis.* 2d ed. Englewood Cliffs, NJ: Prentice-Hall, 1980. 431 p.
Presents techniques of analysis for optimizing the economic outcome of managerial decisions. Topics include methods of evaluating economic alternatives for both private and public enterprise. Also deals with concepts like rate of return, payout criteria, benefit-cost and cost-effectiveness analysis, risk and uncertainty, allowance for variance in estimates, sensitivity analysis, simulation methods, decision trees, and economic decision models.

145. Fellingham, John C., and Newman, D. Paul. "Monitoring Decisions in Agency Setting." *Journal of Business Finance & Accounting (UK)* 6 (2) (Summer 1979): 203–21.
Two major categories characterize the role played by the accounting function: provision of information to support decision making and control over resource utilization. In this article the control function is analyzed using the concept of agency. Investors are viewed as the principals, with the manager acting as their agent in deciding how to employ resources in a productive process so as to provide returns to the principals. The problem considered is whether monitoring, paid for by the manager from his or her resource endowment, can assure the principals of acceptable action on the part of the manager and thus improve the manager's position.

146. Festinger, Leon. *Conflict, Decision, and Dissonance.* Stanford, CA: Stanford University Press, 1964. 163 p.
Psychological aspects of individual and group decision making are examined in this study which also covers topics like preferences, conflict, and alternative choices.

147. Fishburn, Peter C. *Decision and Value Theory.* New York: Wiley, 1964. 451 p.
Deals with the prescriptive theory of choice for individual decision by use of mathematical concepts such as measurement of relative values, probability and decision theory, analysis for pure dominance, valuewise independence of variables, uncertainty, and sequential decision problems.

148. Fisher, B. Aubrey. *Small Group Decision Making: Communication and the Group Process.* New York: McGraw-Hill, 1974. 264 p.
Explains group decision making in terms of individual roles, group preferences, and conflicts. Stresses the importance of communication for effective group decisions.

149. Fisk, George. *The Psychology of Management Decision.* Proceedings of a Symposium of the College on Management Psychology of the Institute of Management Sciences. Lund, Sweden: CWK Gleerup Publishing, 1967. 309 p.
Deals with the structure of individual goals, a human group model of organizations, statistical decision theory and benefit-cost analysis for preferredness of choice among alternative projects. Also covers aspiration levels and utility theory, perceived and "real" organizational behavior, computer-aided planning, heuristic problem solving, and individual attitudes toward risk. Discusses such behavioral concepts as personality

influences on decision making, the two-armed bandit problem, and computer simulation of learning and decision processes in poker.

150. Flamholtz, Eric G. "Toward a Psycho-Technical Systems Paradigm of Organizational Measurement." *Decision Sciences* 10 (1) (January 1979): 71–84.

Develops the notion that measurement in an organizational context must be viewed as a "psycho-technical" system, a technology that has as its goal to influence behavior, including the decisions made by management. To the extent that decision science is concerned with behavior of decision makers, the implications of this new technique must be incorporated into decision theory.

151. Fleming, John E. "A Suggested Approach to Linking Decision Styles with Business Ethics." *Journal of Business Ethics (Netherlands)* 4 (2) (April 1985): 137–44.

This article links management action with business ethics. To examine the important processes of information gathering and information processing, two conceptual models of decision making are advanced: bounded rationality and preferred decision styles. The analysis is then related to the ethical aspects of a business decision in order to explain the differences in the selection of ethical criteria.

152. Ford, Charles H. "The Elite Decision-Makers: What Makes Them Tick?" *Human Resources Management* 16 (4) (Winter 1977): 14–20.

"Elite" decision makers, those who can inevitably get straight to the point and recommend the correct course of action for the solution to problems, have a knack for developing generally accurate "impressions," quickly taking in the total situation and forming rapid interpretive judgments. The first key to this ability is the tendency to evaluate a situation in terms of the effect of the problem. The second key is the ability to go outside familiar constraints for a solution, not allowing anything to be seen as a "constant" simply because it is normally seen as such. The third key is the ability to make decisions quickly and briefly.

153. Ford, Charles H. "Manage by Decisions, Not by Objectives." *Business Horizons* 23 (1) (February 1980): 7–18.

While management by objectives (MBO) is not performing as expected, its goals are still valid. Any system which replaces MBO should be a total decision-making system encouraging timely and responsible decisions and their implementation. The current decision-making system has several defects. The proposed decision-making process would redefine job descriptions to ensure flow of needed decisions, timely response, lower management involvement, coordination of responsibility levels, a fertile environment for setting objectives, adequate communications, easy translation of decisions into action, a basis for performance appraisal, and a system that is easily administered.

154. Fox, R. P. "Agency Theory: A New Perspective." *Management Accounting (UK)* 62 (2) (February 1984): 36–38.

A number of practitioners believe that textbooks on decision making have very little to do with real world decisions. One of the most important reasons for this view is that decisions are, in reality, mainly political, involving some form of ulterior motive other than straightforward profit maximization. A new technique for looking at the decision-making situation is agency theory; its principal advantage is the ability to consider the political element lacking in so many other approaches. Article discusses this theory.

155. Fox, Robert E. "Cost Accounting: Asset or Liability?" *Journal of Accounting & EDP* 1 (4) (Winter 1986): 31–37.
Cost accounting systems are designed to assist management in decision making by linking operating decisions and financial performance measures. However, cost accounting principles are not an accurate linking mechanism due to dependent events and statistical fluctuations.

156. Fredrickson, James W. "Effects of Decision Motive and Organizational Performance Level on Strategic Decision Processes." *Academy of Management Journal* 28 (4) (December 1985): 821–43.
Managers make strategic decisions in response to both problems and opportunities and to whether their firms are performing poorly or well. The effects of these two motives and of organizational performance level on strategic processes are examined.

157. Frederickson, James W. "The Strategic Decision Process and Organizational Structure." *Academy of Management Review* 11 (2) (April 1986): 280–97.
Organizational structure can have a profound impact on strategy through its direct effect on the strategic decision-making process. Article suggests that a structure's pervasive impact offers a reasonable explanation of why a firm develops a particular way of making strategic decisions. Three different structures are discussed, and the prevalent strategic decision process for each is evaluated.

158. French, S. *Multi-Objective Decision Making*. New York: Academic Press, 1983. 325 p.
Based on the proceedings of a conference in April 1982 at Manchester, UK, organized jointly by the Institute of Mathematics and Its Applications and the Department of Decision Theory at the University of Manchester. Paper discusses mathematical modeling in decision making.

159. Frischknecht, Federico. "The Structure of Management Decision Systems." *Interfaces* 5 (1) (November 1974): 11–18.
The history of managerial thought shows a slow but definite shift from an emphasis on doing toward an emphasis on thinking. From managing things we have moved to managing people and hence to managing symbols. Traditional descriptions of management did not pay much attention to symbolic processes. Article discusses hierarchic structure and decision level.

160. Frye, John J. "Consensus Decisions and Analytic Hierarchies—Today's Answers to Tomorrow's Problems?" *Manage* 38 (1) (First Quarter 1986): 25–26.
Consensus decisions are arrived at through use of the total knowledge and experience of a group. Problems tend to be complex when none of the options are clearly superior in all categories. The analytical hierarchy process consists of breaking a problem into its component parts and placing a value on those parts. This is done by determining values, rating options, compiling weighted scores, and selecting the highest value.

161. Fulcher, Claire. "Give Them the Tools to Make Decisions." *Successful Meetings* 25 (2) (February 1976): 60–61, 139.
Decision making is a skill that must be taught to committees. To accomplish this, one must define goals, brainstorm ideas, clarify and pull together similar suggestions, select priorities, refine goals if necessary, choose one priority for real work, analyze any helping and hindering forces, complete an implementation chart assigning specific tasks to specific individuals and setting a timetable, and acquire individual commitment to the decision. Decision making is a complex process involving habit, authority, outside demands, lack of response, and conscious effort. By establishing a procedure for decision making, each person recognizes this process and discovers alternative strategies for action.

162. Gatza, James; Milutinovich, Jugoslav S.; and Boseman, F. Glenn. *Decision Making in Administration: Text, Critical Incidents, and Cases.* Philadelphia, PA: W. B. Saunders, 1979. 289 p.
Intended for use as a supplementary text for courses in managerial decision making, organizational behavior, and principles of management. The incidents and cases have been selected to accommodate a wide variety of needs. They are grouped in the following categories: planning and objective setting, organizing and staffing, controlling, leadership, understanding the social structure, and social issues. The mixture of cases within each section reflects a growing concern with nonprofit organizations.

163. Gelb, Betsy D., and Gelb, Gabriel M. "Strategies to Overcome Phony Feedback." *MSU Business Topics* 22 (4) (Autumn 1974): 5–7.
Phony feedback is useless to the decision maker. Forced feedback results from social pressure, while fuzzy feedback is a substitute for more honest answers, and filtered feedback is a result of organizational filters that soften criticism as it ascends the hierarchy of command. In order to obtain feedback that is potentially useful in decision making, the manager should cultivate feedback rather than force it, reward and act on useful feedback, avoid unnecessary dependence on feedback, and report feedback results.

164. Gemunden, Hans Georg, and Hauschildt, Jurgen. "Number of Alternatives and Efficiency in Different Types of Top-Management Decisions." *European Journal of Operational Research (Netherlands)* 22 (2) (November 1985): 178–90.
A longitudinal study was conducted to assess the determinants of decision-making efficiency and effectiveness for complex strategic decisions. Decision problem complexity was found to be related negatively to decision quality, although decision quality was not significantly improved through information search. Formulation and assessment of decision alternatives were found to improve decision quality.

165. Gleuck, William F., and Willis, Robert. "Documentary Sources and Strategic Management Research." *Academy of Management Review* 4 (1) (January 1979): 95–102.
Strategic management and business policy are concerned with top management decisions that affect the future of the organizations. Research done in strategic management concentrates on single- or several-company case studies. Documentary evidence provides multiple enterprise longitudinal data for hypothesis testing in policy research, but it does not guarantee

objectivity, consistency, or accuracy. Article discusses the strategic management research.

166. Goicoechea, Ambrose. *Multiobjective Decision Analysis with Engineering and Business Applications.* New York: Wiley, 1982. 519 p.
Covers techniques dealing with situations where more than one objective needs to be achieved. Topics discussed include linear multiobjective programming, goal programming, weighting attributes, multidimensional measure of risk, and utility measurement.

167. Gore, William J. *Administrative Decision-Making: A Heuristic Model.* New York: Wiley, 1964. 191 p.
Develops a general model of the decision making process in terms of organizational setting and evaluation and estimation of consequences. Also covers the functions of the decision-making process and the organization theory underlying the decision concept.

168. Gore, William J., and Dyson, J. W., eds. *The Making of Decisions: A Reader in Administrative Behavior.* New York: Free Press of Glenco, 1964. 441 p.
Collection of readings which provide a perspective on the decision-making process. Discusses administrative decisions, rational economic behavior, decision-making strategies such as a behavioral model of rational choice, criteria of choice among risky ventures, group decision making, organizational variables influencing the decision-making process, the normative regulation of authoritative behavior, subjective probability and decision under uncertainty, and interpersonal decision making.

169. Goshen, Charles E. *The Management of Decisions and the Decision of Management.* New York: Vantage Press, 1975. 314 p.
Most individuals have had significant experience in organizational management by virtue of having been a member of a family. This experience becomes inevitably the prototype model for each to either follow or depart from. The book examines the view that much of organizational decision structure is also a reflection of prevailing family patterns. Includes the role of behavior in decision making. The book presents a model for organizational decision making based on behavioral considerations and applies the model to situations such as managing organizational change, morale, communications, and personnel management.

170. Goslin, Lewis N. *Basic Systems for Decision Making.* 2d ed. Dubuque, IA: Kendall/Hunt, 1980. 197 p.
Basic guide that explains systems dynamics and systems approach. It explains the value of classification of models, model building, simulation, and the uses and limitations of models. Other topics include the decision process, decision trees, value of information, and management forecasting.

171. Gottinger, H. W. *Coping with Complexity.* Boston: D. Reidel, 1983. 223 p.
Book explains the structural characteristics in economic models. It covers problem solving, decision rules, complexity, and organizational decision making in terms of structures and performance. The book also covers cost of information processing, and organizational design.

172. Gouran, Dennis S. *Discussion: The Process of Group Decision-Making.* New York: Harper & Row, 1974. 199 p.
This book proposes to provide a basic introduction to the process of small group discussion. The material surveyed includes such topics as types and characteristics of discussion questions, discussion procedure, common obstacles to effective decision making, group environment, the effect of composition on group process, and principles of leadership.

173. Gouran, Dennis S. *Making Decisions in Groups.* Glenview, IL: Scott, Foresman & Co., 1982. 242 p.
This book explains the choices and consequences involved in group decision making. Covers expectations, preferences, group behavior, and individual versus group conflicts.

174. Granick, David. "Use of Corporate and Divisional Headquarters—A Peculiar American Innovation." *MSU Business Topics* 22 (4) (Autumn 1974): 9–17.
Article compares managerial process in American, French, and British companies. It shows how the use of division and company headquarters staff impacts on the decision making in large decentralized American corporations.

175. Grauer, M.; Thompson, M.; and Wierzbicki, A. P. *Plural Rationality and Interactive Decision Processes.* Proceedings, Sopron, Hungary, 1984. New York: Springer-Verlag, 1985. 352 p.
The proceedings include topics like the culture of decision making; the structure, stabilization, and accuracy of the decision process; use of experimental games; group decision making; game and bargaining solutions for group decision problems; interactive group decision making by coalitions; macromodels and multiobjective decision making; interactive multiobjective programming methods; and decision support based on the skeleton method.

176. Green, Thad B., and Lee, Sang M. *Decision Science Process.* New York: Petrocelli Books, 1978. 369 p.
Examines how managers' minds work during the decision process, in terms of analysis from observation, acceptance of scientific recommendations, and management information systems. It offers some dos and don'ts of computer models for planning and decision making and discusses what kind of corporate modeling functions best. Also covers the roles of the manager and management scientist in successful implementation of business decisions.

177. Grove, Andrew S. "Decisions, Decisions." *Computerworld* 17 (38) (September 1983): 1–8.
An essential part of every manager's work is participating in the decision-making process. Authority to make decisions in the traditional organization went with responsibility. However, businesses that deal mainly with information and know-how require a decision-making process that ensures input from knowledgeable personnel. The middle manager is the key to success in this type of decision-making process.

178. Guest, Robert H. "Management Imperatives for the Year 2000—The Creative Potential of Human Beings." *Vital Speeches* 51 (11) (March 15, 1985): 338–41.
Article predicts that in the future individual or group self-determination

will dominate decision making and action. U.S. firms are over-supervised and need to eliminate redundant managers. Greater flexibility and less hierarchical structures will appear along with more decentralization.

179. Guillet De Monthoux, Pierre. *Action and Existence.* New York: Wiley, 1983. 294 p.
Decisions are usually made today in what could be described as a political context. Someone who is weighted down with a structure of intellectual prejudice from another era is likely to find himself at a grave disadvantage in relation to others in this political process. Provides a handbook of self-examination for people of action who are involved in decision-making processes.

180. Gulliver, P. H. *Disputes and Negotiations: A Crosscultural Perspective.* New York: Academic Press, 1979. 293 p.
Explains the process of negotiation and joint decision making. Discusses the impact and role of mediators in the negotiation process.

181. Guzzo, Richard A. *Improving Group Decision Making in Organizations.* New York: Academic Press, 1982. 159 p.
Deals with the applications of group decision making; interpersonal learning and interpersonal conflict reduction in decision-making groups; group remembering; game theory and the structure of decision-making groups; improving the problem-solving process in managerial groups; and creativity, groups, and management.

182. Halter, Albert N., and Dean G. W. *Decisions under Uncertainty.* Cincinnati, OH: South-Western, 1971. 266 p.
Deals with methods for handling risk and uncertainty in managerial decision situations owing to lack of complete information.

183. Hammond, Kenneth R., et al. *Human Judgment and Decision Making.* New York: Hemisphere Publishing, 1980. 258 p.
Regardless of how technology has affected the process of organizational decision making in terms of improved information, analysis, and forecasting, the final task of deciding among many alternatives is left for human judgment. This book discusses the importance of this attribute to managers.

184. Harel, Gedaliahu H. "An Exercise to Simulate Managerial Functions." *Personnel Journal* 62 (6) (June 1983): 464, 466.
The basic management processes of planning, coordinating, decision making, and controlling are best taught by experience. Article discusses an effort to simulate these functions by developing an exercise for groups of managers. Exercise focuses on what steps the group took to achieve its task, how the workload was shared, and whether any attempts were made to use a planning model to evaluate construction problems.

185. Harrell, Adrian, and Klick, Harold D. "Comparing the Impact of Monetary and Nonmonetary Human Asset Measures on Executive Decision Making." *Accounting, Organizations & Society (UK)* 5 (4) (1980): 393–400.
Human resource accounting information can be provided in both monetary and nonmonetary form. A study was recently performed to test whether one had a significant advantage over the other for decision-makers. Two hypotheses which were proposed and later disproved by Flamholtz were retested in this study. Decision makers will put more

emphasis on monetary human asset measures than on nonmonetary measures to arrive at a decision. Decision makers will make different decisions when using monetary human asset measures vs. nonmonetary measures.

186. Harrison, E. Frank. *The Managerial Decision-Making Process.* 2d ed. Boston: Houghton Mifflin, 1981. 391 p.
Explains the nature of the decision-making process, the environment of decision making, values for decision making, the psychology of decision making, the sociology of decision making, techniques for decision making, and implementing the decision.

187. Hart, Lois Borland. *Moving Up! Women and Leadership.* New York: AMACOM, 1980. 228 p.
Compares the performance of women managers as decision makers as opposed to their male counterparts. Studies the accepted notion that female managers focus attention on details, while male managers tend to focus on the whole. Also explains why women managers have no trouble making effective day-to-day decisions but have problems dealing with long-term decisions. Explains the need for women managers to acquire skills in problem solving and risk taking.

188. Hasling, John. *Group Discussion and Decision Making.* New York: Thomas Y. Crowell, 1975. 144 p.
Discusses behavioral concepts relating to group decision making including group preferences, role conflicts, and other psychological factors which must be taken into account before arriving at an appropriate decision.

189. Hayes-Roth, Barbara. *Human Planning Processes.* Santa Monica, CA: Office of Naval Research, 1980. 21 p.
Paper discusses psychological and behavioral factors relating to decision making. While most of the discussion may deal with military applications, it may also be used in corporate decision making.

190. Heinze, David. "The Decision Theory Approach to Managerial Decision Making." *Marquette Business Review* 16 (3) (Fall 1972): 156–62.
An approach to decision making has been sketched, which abstracts from the complexity of reality a useful model that permits the manager to make consistent and satisfactory decisions. In real decision situations there are almost always limitations which prevent the construction of a perfect model.

191. Heirs, Ben J. *The Mind of the Organization.* New York: Harper & Row, 1977. 138 p.
The mind of the organization deals with the relevance of the decision-thinking processes of the human mind to the decision-thinking processes of organizations. Topics discussed include the importance of organizational thinking, the thinking function of the human mind, individual decision making and the mind's four-stage thinking process, the neglect of the mind's thinking process, a systems approach to the problems of organized complexity and the responsibilities of an organization's mind, and some of the barriers to the effective functioning of the organization's mind.

192. Heller, Frank A. *Managerial Decision-Making: A Study of Leadership Styles and Power Sharing among Senior Managers.* London: Tavistock, 1971. 140 p.
One of the major traits of leaders is their skill at making and implement-

ing a decision. However, in exercising this skill, corporate leaders differ vastly in their styles. This book analyzes the effectiveness of different styles on corporate growth and efficiency.

193. Heller, Robert. "The Business of Success." *Management Today (UK)* (January 1983): 50–55, 108.
Successful managers know how to effectively use their powers with the board of directors to promote better and more dynamic decision making. Article discusses this attribute.

194. Henderson, John C., and Nutt, Paul C. "The Influence of Decision Style on Decision Making Behavior." *Management Science* 26 (4) (April 1980): 371–86.
A study was made of cognitive styles measured by the Myers-Briggs indicator to isolate how style influences decision behavior. In the experiment, experienced decision makers from hospitals and companies were asked to assess several capital expansion projects. The experiment revealed that management style was an important determinant of decision behavior.

195. Herbert, Theodore T., and Estes, Ralph W. "The Role of the Devil's Advocate in the Executive Decision Process." *Business Quarterly (Canada)* 46 (2) (Summer 1981): 56–63.
Within the decision-making process, most executives usually delegate the analysis of problems to subordinates and specialists. Where decisions are reached by the consent of a group, there may be additional hazards from group psychology. One technique that can be used to overcome the pitfalls of the executive decision process is the use of formalized dissent. Institutionalizing the dissent function will depersonalize criticism and minimize conflict among persons or groups. The person designated to perform this role can be either an organizational member or someone from outside the corporation. An official dissenter can help ensure that decisions will be more thoroughly researched, and proposed solutions will be more soundly based on reality. The likelihood of marginal or unwise decisions being made is also reduced.

196. Hernandez, William H. "Is the Controller an Endangered Species?" *Management Accounting* 60 (2) (August 1978): 48–52.
Article suggests that management reports become the tools needed to develop proper business decisions. Useful management reports could be developed for internal use only by product or project responsibility, use of time frames more relevant to a particular situation, dealing in cash flow statements directly, establishing return-on-investment-discounted cash flow statements, and using current replacement values.

197. Herron, Sue; Jacobs, Larry; and Kleiner, Brian. "Developing the Right Brain's Decision Making Potential." *Supervisory Management* 30 (3) (March 1985): 16–22.
Managers can enhance their value to the organization by improving their decision-making ability. Right-brain activity is most active in the analysis and preliminary decision stages of the decision-making process. Its intuitive nature is of primary importance. Intuitive abilities can be enhanced by slowing the left brain's activities by such means as physical exercise.

198. Hertz, David Bendel. *Risk Analysis and Its Applications.* New York: Wiley, 1983. 316 p.
Any corporate decision involves the taking of risk because of incomplete information leading to uncertainty. Risk analysis is a mathematical technique designed to help managers choose among many alternatives. This book discusses the application of the technique.

199. Hickling, Allen. *Managing Decision: The Strategic Choice Approach.* Rugby, England: Mantec Publications, 1974. 58 p.
A corporate decision in one area is affected by choices made in others. The book analyzes the interconnected decision areas and presents the process of strategic choice which involves analysis and management of uncertainty, variety, and complexity, as well as discrimination between alternate solutions.

200. Hickson, David J. *Top Decisions: Processes of Strategic Decision-Making in Organizations.* Oxford: Basil Blackwell, 1986. 267 p.
Examines the dynamics of decision making in terms of problems and complexity, interest groups and accommodation, and control and decision processes.

201. Hill, Percy H., et al. *Making Decisions: A Multidisciplinary Introduction.* Washington, DC: University Press of America, 1986. 243 p.
Contains case studies relating to the corporate decision-making process, which includes the following activities: definition of the problem, identification and quantification of alternatives, application of decision aids, and implementation. Also looks at ethical decision making.

202. Hoffer, William. "Being Reasonable Is Not Always Rational." *Nation's Business* 73 (4) (April 1985): 66R–67R, 2.
Most business people like to think their decisions are rational and based on an objective weighing of data. Psychologists reveal, however, that decisions often are not based on all the available data, that decision makers look to the past for help in predicting the future, that negative consequences are weighed more heavily than potential gains, and that decision makers assume a decision's success or failure can be explained rationally.

203. Hogarth, Robin M. *Judgment and Choice: The Psychology of Decision.* New York: Wiley, 1980. 250 p.
While mathematical reasoning provides a sound basis for any business decision, a wise manager does not ignore psychological factors which influence organizational life and structure. This book examines these factors and explains their impact on the decision-making process.

204. Hogarth, Robin M., and Makridakis, Spyros. "The Value of Decision Making in a Complex Environment: An Experimental Approach." *Management Science* 27 (1) (January 1981): 93–107.
The issue of whether the costs of time and effort spent on analyzing decisions are outweighed by the benefits is examined in the context of a competitive business game where human teams are confronted with two kinds of simple-minded arbitrary decision rules, where rules are applied consistently (arbitrary-consistent), and where rules are subject to a random component (arbitrary-random). The former rules outperform, on average,

41 percent of human opponents, the corresponding figure for the latter being 19 percent.

205. Hoh, Andrew K. "Styles of Decision Making." *Supervisory Management* 26 (5) (May 1981): 19–23.

Supervisory or management decisions may be classified into four different types—low quality-high acceptance, high quality-high acceptance, low quality-low acceptance, and high quality-low acceptance. The style of decision making may be democratic, authoritative, or laissez-faire. An effective way of ensuring that a decision receives a high degree of acceptance by employees is for employees to help make the decision as a group. The group approach with management-defined guidelines allows employees to resolve the problem in terms of their own needs.

206. Hollingsworth, A. Thomas. "Improving Managerial Decisions that Affect Human-Resources." *Personnel Journal* 52 (6) (June 1973): 446–50.

In presenting a framework that will enable practicing managers, to improve their decisions concerning use of human resources, this article deals with the controllable and uncontrollable variables that an effective organizational decision maker must identify. It demonstrates some of the problems that can occur when a decision maker fails to analyze all the variables in a decision situation. This is accomplished by describing three incidents observed within industrial organizations.

207. Holloway, Charles A. *Decision Making under Uncertainty.* Englewood Cliffs, NJ: Prentice-Hall, 1979. 522 p.

Uncertainty is at the basis of all corporate decisions. Risk analysis and decision theory to some extent help decision makers handle uncertainty. This book explains the techniques.

208. Hough, Louis. *Modern Research for Administrative Decisions.* Englewood Cliffs, NJ: Prentice-Hall, 1970. 609 p.

Modern decision theory treats managerial problem solving as the selection of the best from a set of weighted alternatives. Such a view calls for a knowledge of analytic methods to be used for handling the uncertainty generally present in predictions, the subjective probability used in Bayesian statistics, research designs which directly lead to administrative action, and system analysis. The book introduces the manager to mathematical concepts in decision research, including model building, parameter estimation, queueing theory, PERT (project evaluation and review technique), network scheduling, linear programming, assignment problem, transformation method, simplex method, and Monte Carlo research techniques.

209. Huber, George P. *Managerial Decision Making.* Glenview, IL: Scott, Foresman & Co., 1980. 225 p.

Basic introduction to the concepts involved in decision process including goal setting, value of information, uncertainty and risk, and evaluation of alternative strategies.

210. Hughes, Robard Y. "A Realistic Look at Decision Making." *Supervisory Management* 25 (1) (January 1980): 2–8.

Most business decisions are not clear-cut and hard-edged. Complicating decision making are the vastness of the information-generating machinery and the fact that information received from colleagues and subordinates is usually biased and incomplete. Managers should not allow hunches to be "educated" out, since hunches are the product of instinct, experience, perceptiveness, and intelligence. An effective manager must understand the steps to decision making, which are definition of the problem, redefinition of the problem in terms of specific objectives, confirmation of goals to those of the overall organization, lining up of alternatives, review of resources, listing and evaluating the consequences of incorrect decisions, preselling the decision, and the decision and action.

211. Humphreys, Patrick; Svenson, Ola; and Vari, Anna, eds. *Analysing and Aiding Decision Processes.* New York: North-Holland, 1983. 510 p.
Explains the concepts of organizational decision making, the structure of small-scale decision problems, and tracing decision processes. Also deals with the validity of studies on heuristics and biases.

212. Hwang, Ching-Lai, and Yoon, Kwangsun. *Multiple Attribute Decision Making, Methods and Applications: A State-of-the-Art Survey.* New York: Springer-Verlag, 1981. 259 p.
The book reviews and classifies the literature on methods and applications of Multiple Attribute Decision Making (MADM). It provides readers with a capsule look into existing methods, their characteristics, and applicability to analysis of MADM problems. The basic MADM concepts are defined, and a standard is introduced.

213. "Identifying Key Decisions for Corporate Management." *Journal of General Management (UK)* 2 (3) (Spring 1975): 67–72.
A general management view of organizational decision making is presented. A framework is developed which identifies the major parts of the organization and the nature of their linkages through various decision processes. Article explains how the framework for decision analysis can be helpful to the manager in a number of ways.

214. Inbar, Michael. *Routine Decision-Making: The Future of Bureaucracy.* Beverly Hills, CA: Sage Publications, 1979. 239 p.
Sheds new light on bureaucracies, describing their present state and mapping their future. Suggests that by using computer science and recent developments in psychology involving heuristics, the major defects of bureaucracy can be transformed into assets. Suggests that it is almost inevitable that a wide variety of decisions can be made by computers in the future, that the technology exists, that errors will be no greater, and that consumer satisfaction will be the same or possibly higher.

215. Isaack, Thomas S. "Intuition: An Ignored Dimension of Management." *Academy of Management Review* 3 (4) (October 1978): 917–21.
Article provides provisional definitions of intuition and intellect. Whereas intellect is the capacity for rational thought, intuition is "that psychological function which transmits perceptions in an unconscious way." Expresses the view that parapsychology might be a potential source of learning more about the role of intuition in the management decision process.

216. Isaack, Thomas S. "Intuition: A Treasury of Knowledge." *Personnel Administrator* 25 (7) (July 1980): 74–78.
Executives state that intuition plays a part in their understanding circumstances and in their decision making. Logical rational thought processes seem to play a dominant part in management development pro-

grams to the point of ignoring the existence of intuition. Article stresses the importance of intuition.

217. Jago, Arthur G. "Configural Cue Utilization in Implicit Models of Leader Behavior." *Organizational Behavior & Human Performance* 22 (3) (December 1978) 474–96.
The manner in which managers employ information concerning four fundamental dimensions of decision making situations in choosing leadership behavior deemed appropriate for those situations was investigated. The results indicated certain similarities and differences between normative and descriptive models of leadership and identified a previously undocumented source of individual differences among managers.

218. Jago, Arthur G. "A Test of Spuriousness in Descriptive Models of Participative Leader Behavior." *Journal of Applied Psychology* 63 (3) (June 1978): 383–87.
Recent research to explore the effects of situational variables on the choice of autocratic vs. participative leader behavior has relied on a measure of behavioral intent in hypothetical managerial decision-making situations. Article develops a new model that offers greater internal validity. It included systematic manipulation of hierarchical levels.

219. Jago, Arthur G., and Ragen, James W. "The Trouble with Leader Match." *Journal of Applied Psychology* 71 (4) (November 1986): 555–59.
Article uses computer simulation to assess and classify leadership situations. Examines the view that managerial effectiveness depends on leadership style and leadership situation.

220. Jameson, Brian. "*Management by Uncertainty.*" *Management Today (UK)* (February 1979): 60–63, 138.
The literature of management techniques often justifies itself by offering managers better predictability, higher stability, and greater control. This situation is antimanagerial. It restricts the scope of management by attempting to make sure that the future holds only situations that need to be administered rather than managed. While stable situations and events are administered, all situations that need to be managed are unstable. Since it is claimed that accuracy can be achieved in predicting the outcomes of managerial decisions, managers study economics, psychology, finance, and marketing. All of this activity serves the purpose of disguising the fact that the market itself is a postulate. Management theory must admit the fact that it cannot predict the future.

221. Janis, Irving Lester, and Mann, Leon. *Decision Making: A Psychological Analysis of Conflict, Choice, and Commitment.* New York: Free Press, 1977. 488 p.
Individual as well as group decision making depends a lot on mathematical analysis in today's complete corporate structure. However, psychological aspects of this job should not be ignored. This book analyzes this aspect and its role in conflict resolution and choice.

222. Jewell, Linda N., and Reitz, H. Joseph. *Group Effectiveness in Organizations.* Glenview, IL: Scott, Foresman & Co., 1980. 164 p.
One of the characteristics of modern organizations of all types is an increasing use of groups for a variety of decision-making activities. Planning, forecasting, policy setting, and problem solving are all activities

traditionally delegated to individuals but now given to research teams, advisory committees, and task forces. This increases time and the cost of decision making. So why give decision making to groups? According to this book, the answer lies in expectations about the quality and acceptance of group decisions.

223. Johnsen, Erik. *Studies in Multiobjective Decision Models.* Lund, Sweden: Denmark Studenlitteratur, 1968. 628 p.
Empirical study of Danish firms which found that the delineation of objectives in decision models is very weak. Managers make their decisions according to several objectives at one time and they want decision models that take this aspect into consideration. The book examines whether it is desirable or possible in practical management as well as in management theory to work with multiobjective models instead of or concurrently with ordinary single objective models. Also examines how such multiobjective models can be formulated so that they become relevant normative elements.

224. Johnson, R. J. *Executive Decisions.* 3d ed. Cincinnati, OH: South-Western, 1976. 641 p.
Case studies dealing with decisions involving control; organizational management, public responsibility; organized labor; and planning, strategy, and policy formulations.

225. Johnston, Wallace R., and Frampton, G. Creighton. "Are You All Tangled up in Problems?" *Management World* 9 (7) (July 1980): 12–14, 32, 36.
Although managers devote much more time and energy to making problem solving decisions, the process of problem solving is not well understood by many managers. Problems seem to be different from company to company; however, the same process or method of analysis is often equally valid in searching for a solution. Decision makers can begin solving their own problems by using the first stage in the problem-solving process, which is a problem recognition and definition.

226. Jones, Manley Howe. *Executive Decision Making.* Rev. ed. Homewood, IL: Richard D. Irwin, 1962. 560 p.
Provides an approach to orderly thinking by the executive as a decision maker. Covers goal setting, creative process, use of premises, anticipatory decisions of others, authority, leadership, communications and training, group decisions, social and economic environment for decision making, and implementing objectives.

227. Kallman, Ernest A.; Reinharth, Leon; and Shapiro, H. Jack. "How Effective Companies Manage Their Information." *Business* 30 (4) (July/August 1980): 35–39.
The jobs at each level of management differ substantially and the kind of information required by each manager must fit the decision-making needs of that level. Strategic decisions, such as introduction of a new product or acquisition of a competing firm, are highly judgmental and unstructured and are undertaken by top management. Middle-level management decisions tend to follow prescribed procedures and deal with structured information. A management information system (MIS) can provide storage and retrieval as well as integration of information for different functional areas and management levels of an organization.

228. Kantrow, Alan M. "The Strategy-Technology Connection." *Harvard Business Review* 58 (4) (July/August 1980): 6–14, 18–21.
Discusses the need to incorporate technological issues within strategic decision making. Technology and strategy are inseparable. Points to logic that must be considered in a firm's strategic planning. This is the process of creating an idea of the business it is in, identifying its goals and objectives and the long-term policies to achieve them, and formulating plans of action. Technology includes the elaborate systems of planning and production through which a firm's abstract capability is changed into the goods and services on which it depends for success. There is an increasing perception by managers of the need to place technological decisions in the context of overall corporate strategy. A review of some of the literature confirms that technological decisions are of fundamental importance to business. The significant message of the past decade's research is that these decisions must be made in the fullest context of the individual firm's strategic thinking.

229. Karasek, Mirek. *The Anatomy of Decision.* New York: Vantage Press, 1985. 177 p.
The book demonstrates how systems analysis is important to rational decision making on all levels, from individual choices to technological processes. Also deals with how not to make decisions.

230. Kassouf, Sheen T. *Normative Decision Making.* Englewood Cliffs, NJ: Prentice-Hall, 1970. 88 p.
Introductory volume which would help undergraduates conceptualize the decision-making process. Deals with applications of normative decision theory, not only in management areas where techniques like linear programming and Bayesian theory are employed, but also in areas where decisions are made in a less formal but more qualitative fashion. The book examines how even in the latter case, ideas like utility, constraints, and probability are of great use.

231. Keeney, Ralph L., and Raiffa, Howard. *Decisions with Multiple Objectives.* New York: Wiley, 1976. 569 p.
Decision analysis looks at the paradigm in which an individual decision maker (or decision unit) contemplates a choice of action in an uncertain environment. It is designed to help the individual make a choice among a set of prespecified alternatives. The book examines such concepts as the structuring of decision objectives, tradeoffs under certainty, unidimensional utility theory, multiattribute preferences under uncertainty preferences over time, and aggregation of individual preferences.

232. Kelley, Neil D. "Business Turns to Graphics." *Infosystems* 27 (11) (November 1980): 51, 54, 56–57, 60.
Computer-based management graphics, or "business graphics," is still relatively new, and those managers considering it should make their decision carefully. Graphics can be useful to every type of manager, but since no standards for data accuracy and layout have yet been developed, managers must be sure that data are accurate in order to avoid false impressions. It must also be ensured that layout does not inadvertently give false impressions, while simultaneously displaying everything pertinent to the data.

233. Kepner, Charles H., and Tregoe, Benjamin B. *The Rational Manager: A Systematic Approach to Problem Solving and Decision Making.* 2d ed. Princeton, NJ: Kepner-Tregoe, Inc., 1976. 263 p.
Presents how the manager can develop his abilities in problem solving and decision making by using information more effectively.

234. Kindlarski, Edward. "Ishikawa Diagrams for Problem Solving." *Quality Progress* 17 (12) (December 1984): 26–30.
The Ishikawa diagram, introduced by Kaoru Ishikawa in the 1960s, is applicable to a wide variety of problems and is highly flexible. It provides a graphical analysis of the causal bonds leading to a final result. The Ishikawa diagram uses a causal nexus for decisions relating to ordering things, events, or actions. The diagrams point from an effect toward the causes. When a problem is large and involves several areas, experts from each area must cooperate in drawing the Ishikawa diagram.

235. Kirkwood, William G. "The Search for Good Ideas." *Supervisory Management* 28 (8) (August 1983): 22–26.
Good ideas are the only way to resolve the decision-making difficulties facing organizations. Four principles that can make the search for good ideas more satisfying and effective are exploring alternate definitions, keeping idea identification and idea evaluation separate, learning to build on ideas as well as to criticize them, and avoiding premature decision solutions.

236. Kmietowicz, Z. W., and Pearman, A. D. *Decision Theory and Incomplete Knowledge.* London: Gower Press, 1981. 121 p.
The decision-making process is characterized as a sequential series of component problems, the basic elements of which are identification of strategies; identification of alternate states of the world in which the chosen strategy will operate; prediction and evaluation of the outcome of every possible strategy in every possible world; viewing the probabilities of the occurence of the different states of nature; and selecting a criterion to evaluate each strategy to identify which one performs the best. The book deals with these components and their applications in capital investment, marketing, and portfolio selection, among other ideas.

237. Koktor, R., et al. *The Implementation of Management Science.* Amsterdam, Holland; New York: North-Holland, 1979. 239 p.
Discusses the components of the decision-making process including the implementation problem, the context of operations research/management systems (OR/MS) implementation, implementation as a change process, risk analysis, the role of intermediaries, integrative complexity and the use of marketing models, and implementing change in very large organizations.

238. Koontz, Harold. "The Management Theory Jungle Revisited." *Academy of Management Review* 5 (2) (April 1980): 175–87.
Article discusses decision theory as one of the approaches to the science of management. It calls for a new understanding of motivation, the melding of motivation and leadership theory, and clarifying semantics.

239. Langton, James F. "Corporate Responsibility and Mainstream Decisions." *Trusts & Estates* 114 (7) (July 1975): 471–73.
Business should be able to recognize social and public policy issues and determine with some degree of assurance its ability to contribute solutions. This cannot be done without a management structure with the power to

make policy decisions. This is where corporate social responsibility influences mainstream management decisions, determining what the firm can do and seeing that it is done.

240. Lapin, Lawrence L. *Management Science for Business Decisions.* New York: Harcourt Brace Jovanovich, 1980. 613 p.

Introductory text covering fundamental quantitative decision concept such as probability, decision theory, decisions with experiments, decisions with normal curve, games, utility, linear programming, queueing, network theory, simulation, and forecasting.

241. Laughhunn, Dan J.; Payne, John W.; and Crum, Roy. "Managerial Risk Preference for Below-Target Returns." *Management Science* 26 (12) (December 1980): 1238–49.

The decision risk preferences are reviewed for below target returns of 224 managers from the U.S., Canada, and Europe. In situations where only nonruinous losses are involved, 7.1 percent of the managers were risk seeking for below-target returns. The distribution of risk preferences tended to be stable over a variety of experimental conditions including diversity of background of the managers, size of the outcomes below target, and context of the decision process, i.e., personal vs. managerial. In cases where ruinous losses were introduced, 6.4 percent switched their behavior to risk adverse actions.

242. LaValle, Irving H. *Fundamentals of Decision Analysis.* New York: Holt, Rinehart & Winston, 1978. 626 p.

An undergraduate textbook which emphasizes the generality of decision analysis. Deals with fundamentals of decision theory analysis, quantification of preference and judgments, normal-form decision analysis, and group decision making and game theory.

243. Lee, Sang M., and Moore, Laurence J. *Introduction to Decision Science.* New York: Petrocelli/Charter, 1975. 589 p.

While some managers approach decision making as an art, there are others who have mastered and used to solid advantage the scientific reasoning of decision models. This book provides a basic introduction to mathematical methods for arriving at corporate decisions.

244. Lee, Sang M., Moeller, Gerald L.; and Digman, Lester A. *Network Analysis for Management Decisions.* Hingham, MA: Kluwer, 1982. 318 p.

Provides a good introduction to network analysis for management. It explains the analytical functions of management, project/venture management, and network models. Also describes the venture evaluation and review technique, network construction and logic, input preparation, outputs and reports, and computer mechanics. Applications of the technique include project management, multiple performance attributes with constraints, new-product development decisions, decision trees applications, and analysis of strategic decisions, like mergers and acquisitions.

245. Leitman, C., and Manzollo, A. *Multicriteria Decision Making.* New York: Springer-Verlag, 1975. 386 p.

A considerable amount of research has been devoted recently to multicriteria decision making, stimulated by the vast number of real business problems, where many decision makers are present or many, possibly conflicting objectives should be taken into account in order to reach some form of optimality. A rough division into two classes may be made between the approaches to multicriterial decision-making problems. The first one deals mainly with the empirical determination of preference structures in some specific problems and seeks methods for their meaningful aggregation in order to arrive at practical, reasonable solutions. The second one is directed toward general and rigorous formulations in order to reduce multicriteria decision problems for which definite solutions algorithms are sought. This book follows mainly the latter line of thought.

246. Lindley, D. V. *Making Decisions.* 2d ed. New York: Wiley-Interscience, 1985. 207 p.
This book is about decision making and the logical processes that need to be used in arriving at a decision. It is not concerned with the ways in which people currently make decisions—the delegation of responsibility, the organization of paper work, and the personality of a decision maker—but, rather, deals with the subject from a scientific viewpoint to see what basic principles there are in any choice of action. It studies the rules of decision making. Topics covered include decision and uncertain events, a numerical measure for uncertainty, the laws of probability, a numerical measure for consequences, the utility of money, Bayes theorem, value of information, and decision trees.

247. Linstone, Harold A. *Multiple Perspectives for Decision Making.* New York: Elsevier Science Publishing Co., 1984. 422 p.
The concept of multiple perspectives is presented in this work as a practical means to bridge the wide gap that exists between analysis and decision making in the realm of sociotechnical systems. It covers risk analysis, forecasting, and corporate planning. The book is of interest to corporate managers and business strategists, policy and system analysts, operations researchers and management scientists, and institutional administrators.

248. Lloyd, D. C. F. "An Introduction to Business Games." *Industrial & Commercial Training (UK)* 10 (1) (January 1978): 11–18.
A short introduction to business (or management) games is given on their use and construction. It is intended to give a background on forms of games, namely the computer operated and the manually operated. Such games may incorporate a full range of decision making, covering many general management activities such as finance, personnel, production, research and development, marketing, forward planning, etc. They may also be functional and cover one specific aspect of an activity, or they may be technical games.

249. Longnecker, Justin G. "Management Priorities and Management Ethics." *Journal of Business Ethics (Netherlands)* 4 (1) (February 1985): 65–70.
Organizational leaders must fully articulate ethical policy and clearly communicate ethical statements and codes. However, communications regarding organizational ethics must be consistently supported by examples of ethical management and decision making and reinforced by sanctions for ethical standard violations.

250. Lyles, Richard I. *Practical Management Problem Solving and Decision Making.* New York: Van Nostrand Reinhold, 1982. 192 p.
There seems to be a definite advantage to following a logical sequence of activities and thought processes when attacking a problem or decision.

This book is most practical in helping managers achieve the best possible results in the vast majority of problem-solving and decision-making dilemmas they face. Discusses the traditional five-step approach to decision making and the Kepner Tregoe method involving the following: identifying everything that could go wrong, describing in detail each potential problem, prioritizing the potential problems according to risk, listing all possible causes for each potential problem, rating the probability each cause is likely to occur, identifying preventative actions and preparing to take contingency actions in case the problem cannot be prevented. The book contrasts these with the Lyles method consisting of the following steps when applied to decision making: definition of the problem, definition of objectives, generation of alternatives, development of action plan, troubleshooting, communicating, and implementing.

251. Mac, Ruth P. *Planning on Uncertainty: Decision Making in Business and Government Administration.* New York: Wiley-Interscience, 1971. 233 p.
Presents the elements of statistical decision theory, including conditional probability and decision trees. Also covers decision agents, value judgments and rational choice.

252. Machol, Robert E., and Gray, Paul, eds. *Recent Developments in Information and Decision Processes.* New York: Macmillan, 1962. 197 p.
Presents papers at a symposium on information and decision processes held at Purdue University in April 1961. Topics include the mathematics of self-organizing systems, dynamic programming, deferred and Bayesian decision theories, and the estimation of reliability.

253. Magee, John F. "Decision Trees for Decision-Making." *Harvard Business Review* 42 (July/August 1964): 126–38.
Explains the role of decision trees in identifying choices, risks, objectives, monetary gains, and information needs for investment decisions.

254. Magnet, Myron. "How Top Managers Make a Company's Toughest Decision." *Fortune* 11 (6) (March 18, 1985): 52–57.
Seven chief executives explain how they made difficult decisions about transforming their companies. The firms include General Motors, Gannett Co., *USA Today*, Rolm Corp., American Can Co., and National Intergroup.

255. Maheshwari, B. L. *Decision Styles and Organizational Effectiveness.* New Delhi, India: Viakas, 1980. 228 p.
Studies styles of decision making commonly used by managers in Indian business organizations, specifically whether it is participative or entrepreneurial. Also studies the impact of the style on organizational effectiveness.

256. Maier, Norman R. F. *Problem Solving Discussions and Conferences: Leadership Methods and Skills.* New York: McGraw-Hill, 1963. 261 p.
Discusses the importance of conference as a decision-making tool.

257. "Management Decisions in Choosing a Computer." *Management Accounting (UK)* 61 (3) (March 1983): 34–35.
Management has begun to view computers as a business tool rather than something to be left to the specialists. The decision to install their systems has been based on management requirements to have direct involvement

with and control of the computer. Management decisions in choosing a computer still involve a fairly time-consuming process of evaluation and elimination based on the business and administrative requirements.

258. "Management for Meetings." *Small Business Report* 5 (11) (November 1980): 15–19.
Many managers rate meetings as the biggest waste of their time. Article discusses alternatives to meetings that should be explored, including one-on-one discussions, circulating a memo to ask for written comments, and conference telephone calls. In planning a meeting, the manager should consider what specific things are to be decided upon and what type of meeting it should be, either ad hoc or scheduled.

259. Marschak, Jacob. *Economic Information, Decision, and Prediction: Selected Essays.* Dordrecht, Holland; Boston: D. Reidel, 1974. 3 vols.
Contains the influential papers of Jacob Marschak in the areas of economics of decision, economics of information and organization, money and other assets, economics measurements, and the logic of economics.

260. Marschak, Jacob, and Radner, Roy. *Economic Theory of Teams.* New Haven, CT: Yale University Press, 1972. 345 p.
Presents efficient ways of providing information allocation among decision makers who constitute a team. Topics include single-person decision problems, team organization problems, and optimality and viability in a general model of organization.

261. Marsland, Stephen, and Beer, Michael. "The Evolution of Japanese Management: Lessons for U.S. Managers." *Organizational Dynamics* 11 (3) (Winter 1983): 49–67.
Management techniques have made Japan a major competitive force in the international economy, and U.S. executives, hoping to emulate this, discuss the three principles that characterize Japanese management: high value placed on information exchange, "bottom-up" decision making, and division of managerial labor. Information is continually traded among employees at all levels of a corporation, and managers always know where to find information they need. Decision making begins at the bottom of the corporate structure with low-level managers, whose proposals are passed upward to successively higher managerial levels for refinement.

262. Martino, R. L., and Stein, Elinor Svendsen. *Decision Patterns.* Wayne, PA: Management Development Institute, 1969. 109 p.
This book develops a total analysis system for planning, allocating and controlling the information flow. The system uses techniques such as critical path analysis and operations research, simulation and decision tables. Using the system, a manager is enabled to make a quantitative evaluation of available alternatives and make a selection after discarding alternatives which are not in keeping with corporate objectives.

263. Marvin, Philip. *Developing Decision for Action.* Homewood, IL: Richard D. Irwin, 1971. 216 p.
Concerns decision-making skills and the conversion of decisions into action.

264. Mason, Richard Owsley. "Dialectics in Decision-Making: A Study in the Use of Counterplanning and Structured Debate in Management Information Systems." Ph.D. dissertation, University of California, Berkeley, 1968. 217 p.
Exploratory study focusing on the information systems by which staff advisors communicate problems and proposals for their solutions to managerial decision makers. Examines how a decision-making approach, which strives for synthesis of information rather than analysis, can be effective in solving organizational problems.

265. Mason, Richard Owsley, and Swanson, E. Burton. "Measurement for Management Decision: A Perspective." *California Management Review* 21 (3) (Spring 1979): 70–81.
The principles of scientific measurement largely ignore a factor that is crucial in measurement for management decision, namely the user. Any managerial measurement system must be designed with primary attention given to the purposes or organizations and their individual members and to the processes by which participants assimilate and act on measurement data. The measure value should increase monotonically as the organization's purpose is increasingly achieved and should decrease in the event of failure to achieve purpose. The measurement of resources may take place at any of three levels within the managerial domain: organizational, individual, and societal. The implementation takes the form of a management information system.

266. McAllister, Daniel W.; Mitchell, Terence R.; and Beach, Lee Roy. "The Contingency Model for the Selection of Decision Strategies: An Empirical Test of the Effects of Significance, Accountability, and Reversibility." *Organizational Behavior & Human Performance* 24 (2) (October 1979): 228–44.
A study was conducted to describe and test a contingency model for the selection of decision strategies. Participants were asked to read descriptions of decision problems and choose the appropriate strategies to solve them. Experiments were designed with differences in the degree of external validity of the task. The participants were full-time managers. The contingency model suggests that when decisions are more significant the decision cannot be reversed, and the decision maker is responsible for the actions. The decision strategy will be more analytic, resulting in a greater investment of time and effort than when the opposite conditions are in effect.

267. McArthur, D. S. "Fantasies, Fundamentals, and a Framework in Corporate O. R." *Interfaces* 10 (4) (August 1980): 98–103.
A gap exists between decision scientists and decision makers. One way to begin closing the gap is to measure it. The decision scientist must develop a rapport with management which allows the free exchange of ideas.

268. McCall, Morgan W., Jr., and Kaplan, Robert E. *Whatever It Takes: Decision Makers at Work.* Englewood Cliffs, NJ: Prentice-Hall, 1985. 132 p.
This book attempts to remove the myth that there is some technique or formula that will ensure good decisions. The most important decision is to strive constantly to build an organization that is better than the one in existence and to make the kinds of decisions daily that are likely to achieve that outcome. There is no shortage of advice for managers on how to make a "proper" decision: marshall all the facts, generate all the

alternatives, evaluate each of them, and make the optimal choice. This book takes the stance that managerial decision making is seldom amenable to such strategies. In modern organizations, decision making requires acting without all the facts, juggling many problems at once, shooting from the hip, and nursing political processes. Major topics include how, from a jumble of facts, events, actions, opinions, and problems are identified in the first place; why, given all the things crying for attention, certain problems are dealt with while others stagnate; how to shoot from the hip without wounding yourself; shepherding complex decision processes through various minefields; discovering how it all came out; and learning from victories and defeats.

269. McClenahen, John S. "Cultural Hybrids: Japanese Plants in the U.S." *Industry Week* 200 (4) (February 19, 1979): 73–75.
Japanese management is characterized by carefully laid groundwork, an emphasis on achieving market stability, and building a solid employee relations foundation. The plants managed by the Japanese are based on a consensus management, in which decisions are made by employees. Although consensus management may be relatively slow in decision making, its proponents feel that such an approach is positive and human oriented and that once a decision is reached it is implemented quickly because people are prepared for it. Japanese management also stresses communication.

270. McGuire, C. B., and Radner, Roy, eds. *Decision and Organization: A Volume in Honor of Jacob Marschak.* New York: American Elsevier, 1972. 361 p.
Deals with the subject of rational choice and the theory of decision and organization. Topics include the structure of alternatives, characteristics of preference orderings, complications associated with time and uncertainty, communication conflict, the theory of teams, and decentralized systems.

271. Meeker, Robert J.; Shure, Gerald H.; and Rogers, Miles S. *A Research Approach to Complex Decision-Making.* Danville, IL: Interstate Printers & Publishers, 1963. 187 p.
The job of decision making involves research as to information availability and use, possible alternatives, and decision implementation. The book stresses the importance of research all through the process.

272. Michalos, Alex C. *Foundations of Decision-Making.* Ottawa, Canada: Canadian Library of Philosophy, 1978. 202 p.
Emphasizes the process of decision making as opposed to an explanation of underlying mathematical concepts. Areas covered include the concepts of preference and indifference; needing, choosing, and deciding; objects of decisions and choices; possibilities, restrictions, and resources; probability and grids of analysis; efficiency and maximization policies; rational decisions and processes; benefits and costs for recipient populations; and estimates, regions, costs, and benefits.

273. Michalski, Richard. "Decentralized Decision-Making: Motivating Managers to Look at the 'Big Picture.'" *Cost & Management (Canada)* 58 (2) (March/April 1984): 55–59.
A divisional manager's specialized knowledge of the problems, threats, and opportunities endemic to a company unit can be used to great advantage in decentralized decision making. The most effective operating decisions are made by managers who are intimately familiar with the environment

within which their divisions operate. Included under decentralized decision-making ideas are that top management can concentrate efforts on ensuring the long-run well-being of the organization and that middle managers can display their decision-making capabilities in response to problems.

274. Miles, Mary. "Getting Bright Ideas from Your Team (Part 1)" *Computer Decisions* 15 (2) (February 1983): 192, 194–95.
In business today, it is necessary to stimulate employees to formulate fresh, creative, and productive ideas to benefit the organization. Employees feel a sense of enthusiasm and commitment if involved in the group approach which allows for input into decision making. Article cautions against the brainstorming approach that allows aggressive employees to gain control of a session, while ideas from less aggressive people may be unheard. Discusses a structured decision method that encourages equal participation and allows well-balanced, informed decisions to be made quickly.

275. Milford, William. "Sharpen up Your Mental Tools." *Supervision* 40 (5) (May 1978): 23–24.
Keeping alert for all new approaches in job functions is a must for career success. Sharp mental capabilities exist for application even in routine decisions while decreased pressures have decided effects on thinking and reasoning capabilities. Article suggests how to sharpen mental capacities.

276. Miller, David Wendell, and Starr, Martin Kenneth. *Executive Decisions and Operations Research.* 2d ed. Englewood Cliffs, NJ: Prentice-Hall, 1969. 607 p.
Examines the structure of decision problems from the viewpoint of an integrated theory of decisions. Within this framework, a logical, rational approach is blended together with the scientific methodology of operations research. Using elementary mathematics, the book analyzes how to determine when an operations research problem exists, how to recognize the appropriate decision classification for that problem, how to approach problems of each class in accord with present theory, when it may be worthwhile to seek specialized assistance, and how the results may be evaluated.

277. Miller, David Wendell, and Starr, Martin Kenneth. *The Structure of Human Decisions.* Englewood Cliffs, NJ: Prentice-Hall, 1967. 179 p.
Examines the structure of decision problems from the viewpoint of an integrated theory of decisions. Within this framework, a logical, rational approach is combined with scientific methodology. Using only the most elementary mathematics, the reader learns how to recognize the appropriate classification for a decision problem and how to approach problems of each class in accord with the present theory. The contents include science and administration, responsibility for decisions, the objectives of decision, the structure of decisions, the analysis of decisions, applied decision theory, and the question of when is a problem worth solving.

278. Miller, James Rumrill. *Professional Decision-Making: A Procedure for Evaluating Complex Alternatives.* New York: Praeger, 1970. 305 p.
The book examines the concept that dollar maximization should not be a normative and descriptive principle of decision behavior because many important consequences of decisions cannot be assessed in dollar terms.

More general and flexible procedures are necessary to capture the real objective held by decision makers and to interpret them in terms of a single nonmonetary unit of worth. The book is devoted to the development of a measure to compare decision alternatives with one another without the restrictive conditions imposed by profit maximization, by using statistical decision theory, operations research, and systems analysis.

279. Mintzberg, Henry. "Patterns in Strategy Formation." *Management Science* 24 (9) (May 1978): 934–48.

By defining strategy as "a pattern in a stream of decisions," it is possible to research strategy formation in a broad descriptive context and study both strategies that were intended and those that were realized despite intentions. Studies show that strategy formation can be fruitfully viewed as the interplay between a dynamic environment and bureaucratic momentum, that strategy formation over time appears to follow some important patterns in organizations, notably life cycles, and that the study of the interplay between intended and realized strategies may lead us to the heart of this complex organizational process.

280. Mode, V. Alan, and Breeze, Jack E. "Planning: Forward or Backward?" *Canadian Manager (Canada)* 7(5) (October 1982): 15–16.

Planning is difficult for many managers because it involves looking into the future when everything they know about is in the past. However, if successful decisions in the past were not part of a coordinated plan for the future, then past success might be nothing more than luck. Planning is the solution to a multidimensioned problem which is simultaneously influenced from several directions.

281. Moody, Paul E. *Decision Making.* New York: McGraw-Hill, 1983. 192 p.

Presents a guide to how decisions should be made and the factors which influence decisions and decision makers. The techniques covered include PERT (project evaluation and review technique), force field analysis, decision trees, utility theory, probability, and statistics.

282. Moore, Peter G., et al. *Case Studies in Decision Analysis.* Harmondsworth, England: Penguin, 1976. 167 p.

Decision analysis is a systematic approach to decision making in situations where there are a number of alternative courses of action and some uncertainty as to the precise outcomes of the various possible options. This book provides a series of case studies or case histories relating to the application of the tools of decision analysis.

283. Moorehead, Gregory. "Groupthink: Hypothesis in Need of Testing." *Group & Organization Studies* 7 (4) (December 1982): 429–44.

Irving Janis proposed that groupthink, a tendency in decision-making groups to focus on group involvement rather than on group function, seriously jeopardizes the effectiveness and adequacy of group decision processes. Symptoms of groupthink include extreme cohesiveness of group members, illusions of morality, invulnerability and unanimity, self-censorship, and stereotyping of group opponents. Article emphasizes that empirical research is needed to determine the validity of the groupthink concept.

284. Morell, Robert William. *Managerial Decision-Making: A Logical Approach.* Milwaukee, WI: Bruce Publishing Co., 1960. 201 p.
This is a textbook for an advanced undergraduate course in business policy or for management development programs. It examines the nature and patterns of corporate decision making. The case studies examine the antecedents of decision, logical properties of assumptions, and inductive and deductive techniques. The book cautions that while many mathematical concepts have a lot of potential value to the decision makers they should set more store on techniques where the effects of a large number of controlled variables must be considered, where the number of uncontrolled variables are small, and where there is reason to believe that past relationships will continue into the future.

285. Morris, William Thomas. *Management for Action: Psychotechnical Decision Making.* Reston, VA: Reston Publishing Co., 1972. 223 p.
No decision can ever be truly objective because it is made by an individual, and each individual has a personal style of decision making. While much has been written to give the manager help in making decisions, almost nothing has been said about the most significant source of help—the decision-making process itself. Thus, if managers look objectively at themselves and how they make decisions, and if they come to understand the process, they will be able to improve on that process and make more satisfying decisions. This book deals with the content of psychotechnics, which refers to the practical or technical use of psychology in decision making, and thus describes the work of making decisions that are more satisfying. It is used, quite frankly, as a way of getting the attention of those who are sufficiently innovative in their outlook as to be afraid of missing something.

286. Morrison, J. Roger, et al. *Decision Making: The Chief Executive's Challenge.* London: British Institute of Management, 1972. 44 p.
Consists of three papers: "The Chief Executive's Decision-Making Dilemmas"; "Management Science and the Chief Executive"; and "Can Strategic Planning Pay Off?"

287. Murray, Edwin A., Jr. "Strategic Choice as a Negotiated Outcome." *Management Science* 24 (9) (May 1978): 960–72.
With increasing pressures for public accountability by private enterprise, the zone of strategic discretion for top-level corporate managers is being reduced. Preliminary evidence from recent field research in a major electric utility demonstrated that corporate decisions of major strategic significance were not only formulated (within the company), but negotiated (implicitly if not explicitly) with external parties.

288. Murray, Michael. *Decisions: A Comparative Critique.* Marshfield, MA: Pitman Publishing, 1986. 260 p.
The purpose of this book is to discuss and discredit the illusions that the business sector follows only a quantitative approach, that public administrators are purely political, and that legalists do not exercise discretion. A further intention is to build a framework that outlines an integrated approach to decision making based on the tools or methods of these three approaches.

289. Neave, Edwin H., and Petersen, Edward H. "A Comparison of Optimal and Adaptive Decision Mechanisms in an Organizational Setting." *Management Science* 26 (8) (August 1980): 810–22.
Simulation experiments are used to compare optimal and adaptive decision mechanisms for firms operating in a duopoly. Optimal decision policies are derived making use of a dynamic programming approach based on the Cyert-Degroot duopoly models, and the adaptive decision mechanism uses the Cyert-March behavioral theory of the firm. The simulations suggest that good organizational performance requires good decision-making processes and efficient operation of the organization.

290. Newman, William Herman. *Contemporary Adjustments in Managerial Decision Making and Planning.* Austin, TX: Bureau of Business Research, University of Texas, 1962. 29 p.
Discusses decision-making processes such as problem identification, diagnosis and simplification of -isms, search for alternatives, estimation of the consequences of various alternatives, evaluation, and making a choice. Application of these ideas to managerial planning is also discussed.

291. Nickerson, R. S., and Feehrer, C. E. *Decision Making and Training: A Review of Theoretical and Empirical Studies of Decision Making and Their Implications for the Training of Decision Makers.* Cambridge, MA: Bolt Beranek and Newman, 1975. 218 p.
Decision making is conceptualized here as a type of problem solving, and the review is organized in terms of the following component tasks: information gathering, data evaluation, problem structuring, hypothesis generation, hypothesis evaluation, preference specification, action selection, and decision evaluation. Implications of research findings for training are discussed in the context of description of each of these tasks. A general conclusion drawn from the study is that decision making is probably not sufficiently well understood to permit the design of an effective general-purpose training system for decision makers. Systems and programs could be developed, however, to facilitate training with respect to specific decision-making skills. The development of more generally applicable training techniques or systems should proceed in an evolutionary fashion. Training is one way to improve decision-making performance; another is to provide the decision maker with aids for various aspects of the task. Because training and the provision of decision aids are viewed as complementary approaches to the same problem, the report ends with a discussion of several decision-aiding techniques that are in various stages of study or development.

292. O'Connell, Jeremiah J., and Zimmerman, John W. "Scanning the International Environment." *California Management Review* 22 (2) (Winter 1979): 15–23.
A firm may scan the international environment for trends, events, and expectations which will influence the decisions that shape the nature and direction of the business. Executives must search the external environment for information relevant to administrative and operational decisions. Article reveals the results of a survey of how well the environmental process is managed by American and European executives.

293. Odiorne, George S. *Management Decisions by Objectives.* Englewood Cliffs, NJ: Prentice-Hall, 1969. 252 p.

This book will help managers improve their decision-making ability by explaining how to define a problem in very specific form. Other topics dealt with are the use of analytical tools, evaluation of options, and implementation of objectives.

294. Olson, Philip D. "The Overburdened Manager and Decision Making." *Business Horizons* 22 (5) (October 1979): 28–32.

Top managers do not have the time for reflective, careful planning, and they tend to prefer verbal information rather than formal information provided by management information systems. Article suggests that error analysis can be used directly by senior managers as an alternative to management analysis. This is a method of statistical hypothesis-testing logic used in situations where information is not obtained from random samples. Each strategy is weighed to see how likely it is that it contains errors and what the consequences would be.

295. Oxenfeldt, Alfred Richard, et al. *A Basic Approach to Executive Decision Making.* New York: AMACOM, 1978. 229 p.

Text deals with decision-making processes including collection of data, goal setting, evaluation of alternatives, cost-benefit analysis, and decision implementation.

296. Palmer, David D.; Veiga, John F.; and Vora, Jay A. "Personal Values in Managerial Decision Making: Value-Cluster Approach in Two Cultures." *Group & Organization Studies* 6 (2) (June 1981): 224–34.

Interest in the role of personal values in decision making has recently grown. Improved understanding of the relationship between managers' personal values and decision making in crosscultural settings is particularly important, given the expansion of multinational corporations and international trade. Much of the research on managerial decision making in crosscultural settings has depended heavily on overall differences in values to explain variance in decision preferences. Although the research has been valuable to identify cultural differences, it has not centered enough on the similarities among cultures, particularly in occupational subgroups. Article reports a cluster-analytic approach to developing value profiles as a technique for identifying value similarities in managerial subgroups. The results from a sample of Indian and American managers illustrate that two dominant value profiles, designated "pragmatic" and "altruistic," were present and that these value profiles helped explain variances in decision preferences.

297. Pattanaik, Prasanta K. *Voting and Collective Choice. Some Aspects of the Theory of Group Decision-Making.* New York: Cambridge University Press, 1971. 184 p.

Assuming knowledge of set theory, this book presents three different methods of solving problems. A social ordering of preferences based on restricted individual preference, it provides the substitution of a best alternative social ordering for the complete social ordering requirement and the inclusion of preference intensities as a factor underlying social choice.

298. Patton, B. R., and Giffin, Kim. *Decision-Making Group Interaction.* 2d ed. New York: Harper & Row, 1978. 259 p.
Discusses group decision making in terms of the orientations and attitudes of people in groups; interpersonal behavior in groups; leadership; group characteristics and their effects; conflict and its resolution; communication within the group; identifying, analyzing, and evaluating proposed solutions and implementing a decision; evaluating interpersonal relations; and improving ability by observing other groups.

299. Patz, Alan L., and Rowe, Alan J. *Management Control and Decision Systems: Texts, Cases, and Readings.* Santa Barbara, CA: Wiley, 1977. 453 p.
The role of a manager is comparable to that of a catalyst: to bring about results from actions of the components and constituents in an organization, and to utilize resources in the most effective manner possible. Unfortunately when dealing with human beings, there are no simple formulas or rules that best determine how a manager should interact with members of the organizations to achieve desired results. Many prescriptive approaches have been suggested by which the manager could make appropriate decisions leading to effective control. Contingency theory is one of the approaches which has clearly demonstrated there is no "one best way" and that situational variables often determine the outcome in a given circumstance. How then is the manager to exercise control? How should decisions be made to achieve organizational objectives? This book is an attempt to answer these questions.

300. Pearce, M. R., et al. *An Introduction to Business Decision Making.* New York: Methuen, 1977. 507 p.
This is a book of case studies relating to business decision making, with particular reference to Canadian management practices.

301. Pennings, Johannes M. *Decision Making: An Organizational Behavior Approach.* 2d ed. New York: Markus Wiener, 1986. 340 p.
Shows how the individual, organizational, and strategic areas of decision making are mutually relevant for a general organizational behavior theory and how they cross-fertilize each other. The selected articles deal with microorganizational behavior, macroorganizational behavior, and organizational strategy.

302. Persek, Stephen C. "Consulting: An Overview." *Review of Business* 4 (1) (Summer 1982): 19–22.
In today's rapidly changing business environment, managers must frequently make decisions in a short timeframe and expanded information structure. The firm's chief external source to help cope with these problems is the consultant. Article discusses areas where consultants can be effective such as inventory management, materials requirement planning, production scheduling, and quality control.

303. Pettigrew, Andrew M. *The Politics of Organizational Decision-Making.* London: Tavistock; distr. by Harper & Row, 1973. 302 p.
Deals with power and conflict in organizational life. Studies organizational decision as a political process in the context of a specific firm whose executive made a series of innovation decisions. The book uses longitudinal research designs for highlighting social process in organizations.

304. Pike, R. "No Accounting for Intuition." *Management Accounting (UK)* 57 (7) (July–August 1979): 20–21.
Intuition and critical analysis are not contradictory but complementary in the majority of cases. An analytical approach involves a systematic breakdown of the decision into its component steps. Intuition may be defined as the immediate apprehension by the mind without reasoning. In accounting for intuition, accountants can cultivate an awareness that focuses on the whole, and not merely on the parts easily quantifiable. Accountants can recognize that in an uncertain world there is no neat formula or programmed sequence of steps that guarantees successful outcomes.

305. Plunkett, Lorna C., and Hale, Guy A. *The Proactive Manager: The Complete Book of Problem Solving and Decision Making.* New York: Wiley, 1982. 221 p.
The term "proactive management" describes a set of analytical skills used to resolve the uncertainties facing managers. The skills or processes are different for each different form of uncertainty. Perhaps the easiest method of classifying the processes is the use of a timeframe. A manager has several basic timeframes to manage: the past, the present, the future and the past, present, and future all together. This book examines the uncertain situations in early stages and explains how to solve them by decision analysis.

306. Prescott, Bryan D. *Effective Decision-Making.* London: Gower Press, 1981. 90 p.
Deals with decision-making processes such as data collection, goal setting, evaluation of alternatives, choice of a solution, and its implementation.

307. Puxty, Anthony G. "Recent Research in Financial Control." *Managerial Finance (UK)* 6 (1) (1980): 3–8.
Financial control is the use of primarily financial information in order to induce decisions which lead to the control of the organization concerned. This definition has three elements: the nature of the information itself, the way in which decision makers react to and create it, and the nature of the concept of "being in control." Research into decision makers and the process of decision making has taken on the title "behavioral accounting." It implies a distinction between a certain kind of accounting research and other kinds. It is the nature of control which is the crucial area and which should be the focus of the other.

308. Qubein, Nido R. "How to Make Decisions—Fast." *Management World* 14 (8) (September 1985): 17–19.
Gives guidelines that will help simplify the decision-making process. Successful managers learn to choose what decisions they will make, and they focus their energies on those decisions essential to accomplishing goals. Decision making involves assuming responsibility. Good decisions are made on the basis of an assessment of the whole situation. It helps to consult with other people before making a decision. One should not be afraid to make decisions because of the fear of making mistakes. When the decision has been made, go on to other tasks.

309. Quinn, James Brian. "Strategic Change: Logical Incrementalism." *Sloan Management Review* 20 (1) (Fall 1978): 7–21.
Strategy formulation in major companies is often perceived as following a formal systems planning approach. However, interim decisions inexorably shape the future strategic posture. Recognizing the inability of companies

to foresee the timing, severity, or nature of precipitating events, top executives consciously deal with these events in an incremental fashion.

310. Radford, K. J. *Complex Decision Problems.* Reston, VA: Reston Publishing Co., 1977. 208 p.
Discusses how complex problems are analyzed and solutions decided upon by use of quantitative decision-making techniques like modeling and simulation.

311. Radford, K. J. *Modern Managerial Decision Making.* Reston, VA: Reston Publishing Co., 1981. 258 p.
Considers decision problems in terms of four major characteristics which have a major effect on methods of resolution, rather than in other categories frequently used previously. The characteristics are (1) whether the power to make decisions is in the hands of individual, organization, or entity or whether many participants have the power to influence; (2) whether single or multiple objectives are involved; (3) whether benefits and costs of all choices can be measured; and (4) whether uncertainty exists in the decision situation.

312. Radford, Les G. "The Positive Side of Unpopular Decisions." *Supervisory Management* 27 (11) (November 1982): 10–12.
Work situations sometimes require supervisors to make unpopular decisions, preferably in a way that will not create more problems. Those who refuse to make such decisions can undermine their own managerial role by jeopardizing management's objectives or threatening harmonious working relationships. Article describes how to handle unpopular decisions.

313. Raiffa, Howard. *Decision Analysis: Introductory Lectures on Choices under Uncertainty.* Reading, MA: Addison-Wesley, 1968. 309 p.
Decision problems under uncertainty requires the following actions: listing viable options for gathering information for experimentation or action; listing events which may recur; deciding the utility of consequences; and judging the probability of occurence of the uncertain event. This book contains a series of lectures dealing with this process. It covers among other things, sampling, risk sharing and group decision, the art of implementation, game theory, systems analysis, and operations research.

314. Ramstrom, Dick. *The Efficiency of Control Strategies: Communication and Decision Making Organizations.* Stockholm, Sweden: Almquist & Wiksell, 1967. 442 p.
Concentrates on the cognitive aspects of decision making and information processing in organizations. Discusses among other things, the general nature of the decision-making system, the decision behavior of the system, and the various methods used for estimating the rationality level of decisions, the content of information available to decision makers, and the general properties of decision process in organizations.

315. Rappaport, Alfred. "A Fatal Fascination with the Short Run." *Business Week* 2686 (Industrial edition) (May 4, 1981): 20, 22.
Decisions based primarily on short-term results, without consideration of long-term consequences, can be economically inefficient for both the company and the economy. Since corporate policy is shaped by managers who assess decisions in terms of personal economic rationality, incentive systems are necessary to motivate executives to make decisions consistent with the long-term interests of the company.

316. Raymond, Thomas Cicchino. *Problems in Business Administration: Analysis by the Case Methods.* 2d ed. New York: McGraw-Hill, 1964. 331 p.
Describes the case study approach to management decision making and supplies cases for analysis.

317. *Readings in Decision Analysis.* 2d ed. Menlo Park, CA: Decision Analysis Group, Stanford Research Institute, 1977. 613 p.
Collection of readings designed to provide a perspective on the "Stanford School of Decision Analysis." The term "decision analysis" is used to mean the discipline concerned with the practice of rational decision making, relating to any problem of resource allocation. *Readings* represents most of the current written materials that reflect the Stanford approach to decision analysis.

318. Research Conference on Subjective Probability, Utility, and Decision Making, 4th, Rome, 1973. *Utility, Probability and Human Decision Making.* Dordrecht, Holland; Boston: D. Reidel, 1975. 415 p.
Aims to develop a theoretically sound technology for the optimal solution of decision problems and to formulate a descriptive theory of human decision making to protect decision makers from being caught in the traps of their own limitations and biases. Topics covered include experimental applications of multiattribute utility models, the notion of semiorders to build outranking relations in multicriteria decision making, subjective preference orderings for multiattributed alternatives, judgment under uncertainty, heuristics and biases, and subjective probability forecasting.

319. Research Conference on Subjective Probability, Utility, and Decision Making, 5th, Darmstadt, 1975. *Decision Making and Change in Human Affairs.* Edited by Helmut Jungermann and Gerard de Zeeuw. Dordrecht, Holland; Boston: D. Reidel, 1977. 527 p.
Papers that provide European perspectives on decision theory and its applications. Topics include measurement and interpretation of beliefs, decision making and cognition, cognitive functions in decision making, decision making and numerical structuring, and Bayesian statistics and efficient information processing constrained by probability models.

320. Rice, George H., Jr. "Idealism and Management Decision-Making." *Journal of General Management (UK)* 5 (2) (Winter 1979/ 1980): 14–21.
Discusses how managers make decisions and just what they make decisions about. It is possible that managers approach their decision making behavior on the basis of either determinism or idealism. Each can serve as a foundation for a theory of decision making; however, idealism seems to afford a more appropriate foundation from which to construct a model of managerial decision-making. Traditional theories of problem solving or decision making rely heavily on a simplified philosophy of determinism— the belief that everything is caused by something. Article examines this and finds most business education presently centers on the technical methods (determinism) rather than on the creativity (idealism) required for business operations.

321. Rice, George H., Jr., and Hamilton, Richard E. "Decision Theory and the Small Businessman." *American Journal of Small Business* 4 (1) (July 1979): 1–9.
Discusses a field study done to determine the extent to which small business people use scientific decision making. It was found that they primarily used a very informal approach to decision making, as the rational model seemed to be too ambitious an undertaking. These businesspeople operate in a manner described by the social model. Further studies, acting on the assumption that it is this model which is applicable, should be able to describe the processes at work in the small business person's decision behavior.

322. Richards, Max De Voe, and Greenlaw, Paul S. *Management: Decisions and Behavior.* Rev. ed. Homewood, IL: Richard D. Irwin, 1972. 655 p.
Views the business organization as an information-decision system in which decision making represents the focus of activity performed by managers. It emphasizes that in dealing with problems in all areas of organizational endeavor, from those involving personal relationships to those requiring an economic analysis of costs, revenue, and profits, the manager is faced with choice situations in which numerous courses of action are possible and for which certain information is prerequisite for decision making. Specific topics covered include individual behavior, group behavior, leadership process, organizational process, organizational change, and allocation of resources.

323. Rome, Beatrice K., and Rome, Sydney C. *Organizational Growth through Decision Making: A Computer-Based Experiment in Eductive Method.* New York: American Elsevier, 1971. 242 p.
Develops a humanistic approach to organizations and organizational growth. Explains managerial responsibility and its classification, gaining operational control, gaining administrative control over operational control, establishing moral authority, and innovative planning.

324. Ross, Kenton E. "The Place of the Manager and the Systems Analyst." *Office* 81 (1) (January 1975): 74, 78.
There are two significant differences between management and systems analysis. The first is authority. The systems department operates only with the authority granted to it. The second difference is that the systems analyst does not have the responsibility that the manager has. Managers must make the final decision, since they will be held responsible. The systems professional can make only suggestions and recommendations. It is important to the success of systems management to have the participation and involvement of others within the organization.

325. Rowe, Alan J. "Decision Making in the '80s." *Los Angeles Business & Economics* 6 (1) (Winter 1981): 7–9.
One of the challenges that managers will be confronted with in the 1980s will be how to make effective decisions in a continually changing environment. To answer this challenge, managers will need to know how to improve their decision-making skills, how to adapt to new and altering situations, and how to predict the future more accurately. Article discusses one approach to decision styles that has been used by some business organizations. Also describes a "cognitive-contingency" model.

326. Rowe, Alan J. "The Myth of the Rational Decision Maker." *International Management (UK)* 29 (8) (August 1974): 38–40.
Most executive decisions are based on personal preference rather than rational deliberation. The idea of an executive gathering all pertinent facts, weighing them carefully, and then making a decision in the best interests of the organization is largely a myth. Article contends that executives must understand the influence of personal preference in decision making, in order to improve the quality and rationality of their own decisions and predict the decisions of their subordinates, colleagues, and superiors. Eight basic guideposts are offered to help the individual manager gain insight into the role that personal preference plays in decision making.

327. Ruskin, Arnold M. "The Nature of Strategy and Tactics, Executives and Managers, and Executive Managerial Decisions." *Managerial Planning* 33 (5) (March/April 1985): 11–15, 21.
Relationships between strategy and tactics, executives and managers, and executive decisions and managerial decisions are examined. Strategies are defined as organizational state vectors that can ensure the organization's future; tactics are defined as paths for reaching a strategy from a prior state vector. Executive decisions are equated with choosing tactics.

328. Saaty, Thomas L. *The Analytic Hierarchy Process.* New York: McGraw-Hill, 1980. 287 p.
Most corporate decisions involve planning for goals, setting priorities and deciding on how to allocate limited resources for optimum effectiveness. The job involves a hierarchy of various steps all of which are explained in this book.

329. Saaty, Thomas L. *Decision Making for Leaders.* Belmont, CA: Wadsworth, 1982. 290 p.
Because of the interaction among the multitude of factors affecting a complex decision, it is essential to identify the important ones and determine the degree to which they affect each other before a clear decision can be made. This book addresses the issue of how to structure a complex situation, identify its criteria and other facts, whether intangible or concrete, measure the interactions among them in a simple way, and synthesize all the information to obtain priorities. The priorities can then be used in a benefit/cost setting to develop portfolios of activities, one of the major concerns of corporations today. Topics covered include the analytic hierarchy process, analyzing and structuring hierarchies, practical examples of hierarchies, resolving conflict, and making group decisions.

330. Sadek, Konrad E., and Tomeski, Edward A. "Set Theory and Management." *Journal of Systems Management* 30 (10) (October 1979): 6–11.
Not all managers on a given hierarchical level have an equal say in all interdepartmental decision making. Some managers become leaders while the others follow. With the aid of set theory, the interplay between managers on interdepartmental decision making and the influence they have on an organization and systems design can be analyzed.

331. Sathe, Vijay. "The Controller's Role in Management." *Organizational Dynamics* 11 (3) (Winter 1983): 31–48.
Corporate controllers are subject to seemingly contradictory pressures in performing their jobs. On one hand, they are responsible for taking an active role in business decision making. They must also closely monitor

the accuracy and completeness of financial information reporting. Article examines whether one person can or should perform both roles effectively.

332. Sawyer, Lawrence B. "Consultant to Management: The Internal Auditor's Emerging Role." *Internal Auditor* 38 (3) (June 1981): 30–38.
Internal auditors can be helpful to the decision makers by reviewing information developed by others on the availability of people, materials, money, and machines; the amount of risk; the costs of achieving the hoped for results; the constraints; and the timeframe within which the decision will be implemented.

333. Scanlan, Burt K., and Atherton, Roger M., Jr. "Participation and the Effective Use of Authority." *Personnel Journal* 60 (9) (September 1981): 697–703.
Participative management consists of more two-way communication, more opportunity for subordinates to assist in decision making, and less stress on management's authoritative posture. Changing management's approach to using authority brings about more employee participation and the gains associated with it. As long as employees are mentally and emotionally involved in their job objectives, they will produce more effectively.

334. Scholz, Roland W. *Decision Making under Uncertainty.* New York: North-Holland; distr. Elsevier Science Publishing Co., 1983. 445 p.
This book is of interest to theoretical or empirical researchers in those disciplines that are concerned with the adequate modeling of decision making. Covers cognitive decision research, social interaction and development and epistemology, the role of heuristics in models of decision, problem structuring calculi and levels of knowledge representation in decision making, biases in group decision making, decision-theoretic paradoxes, and individual decision making and social psychology.

335. Schroeder, Roger G. *Operations Management: Decision Making in the Operations Functions.* New York: McGraw-Hill, 1981. 680 p.
Some managerial decisions relate to the corporation's long-range goal. But decisions have to be made on a day-to-day basis for the operation of the enterprise by managers at different levels and departments. This book explains how these decisions are different in nature and how they are made.

336. Schwartz, R. Malcolm. "Preparing Decision Packages—And Just Making Decisions." *Management World* 7 (6) (June 1978): 30, 32–33.
Among the most important tools for managers to use in making decisions or preparing decision packages are analytical tools such as standard cost, fixed and variable cost, and performance ratios. Performance measurements such as allocation of time, reports on performance, and effective standards are other vital tools. Developing standard costs and cost analyses are also major considerations for the manager. Two key steps to create an effective decision package are analyzing alternatives and analyzing service levels.

337. Schwarz, LeRoy B., and Johnson, Robert E. "An Appraisal of the Empirical Performance of the Linear Decision Rule for Aggregate Planning." *Management Science* 24 (8) (April 1978): 844–49.
More than twenty years after the publication of the Linear Decision Rule by Holt, Modigliani, Muth and Simon, it remains an implementation failure with no firm reported to be using it. This study hypothesizes that the reason for the failure may be that the incremental benefit of aggregate planning over improved aggregate inventory management alone may be quite small.

338. "Selling a Decision." *Small Business Report* 5 (9) (September 1980): 26–27.
In most situations, the best decision-implementing method for handling conflicts is the win-win method in which the manager "sells" the decision through open communication with subordinates. Win-win gains consensus through the use of participative management to gain commitment from all parties. Goals are identified and obstacles to reaching the goals are defined. Successful situations occur when the group spends more time in defining the problem than on pondering the solutions.

339. Sengupta, Jati K. *Decision Models in Stochastic Programming.* New York: Elsevier Science Publishing Co., 1982. 189 p.
Provides operational methods of decision making under uncertainty. Covers systems science and engineering.

340. Sengupta, Jati K. *Optimal Decisions under Uncertainty.* New York: Springer-Verlag, 1981. 156 p.
The theory of optimal decisions in a stochastic environment has seen many new developments in recent years. The implications of such theory for empirical and policy applications are several. This book attempts to analyze some of the important applied aspects of this theory and its recent developments. The stochastic environment is considered here in specific form, for example, linear programs with parameters subject to a probabilistic mechanism, decision models with risk aversion, and resource allocation in a team. Methods of optimal decision rules developed here for quadratic and linear decision problems are applicable to operations research models in management decisions involving portfolio analysis and stochastic programming, and systems sciences models in stochastic control and adaptive behavior.

341. Sherwood, John J., and Holyman, Florence M. "Individual versus Group Approaches to Decision Making." *Supervisory Management* 23 (4) (April 1978): 2–9.
There are five factors to consider when one is faced with deciding whether to assign a particular task to an individual for solution or to a group of people for their combined consideration. These are the nature of the task itself, the importance of general acceptance of or commitment to a solution for its implementation, the value placed on the quality of the decision, the role in implementation of each person involved, and the anticipated operating effectiveness of the group.

342. Shields, Michael D. "Effects of Information Supply and Demand on Judgment Accuracy: Evidence from Corporate Managers." *Accounting Review* 58 (2) (April 1983): 284–303.
The choice of information is an important problem in many organizations. This empirical study examines the relationships between supply, demand,

and judgment accuracy observed when corporate managers analyzed information in performance reports and made diagnostic judgments. This evidence will shed light on the information-choice problem of accountants. A predecisional research method is used for this investigation.

343. Shields, Michael D. "A Predecisional Approach to the Demand for Information in a Performance Report." *Accounting Organizations & Society (UK)* 9 (3) (1984): 355–63.
A major concern of accountants is what information decision makers demand to solve problems. A predecisional research approach—one used by psychologists to measure the cognitive processing of information—is used to provide empirical evidence regarding the demand for information in performance reports.

344. Shull, Fremont A.; Delbecq, Andre L.; and Cummings, L. L. *Organizational Decision Making.* New York: McGraw-Hill, 1970. 320 p.
This book is an attempt to improve decision making within formally structured and administered organizations. It treats decision making within the organization as a major dependent variable in administration. Looks at psychological perspectives, small group behavior, and strategies for administrative role conflict.

345. Silhan, Peter A. "Management Accounting Is Research." *Management Accounting* 64 (3) (September 1982): 38–42.
Management accounting is distinguished from other areas of accounting by its emphasis on financial information for management decisions. Viewing management accounting as research could help unify the diverse activities of management accounting under a single framework.

346. Simon, Herbert Alexander. *The New Science of Management Decision.* Rev. ed. Englewood Cliffs, NJ: Prentice-Hall, 1977. 175 p.
Provides an introduction to computers in management decision. Explains the process of management decisions, impact of computers, organization design, and man-machine systems for decision making.

347. Simon, Julian L. "Unnecessary, Confusing, and Inadequate: The Marginal Analysis as a Tool for Decision Making." *American Economist* 25 (1) (Spring 1981): 28–35.
Article examines the technique of marginal analysis as used in managerial decision making. The major problem with it is that it cannot handle certain business problems easily solved with tables. It is incapable of determining price when pricing has a lagged effect on sales. Also, marginal analysis does not help in price lining. Simultaneously choosing a plant or production method, a price and a promotion policy is another situation where marginal analysis would fall short.

348. Siu, Ralph G. H. "Management and the Art of Chinese Baseball." *Sloan Management Review* 19 (3) (Spring 1978): 83–89.
Subjective and sensed unknowables play a major role for important executive decisions. Everything is continually changing—not only the events themselves but also the rules governing those events. Article explains how decision makers can handle this situation.

349. Smith, August W. "Choosing the Best Decision Making Style for Your Job." *Supervisory Management* 30 (5) (May 1985): 27–33.
Decisions can be sorted by the degree of uncertainty involved and the need for immediate or prolonged attention. Intentions tell what a decision is about and who makes it; interventions explain when it is needed and how it is carried out. The interplay of the two are reflected in decision-making styles in supervisory positions and higher level management.

350. Staats, Wayne L. "Micrographic Systems: Selling Management and Users." *Journal of Micrographics* 13 (3) (January/February 1980): 123–26.
Before making a decision, the presenter should determine current operating procedures, current costs, problems with current systems, possible alternatives, and costs of each alternative. Economic decision-making tools are cash flow (or present value) analysis, return on investment, and payback period required. Other decision-making tools include measuring the problem-solving capability of alternatives, measuring need fulfillment of alternatives, listing other advantages/disadvantages. Using these tools, the proposer recommends a particular alternative which usually requires making some value judgment.

351. Stonich, Paul J., and Zaragoza, Carlos E. "Strategic Funds Programming: The Missing Link in Corporate Planning." *Managerial Planning* 29 (2) (September/October 1980): 3–11.
Discusses Strategic Funds Programming which is a management system designed to help organizations identify potential programs having an impact on the future of the business and then to make decisions about what programs to undertake.

352. Stout, Russell, Jr. "Formal Theory and the Flexible Organization." *Advanced Management Journal* 46 (1) (Winter 1981): 44–52.
Formal theories of management generally have little resemblance to the daily problem in real organizations. Frequently, they only serve to confuse the task of managing, making the structure of an organization too rigid, and ignoring the informal decision-making processes that naturally arise to accommodate the unexpected. An organization that is dominated by formal theory may exercise absolute control within its structure, but it is the kind of control that strangles creativity and reduces the organization's capacity to adapt to change.

353. Sutherland, J. W. *Administrative Decision-Making.* New York: Van Nostrand Reinhold, 1977. 315 p.
Explains the concepts of suboptimality as opposed to optimum benefit, structure of decision responsibilities and accountability, performance measurement, method audits, and value analysis.

354. Swap, Walter C. *Group Decision Making.* Beverly Hills, CA: Sage Publications, 1984. 315 p.
Provides a social-psychological perspective of group decision making. Also studies the destructive effects of groups on individuals, a fair and rational method of voting ethical aspects of group decision making and social risk assessment and group process.

355. Szidarovszky, Ferenc, et al. *Techniques for Multiobjective Decision Making in Systems Management.* New York: Elsevier Science Publishing Co., 1986. 506 p.
Published as a volume in the Advances in Industrial Engineering Series, this book discusses the mathematical concepts involved in handling decision situations when more than one goal is involved.

356. Tainiter, M. *The Art and Science of Decision Making.* New York: Timetable Press, 1971. 81 p.
This book is an introduction to the structure, common features, methods, and criteria for decision making, including basic ideas of probability theory. Contains examples of decision problems and decision-making criteria.

357. Taylor, Derek. "Coping with Change." *Management Today (UK)* (October 1977): 80–83.
A central aspect of strategic planning is to develop an understanding of a company's situation in relation to its environment. Another key task is to identify and make decisions on the problems created by mismatches between the environment and the company's norms and organization.

358. Taylor, R. N. *Behavioral Decision Making.* Glenview, IL: Scott, Foresman & Co., 1984. 254 p.
While there are numerous mathematical aids to decision making, managers still need to take into account the impact of individual and group behavior in an organizational context. This book discusses the types of conflicts which may arise in decision making because of behavioral considerations.

359. Taylor, Ronald N. "Age and Experience as Determinants of Managerial Information Processing and Decision-Making Performance." *Academy of Management Journal* 18 (1) (March 1975): 74–81.
Investigation of differences in managerial decision-making performance due to age and decision-making experience reveals that age influences performance more than it does prior decision-making experience. Little evidence is available to support the notion that older managers are less facile information processors and decision makers.

360. Thiriez, H., and Zionts, S. *Multiple Criteria Decision-Making: Proceedings of a Conference Jouy-en-Josas, France, May 21–23, 1975.* New York: Springer-Verlag, 1976. 409 p.
Discusses current state of the art with respect to theory and practice of multiple criteria decision making. Considers such developments as models, behavioral aspects, and practical applications. Topics concerned include goal setting and linear programming and research and development project selection.

361. Thomas, H. *Decision Theory and the Manager.* London: Pitman, 1972. 137 p.
Discusses the methodology for structuring and analyzing risky or uncertain decision situations. Includes concepts such as "acts" or strategies, "states of nature," "pay-off," and "criterion" for choice.

362. Thornhill, William T. "Management Kiting." *Internal Auditor* 38 (5) (October 1981): 21–29.
Management auditing, as distinguished from financial and operating auditing, has a distinctive but not readily identifiable problem. This is manage-

ment kiting, defined as management manipulation or management of misobjectives. Article explains how, by categorizing management decisions and using a stratified review approach, it is possible to detect types of management kiting, such as taking quick action on a criticism to discourage further reviews, issuing a retroactive policy directive, changing management quickly when deficiencies are identified, avoiding materiality, favoring a particular position, managers acting on the behalf of another, and changing related procedural instructions immediately upon identification of a problem.

363. Tietz, Reinhard, ed. *Aspiration Levels in Bargaining and Economic Decision Making.* New York; Tokyo: Springer-Verlag, 1983. 406 p. Proceedings of the Third Conference on Experimental Economics, Winzenhol, Germany, August 29–September 3, 1982. Published as a volume in the Lecture Notes in Economics, Mathematical Systems and Experimental Economics, this is a collection of papers dealing with mathematical models in game theory, negotiation, and decision making.

364. Trautman, Lawrence J. "The Case for Strategic Planning." *Mortgage Banker* 38 (10) (July 1978): 52–54. Business community's dedication to the concept of strategic planning is growing rapidly. Planning includes isolating major strategic factors that are dominant contributors to a firm's long-term success and stating corporate goals and objectives to help make decisions on an implementation plan. Article explains the application of strategic planning by mortgage bankers.

365. Tregoe, Benjamin B., and Zimmerman, John W. "The New Strategic Manager." *Business* 31 (3) (May/June 1981): 15–19. The strategic manager of the future who will do well will be one whose operational decisions are supported by a clear strategy arrived at through a logical step-by-step process. No longer is decision making just a gut level, intuitive action. Intuitiveness and creativity will be backed by a decision-making methodology. Article explains that the strategic manager must recognize that there are two decision levels—strategic and operational. The first guides the organization's direction, and the latter concerns daily decisions. It is necessary for managers to become conscious of their own decision-making processes. Without a clear understanding of the mental processes involved in decision making, there is a tendency to confuse problem solving with decision making.

366. Tuite, Mathew, et al. *Interorganizational Decision Making.* Chicago: Aldine, 1972. 298 p. Deals with the concept of interorganizational decision making. Provides a framework for solving joint decision problems. Other topics covered include interorganizational decision making in a business context, decision making at the government/business interface, and interorganizational decision making in government.

367. Turner, Samuel H. "How Not to Run a Life Company." *Best's Review (Life/Health)* 78 (6) (October 1977): 94, 96. Life insurance business cannot be managed with the same time perspective one might utilize in running other enterprises. Many decisions must reach far into the future, and other decisions involve risks over which management has little or no control. The key is to identify risks. Affordability depends on the size of the mistake and the resources available to cover it. Some common pitfalls and mistakes are identified.

368. Ungson, Gerardo Rivera, and Braunstein, Daniel N. *Decision Making.* Boston: Kent Publishing Co., 1982. 376 p.
Based on a conference on "New Directions in Decision Making: An Interdisciplinary Approach to the Study of Organizations," sponsored by the Office of Naval Research and the Graduate School of Management, University of Oregon, held at Eugene, Oregon, March 1–3, 1981. Papers provide an interdisciplinary inquiry into decision making. Topics covered include behavioral decision theory, human problem solving, organizational decision making, and applications of information processsing and decision-making research.

369. Ungson, Gerardo Rivera; Braunstein, Daniel N.; and Hall, Phillip D. "Managerial Information Processing: A Research Review." *Administrative Science Quarterly* 26 (1) (March 1981): 116–34.
Recent research attempts to elaborate on the types of cognitive processes used by individuals, particularly how these processes apply to decision-making behavior in organizations. An examination is made of the various mainstreams in information-processing research as they relate to cognitive processes. There are three issues pertinent to managerial information processing: how problems in managerial decision-making contexts can be described, the types of cognitive processes used in these decision-making contexts, and the research problems and direction that need to be addressed in order to improve the understanding of and training for decision making in organizations.

370. Van de Ven, Andrew H. *Group Decision Making and Effectiveness.* Kent, OH: Kent State University Press, 1974. 110 p.
Presents value judgment procedures and limitations inherent in an experimental comparison of group decision-making techniques. Also calls attention to and demonstrates the application of important new methodological procedures that enable researchers to properly apply classical hypothesis-testing methodology for making decisions. Explains the application of the nominal group technique in a wide variety of public and private organizational settings and of the Delphi technique for group decision making.

371. Verderber, R. F. *Working Together: Fundamentals of Group Decision Making.* Belmont, CA: Wadsworth, 1982. 194 p.
Introductory text dealing with the behavior of individuals and groups in an organizational context and their impact on decision making.

372. Verge, Robert W. "Accounting: A Language out of the Mainstream." *CA Magazine (Canada)* 118 (6) (June 1985): 46–49.
There are several problems with using accounting data for decision making. First, accounting has a historical perspective, while business is dynamic. In addition, access to capital is viewed as the major limiting factor for a business, but in the future, access to information will be the major factor. Moreover, by the use of numbers, accounting is thought to be objective and verifiable; however, numbers can be manipulated to obtain desired results. Finally, accounting rules and procedures are slow to respond to change.

373. Vira, Chankong. *Multiobjective Decision Making.* Amsterdam, Holland; New York: North-Holland, 1983. 406 p.
Deals with situations when there is more than one goal for the corporation to be achieved at the same time. How it can be achieved without sacrific-

ing the corporate purpose is discussed in this book with the help of mathematical models.

374. Vogel, Ezra F. *Modern Japanese Organization and Decision Making.* Berkeley: University of California Press, 1975. 340 p.
Papers presented at a conference held January 5–10, 1973, at Maui, sponsored by the Joint Committee on Japanese studies of the American Council of Learned Societies and Social Science Research Council. It examines the economic organization of Japanese internal and multinational business enterprises and its impact on managerial decision making in Japan. The book also delves into western concepts of Japanese organizations and examines how closely they conform to reality.

375. Vroom, Victor Harold, and Yetton, Philip W. *Leadership and Decision Making.* Pittsburgh, PA: University of Pittsburgh Press, 1973. 233 p.
Deals with situational factors that influence managers to adopt one leadership style versus another in their decision making. Develops a normative model of leadership styles. Also covers the importance of participation in decision making.

376. Wakin, Eleanor. "Attribute Listing: Cutting Problems down to Size." *Today's Office* 19 (11) (April 1985): 20.
Attribute listing is a problem-solving technique that can help give managers an objective view of the situation and show ways to a decision resolution. It works best in areas that need improvement, modification, or updating, rather than those that require total redesign, and can be used by managers either singly or in groups.

377. Wallsten, S. T. *Cognitive Processes in Choice and Decision Behavior.* Hillsdale, NJ: Erlbaum Associates, 1980. 285 p.
The book deals with the process of learning from experience and suboptimal rules in decision making. It discusses the external validity of decision-making research. Other topics include decisions that might not get made, analyzing decision behavior, the use of probabilistic information for making decisions, information processing theory, measuring values, and a study of risk.

378. Wanner, C. *Managerial Decision Making.* New York: Irvington, 1983. 95 p.
Provides an introduction to the process of decision making in a firm. Covers goal setting, data collection, forecasting, simulation, choosing among alternatives, and decision implementation.

379. Warren, Ben H. "Constant Values in a Changing World." *Vital Speeches* 46 (6) (January 1, 1980): 183–87.
Businesses have to be concerned with ethics, which affects management decisions in many ways. It is essential to the free enterprise system that business face ethical questions head on. Businesses also have a great deal of power to create ethical norms, but they also have an awesome responsibility. Businesses must be aware that profit alone is no longer justification for the free enterprise system.

380. Weiss, W. H. "Cutting down the Risks in Decision-Making." *Supervisory Management* 30 (5) (May 1985): 14–16.
Decision making entails risks. Article suggests some tests which can help predict how great the impact may be if the outcome is favorable.

381. Weiss, W. H. *Decision Making for First-Time Managers.* New York: AMACOM, 1985. 179 p.
Comprehensive guide which stresses the notion that decision making is a supervisory responsibility, explains what is involved in delegating responsibility, and recommends when a decision should not be made. Also analyzed are the factors that influence decisions, deterrents and hindrances to decision making, communication (which is a key to making decisions), analysis procedures in making a choice, and, finally, implementing the decision and following up.

382. Weisselberg, Robert C., and Cowley, Joseph G. *The Executive Strategist; An Armchair Guide to Scientific Decision-Making.* New York: McGraw-Hill, 1969. 249 p.
A successful executive is one who is said to be not afraid to make a decision. But this ignores "time" discussion in decision making because the decision process starts long before and continues long after the instant of choice. Decision making is not simply a matter of "go or no go" action. This work expands on this idea and explains the concepts and terminology of decision theory, statistical analysis, sampling, probability, network analysis, queueing, Monte Carlo simulation, and the application of all these techniques to real business problems.

383. Wellens, John. "Training: The Choices Ahead." *Industrial and Commercial Training (UK)* 11 (7) (July 1979): 273–77.
It is necessary to make the distinction between the two aspects of management policy formation and policy execution. How much influence executives should have over the policy-forming process is debatable. However, if a system is to be accountable, executives must be free, within the boundaries determined by the policy formation process, to determine their own means of achieving policy objectives. Interference with executive management risks destroying accountability.

384. Werther, William B., Jr. "Quality Circles: Key Executive Issues." *Journal of Contemporary Business* 11 (2) (1982): 17–26.
A quality circle is a group of employees and their supervisor who voluntarily meet to solve work-related problems affecting performance. It is a commitment on the part of management to increase employee involvement. Article discusses how quality circles help in group decision-making situations.

385. Wheeler, Daniel D., and Janis, Irving Lester. *A Practical Guide for Making Decisions.* New York: Free Press, 1980. 276 p.
Step-by-step analysis of each individual process involved in organizational decision making, including goal setting and evaluation of alternatives.

386. White, Douglas John. *Decision Methodology: A Formalization of the OR Process.* New York: Wiley, 1975. 274 p.
Deals with the general origin and nature of decision analysis with reference to system components, technical content, and analysis procedures. Also covers the phases of decision analysis, namely, formulating the problem, constructing the model, and deriving the solution. Testing and controlling the solutions and models have been included as part of model construction reflecting the fact that modeling is an ongoing process, and testing and controlling are integral parts of modeling.

387. White, Douglas John. *Decision Theory.* Chicago: Aldine, 1969. 185 p.
Presents results of a research project which ascertains the content of decision theory. Topics include theories of choice, value, and uncertainty; decidability; practical considerations in decision analysis; information for decision; pragmatic aspects of decision theory; and mathematical models and decisions.

388. Wiest, J. D. "Heuristic Programs for Decision Making." *Harvard Business Review* 44 (September/October 1966): 129–43.
Considers the role of heuristic programs in decision making with examples from chess playing, inventory control, engineering design, and scheduling. Also considers their role in management.

389. Wilcox, Jarrod W. *A Method for Measuring Decision Assumptions.* Cambridge, MA: MIT Press, 1972. 252 p.
Assumptions are a necessary part of any decision-making activity, even though enough information is available relating to the decision situation. The book discusses some mathematical models that will help evaluate the validity of these assumptions.

390. Wild, Ray. "Decision-Making in Operations Management." *Management Decision (UK)* 21 (1) (1983): 9–21.
While much of the literature about operations management concerns a form of decision making and the solving of particular problems, little attention has been given to the broader decision-making process. Article discusses the formulation of overall strategies for operations, then making decisions in pursuit of those strategies, all within the wider context of business. Operations management decision making is viewed as a process in which outcomes are influenced by feasibility, desirability, and preference factors.

391. Wild, Ray. "Survey Report: The Responsibilities and Activities of UK Production Managers." *International Journal of Operations and Production Management (UK)* 4 (1) (1984): 69–74.
A small and simple questionnaire survey of UK production managers was conducted in 1983 for the purpose of collecting information to aid in curriculum design. Data were obtained from production managers employed in manufacturing. It was found that production managers contribute substantially to their organizations' decisions on the use of plant and facilities and upon the nature and control of production work.

392. Williams, K. *Dynamic Programming: Sequential Decision-Making.* London: Longman, 1970. 64 p.
Explains techniques applicable to solving certain types of sequential decision problems. Analyzes how to establish a procedure for determining the set of sequential decisions which optimize some measure of value in situations where each decision affects future decisions by changing the sequence of situations.

393. Williams, R. E. *Anatomy of the Creative Decision.* Kent, OH: Kent State University Press, 1966. 35 p.
Deals with information, goal setting, evaluation of alternatives, forecasting, decision implementation, and evaluation. Analyzes how creative decisions can be achieved.

394. Wright, G. *Behavioral Decision Theory.* Beverly Hills, CA: Sage Publications, 1984. 129 p.
Discusses the theories and the impact of individual and group behavior on organizational decision making. Analyzes characteristics of individual and group preferences and conflicts and their ways to deal with them.

395. Wright, Norman B. "Leadership Styles: Which Are Best When?" *Business Quarterly (Canada) 49* (4) (Winter 1984/1985): 20–23.
Effective leadership style depends upon the individual situation. Article describes the similarities and differences of five leadership styles whose components include adequate information, commitment, goal congruences, and conflict over alternatives. By combining the variables applicable to a situation, a flowchart can be used to determine which of the five leadership styles might be appropriate. This method of choosing leadership style helps to determine who, how, and when to involve others in a decision.

396. Young, Stanley. *Management: A Decision-Making Approach.* Belmont, CA: Dickenson Publishing Co., 1968. 146 p.
Collection of articles which attempt to analyze managerial decision making from an interdisciplinary point of view. Topics covered include studies and theories of decision making, deliberation and foreknowledge, using brains, organizational creativity, quest for subjective certainty in decision making, and ethics of rational decision making.

397. Yukl, Gary A. *Leadership in Organizations.* Englewood Cliffs, NJ: Prentice-Hall, 1981. 278 p.
An important study devoted to participatory decision-making process. Covers the well-known Vroom and Yetton model of decision participation. Among other things, the book examines the concept of leadership in decision-making groups, including such ideas as determinants of effective group decisions, leadership functions in decision groups, role of conference leader, leader facilitation of group problem solving, procedures for increasing idea generation, and leader facilitation of group decision.

398. Ziegler, Raymond J. *Business Policies and Decision Making.* New York: Appleton, 1966. 260 p.
Policy formulation is an aid to the business manager in guiding the company, promoting its objectives, and making decisions. It enables the executive to plan and determine objectives. This book contains actual case studies of how policy information and managerial decision making are interrelated.

399. Ziontis, Stanley. "MCDM—If Not a Roman Numeral, Then What?" *Interfaces 9* (4) (August 1979): 94–101.
MCDM stands for multiple criteria decision making, which is problem solving with multiple conflicting objectives. Although managers perform MCDM all of the time, most of the work done on multicriteria problem solving is incomprehensible to managers. Three assumptions usually made in management decision making are that there is a fixed set of alternatives from which one alternative is to be chosen, that there is a decision maker who knows the alternatives and chooses one, and that the alternative selected is in some sense optimal or best. MCDM methods have been helpful in capital budgeting, in planning, and in corporate strategy.

Applications

400. Aggarwal, Raj, and Khera, Inder. "Using Management Science Models: A Critique for Planners." *Managerial Planning* 28 (4) (January/February 1980): 12–15, 19.
Scientific techniques are applied to decision making in the business world. Management models help management to optimize their use of available resources. Models may be descriptive and used for explaining or predicting, or they may be decision models to help evaluate expected outcomes. Management science models have limits to their usefulness. Managers must decide how, when, and where to apply such models and how to modify the results to correct for some assumptions.

401. Agor, Weston H. "Using Intuition to Improve State Government Productivity." *State Government* 57 (4) (1984): 125–28.
Gives the result of a major field study conducted of over 2,000 managers in both the public and private sectors across the U.S. to determine managers' ability to use intuition. Results showed that there is a great deal of variance in that ability and that intuition is more prevalent as one moves up the management ladder.

402. Allen, George R. "Liberty, Equality and Anxiety as Worker-Run IGP." *Business & Society Review* (24) (Winter 1977–78): 43–46.
In 1969, J. Gibbons became the sole owner of International Group Plans (IGP), a holding company with four separate corporations. A management decision was made to establish two goals: to help satisfy the needs of clients and to build an institution which maximizes the "humanness" of everyone involved. How this may be done is examined in this article.

403. *Applied Decision Analysis and Economic Behaviour.* Dordrecht, Holland: Nijhoff, 1984. 331 p.
Deals with econometric models in decision making. Concepts analyzed include expectations, uncertainty, policy analysis and decision models, market management, and decentralization and multisector planning.

404. Arnold, John. *Pricing and Output Decisions.* London: Accountancy Age Books, 1973. 181 p.
Practice in managerial accounting has changed dramatically during the last twenty years. Traditional accounting methods of cost analysis for decision purposes have had to be adapted to new procedures. A primary influence has, perhaps, been that of the operational researcher, who studies business problems by developing mathematical models that describe the relationships between the relevant variables. The book is intended to help accountants learn and use those techniques.

405. Arrow, Kenneth J. *Social Choice and Multicriterion Decision-Making.* Cambridge, MA: MIT Press, 1986. 124 p.
This study comes to grips with industrial outranking problems: given a large but infinite set of criteria and a large but finite number of alternatives, how can the criteria be ranked in priority order, and how should the alternatives be ranked from best to worst consistent with the ordering of criteria that may be conflicting or incommensurable? There have been many proposed solutions to the problem. Numerous empirical recipes, among them the majority method, have been submitted, based in large part on the subjective judgments and biases of various observers. In this book it is argued that the axiomatic formulation offers the surest path to a solution that is as objective as possible, minimally distorted by the unwitting.

406. Atkinson, Anthony A. "Standard Setting in an Agency." *Management Science* 24 (13) (September 1978): 1351–61.
The decision to hire an agent (manager) to transact business on the principal's behalf reflects (and results) in the agent's use of specialized skills and information in managing the agency's activities. Considered here is a relationship where the principal and the agent have differing beliefs regarding the uncertain economic returns to the agency. Article discusses how to deal with this situation.

407. Baccour, Abdelmajid. "Product Deletion Decisions: A Systematic Approach and An Empirical Analysis." Ph.D. dissertation, University of Illinois at Urbana-Champaign, 1971. 226 p.
Empirical study of the decision processes used by corporations relating to how and when to abandon existing products.

408. Baker, Alan J. *Business Decision Making.* New York: St. Martin's Press, 1981. 266 p.
Explains the quantitative concepts and applications of decision making including probability, decision theories, linear programming, acquiring and valuing information, capital structure and cost of capital, aspects of capital budgeting, and capital market theory.

409. Baker, H. Kent, and Pettit, Glenn. "Management's View of Stock Exchange Listing." *Akron Business & Economic Review* 13 (4) (Winter 1982): 12–17.
Each year many financial managers must decide whether their companies should opt to list their common stock. This study examined management perceptions in an attempt to ascertain the motivations held by management for listing and why companies that are qualified for listing have chosen not to list.

410. Ballassie, Eugene G. "Planning Must Begin with Marketing Opportunities." *Managerial Planning* 22 (2) (September/October 1973): 21–25.
It is very difficult bringing new products to new markets. As in most business-oriented activities, it is the caliber of the men and women involved that outweigh all other inputs in importance. These people must establish whether a valid marketing opportunity truly exists. They must identify the characteristics of this marketing opportunity, and they must be able to make the decision based upon business judgment as to whether this opportunity should be pursued.

411. Ballot, Michael. *Decision-Making Models in Production and Operations Management.* Malabar, FL: R. E. Krieger, 1986. 294 p.
Introduction to applications of qualitative models for solving production and operations management problems. Topics include cost-profit-value analysis, capital budgeting, decision trees, pay-off matrices, simulation techniques, resource allocation by linear programming techniques, forecasting, scheduling, and inventory management.

412. Barish, Norman N. *Economic Analysis for Engineering and Managerial Decision-Making.* New York: McGraw-Hill, 1962. 729 p.
A textbook covering the fundamental material on project and equipment evaluation traditionally included in courses in engineering economy, this book contains the traditional material on decision making under certainty to minimum-cost and maximum-profit determinations, the managerial economic problems of capital budgeting, risk, uncertainty and intangibles in economic analysis, and elements of economic measurement and analysis and the managerial economic problems of forecasting sales, costs, and profits. Applications include the costs of operating an enterprise, interest and the time value of money, depreciation, profits, interest, and return on investment, income taxes, annual-cost comparisons, present-worth and premium-worth comparisons, determination of rate of return and investment, and theory of planning.

413. Barket, Kenneth J., and Coggins, Patrick E. "Attitudes of Foremen in the Petroleum and Automotive Industries." *Sloan Management Review* 16 (1) (Fall 1974): 57–68.
In studies of both petroleum and automotive foremen, communication was the primary source of dissatisfaction. In both industries, the foremen expressed concern that their input into management decisions was less than what they thought it should be. In general, the foremen were satisfied with the relationship they had with immediate supervisors. In the case of the automobile industry, the respondents felt that the prestige and importance of the foreman's job were deteriorating over time. The more serious dissatisfactions occurred when foremen found their decisions on discipline reversed by management without prior consultation with them. Article suggests how to deal with these problems.

414. Basil, Douglas Constantine, and Cone, Paul R. *Executive Decision-Making through Simulation; A Case Study and Simulation of Corporate Strategy in the Rubber Industry.* Columbus, OH: Charles E. Merrill Publishing Co., 1965. 213 p.
Designed to give readers the opportunity to develop decision-making skills and an awareness of the interrelationship of the functional fields which constitute the administration. Aims to illustrate the dynamic interplay in the management of internal resources of the firm, taking into consideration the effect of external environment and the actions of the competitors. The functional fields mentioned above include marketing, production, and finance.

415. Batstone, Eric. "What Have Personnel Managers Done for Industrial Relations?" *Personnel Management (UK)* 12 (6) (June 1980): 36–39.
Gives the results of a British survey which indicates personnel managers have formalized and centralized industrial relations procedures and decision making but have not influenced the content.

416. Beckman, Martin J. *Dynamic Programming of Economic Decisions.* New York: Springer-Verlag, 1968. 143 p.
Basic idea of dynamic programming as applied to economic analysis, operations research, and decisions in general are illustrated. Topics include discrete and continuous sequences and decision variables; certainty, risk, and uncertainty; and applications to automobile replacement, inventory control, adaptive programming, machine care, and the maximum principle.

417. Behn, Robert D., and Vaupel, James W. *Quick Analysis for Busy Decision Makers.* New York: Basic Books, 1982. 403 p.
An excellent introduction to the concepts of analytical thinking. Deals with uncertainty as a double-risk situation, analyzing range-of-risks, conflicting consequences, and trade-offs. Actual applications are also presented.

418. Bell, Peter. "How to Cope with Uncertainty." *Management Today (UK)* (April 1978): 66–69, 126.
The following rules constitute good practice in handling uncertain information and can improve managerial performance: managers should be comfortable making decisions with less than perfect data. How well managers perform depends not only on how good they are at making decisions, but also on how well they cope with uncertainty of information or performance. Managers must develop a management approach that takes into account the uncertainties surrounding each decision. Managers can minimize the uncertainties of the future through forecasting. The company's day-to-day existence depends on the routine generation of forecast information.

419. Bennett, E. D., et al. *Administrative Policy: Cases in Managerial Decision Making.* 2d ed. Columbus, OH: Charles E. Merrill Publishing Co., 1974. 766 p.
Case studies relating to decision-making situations in areas like personnel, management development, administrative services, and system and information management.

420. Bennett, E. D.; Brandt, Floyd S.; and Klasson, Charles R. *Business Policy: Cases in Managerial Decision Making.* Columbus, OH: Charles E. Merrill Publishing Co., 1970. 757 p.
A book of case studies relating to the major decision problems confronting management. Cases are oriented toward the development of competitive and administrative policies and their implementation, related, or operational problems, leading to the reappraisal of operational policies.

421. Bently, Trevor. "Who Controls Costs?" *Management Accounting (UK)* 56 (5) (May 1978): 195–97.
To find out who controls costs in any organization requires a detailed analysis of costs and the activities of the business. Cost control means the prevention of waste. People cause waste of time, materials, and energy. Responsibility must be delegated to individuals who are in a position to make decisions to prevent waste. One of the biggest problems in the control of equipment utilization is the gap between the level where the decision is made and the user. Accounting for these costs requires an approach based primarily on common sense and understood by all involved. There should be a sound system for recording information on the use of resources and providing information on how costs change.

422. Bicksler, James L., and Samuelson, Paul A. *Investment Portfolio Decision Making.* Lexington, MA: Lexington Books, 1974. 368 p.
Discusses the theory of portfolio choice and capital market behavior. Other topics include uncertainty and indifference curves, risk, ambiguity, risk aversion, portfolio choice framework, and the accumulation of risky capital.

423. Biddle, Gary C. "Accounting Methods and Management Decisions: The Case of Inventory Costing and Inventory Policy." *Journal of Accounting Research* 18 (Supplement) (1980): 235–80.
A choice among inventory costing methods, especially between the last-in/first-out (LIFO) and the first-in/first-out (FIFO) cost-flow assumptions, can generate potentially large changes in a firm's cash flow due to its impact on taxable earnings. These cash flows depend, in part, on the levels of year-end inventories. Article gives the results of a study which found, that while generally insignificant preadoption date differences were found between firms that adopted LIFO and those that did not, there were significant differences in the postadoption periods.

424. Binder, Hamlyn Fry and Co. *Forecasts for Decision-Making.* London: 1977. 110 p.
Deals with forecasting techniques needed for decision makers. Areas covered include sales targets, budgets, prices, production capacity, capital investment, and stock levels.

425. Blanning, Robert. W. "How Managers Decide to Use Planning Models." *Long Range Planning (UK)* 13 (2) (April 1980): 32–35.
An increasing number of corporations are using decision models for lower level scheduling and resource allocation. In addition, they are using such models for short-range and long-range planning. However, the literature has not paid much attention to the way in which managers decide whether to use these models. An examination, through case studies, suggests that the decision to use planning models is made by the use of a reference model rather than by performing a comprehensive cost-benefit analysis.

426. Bonczek, Robert H.; Holsapple, Clyde W.; and Whinston, Andrew B. "Aiding Decision Makers with a Generalized Data Base Management System: An Application to Inventory Management." *Decision Sciences* 9 (2) (April 1978): 228–45.
Examines the attributes of a generalized database management system with respect to the impact that it has on managerial decision making. The discussion focuses on two primary considerations: the organization of data within a database such that all intricate relationships are respected and the utilization of a facile method for nonprogramming users to interrogate the database. Examples are cited from the field of material requirements planning, and they are used to illustrate the concepts and potential of the generalized database management system.

427. Borch, Karl Henrik, and Massin, Jan, eds. *Risk and Uncertainty: Proceedings of a Conference Held by the International Economic Association.* Conference on Risk and Uncertainty, Smolenice, Czechoslovak Republic, 1966. London; Melbourne, Australia: Macmillan; New York: St. Martin's Press, 1968. 455 p.
The conference papers cover topics such as economic decision under uncertainty, measuring the perception of risk, investment behavior with

utility, a concave function of wealth, uncertainty and the communication of information, questions in statistical decision theory, binary decisions, programs for human decision making, group decisions and market mechanisms, and sequential decision problems.

428. Brandt, William K., and Hulbert, James J. "Headquarters Guidance in Marketing Strategy in the Multinational Subsidiary. *Columbia Journal of World Business* 12 (4) (Winter 1977): 7–14.
Managing a multinational enterprise to achieve corporative objectives requires some integration and cohesion among foreign subsidiaries. Two patterns of control of market decisions are employed by headquarters: a hierarchical authority which limits the autonomy of subsidiary management, and an integration of global activities through standardized marketing strategies. This study concentrated on the role of the home office as perceived by subsidiary management.

429. Brewer, Garry D. *An Analyst's View of the Uses and Abuses of Modeling for Decision Making.* Santa Monica, CA: Rand Corp., 1975. 26 p.
Paper dealing with mathematical concepts involved in construction of decision models. Also talks about their likely applications.

430. Bridge, John. *Managerial Decision Making.* New York: Wiley, 1975. 309 p.
Deals with the concepts in economic theory as applied to the firm and managerial decisions. Covers imperfections in knowledge, production functions and linear programming, cost analysis, demand analysis, market structure, and pricing and investment decisions.

431. Brockett, Patrick L.; Cox, Samuel H., Jr.; and Witt, Robert C. "Self-Insurance and the Probability of Financial Regret." *Journal of Risk Insurance* 51 (4) (December 1984): 720–29.
The decision of whether a firm should self-insure a group of exposure units is a complex but very important one. Risk management decisions are similar to other financial decisions, but the main focus of risk management is on pure, rather than speculative, risk. Article uses a statistical framework to analyze the probability of financial regret in the decision to self-insure.

432. Brown, Robert Goodell. *Decision Rules for Inventory Management.* New York: Holt, Rinehart & Winston, 1967. 398 p.
Applies economic order quantity concept to the problem of inventory control. Topics include demand and forecast of sales, quantity discounts, shipping costs, shop scheduling, and other factors in inventory control.

433. Brown, Robert Goodell. *Management Decision for Production Operations.* Hinsdale, IL: Dryden Press, 1971. 683 p.
Planning for production operations is a complicated task. This book on industrial management and production control discusses certain decision-making techniques in this area.

434. Burr, Pat L., and Heckman, Richard J. "Why So Many Small Businesses Flop and Some Succeed." *Across the Board* 16 (2) (February 1979): 46–48.
The major cause of failure is believed to be a general lack of management ability and a lack of experience and training. New business owners tend to make potentially fatal decisions in the areas of site selection, relationships with financial sources, budgeting for the first months of business operation,

extending long-term credit to buyers, creating a cash flow problem, and investing in long-term commitments and acquisitions, further draining the cash flow.

435. Byrne, R. F., et al. *Studies in Budgeting: Budgeting Interrelated Activities—2.* New York: American Elsevier, 1971. 392 p.
Collection of nine papers dealing with topics like capital budgeting under risk, a chance-constrained approach to capital budgeting, the payback period and capital budgeting decisions, and an empirical study of the congressional approach.

436. Calantone, Roger, and Darmon, Rene. "Sales Force Decisions: A Markovian Approach." *Journal of the Academy of Marketing Science* 12 (4) (Fall 1984): 124–44.
The use of a Markov model for macro-salesforce planning and control is described. The model depicts the succession of levels of salesforce members from application to all possible outcomes, including firing, voluntary departure, and promotion. The effects of several decision states, including recruiting, training, and promotion, are then evaluated, and the implications are assessed through the use of data from two large pharmaceutical firms.

437. Canada, John R. *Capital Investment Decision Analysis for Management and Engineering.* Englewood Cliffs, NJ: Prentice-Hall, 1980. 528 p.
In addition to covering the basic principles of interest computations and basic analysis methods, this book extensively treats techniques for the quantitative analysis of investment problems involving risk and uncertainty. Includes discussions of quantitative techniques, particularly mathematical programming for handling capital budgeting problems, sensitivity and risk analysis techniques, and basic capital project evaluation techniques.

438. Cane, Paul R., et al. *Executive Decision Making through Simulation.* 2d ed. Columbus, OH: Charles E. Merrill Publilshing Co., 1971. 264 p.
Presents industry and company case studies, a computer-based simulation management game, and a behavioral lab. The various topics consist of elements of strategy, learning through case study and simulation, the industry and its environment, company cases, and the simulation and decision forms. Decisions are of three major types: repetitive year-by-year decisions involving both long-range and short-run planning, repetitive quarter-by-quarter decisions involving the planning of the next quarter's operation, and nonrepetitive decisions to meet unusual situations such as strikes, fire or accident, antitrust actions, recall of tires, pollution control, and so on.

439. Cannon, Tom. "New Product Development." *European Journal of Marketing (UK)* 12 (3) (1978): 215–48.
There are many aspects to a decision to develop a new product. Launching a new product represents the final stage in the long process of product development and innovation. Article examines decision making in this process.

440. Capettini, Robert Joseph. "Some Social Influence Variables Affecting the Internal Allocation of Capital Resources." Ph.D. dissertation, University of Illinois at Urbana-Champaign, 1975. 115 p.
Relates the impact of social factors on corporate decision making in the area of resource allocation.

441. Carson, D. "Political Factors as Managerial Decision Elements in Formulating Multinational Strategies." *Management International Review (Germany)* 19 (1) (1979): 71–79.
A general strategy was developed for managers of multinational corporations in dealing with rapidly changing political situations. The strategy, which was developed from an analysis of forty-one sub-Saharan countries in Africa, involves the analysis of key characteristics of a country to see if investment in the country would be profitable.

442. Catt, C. C., and Rivett, D. W. "Fixed Asset Prices and Economic Production Theory." *Abacus (Australia)* 15 (2) (December 1979): 128–35.
A key consideration in the controversy over alternate asset valuation methods is their relevance to management decisions. Barton has argued that the current cost of assets owned by a firm is essential information for business decisions on operating efficiency. However, a model is developed here which is based on the economic theory of production. This theory defines long-run production plans in terms of establishing utilization of fixed and variable inputs of production and short-run plans which define utilization rates.

443. Chambers, John Carlton; Mullick, Satinder K; and Smith, Donald D. *An Executive's Guide to Forecasting.* New York: Wiley, 1974. 308 p.
Explains the strategic importance of forecasting in decision making and the manager-analyst's roles in forecasting. Also covers topics such as decision making during the product life cycle, product testing, tracking and warning, inventions, innovations, and forecast management.

444. Chapman, Christopher. *Modular Decision Analysis: An Introduction in the Context of a Theoretical Basis for Consumer Demand Analysis.* Farnborough, Hants, England: Saxon House, 1975. 292 p.
Discusses mathematical models in marketing relating to the analysis of product demand by consumers.

445. Childress, Robert L. "Optimal Planning—The Use of Sales Forecasts." *Decision Sciences* 4 (2) (April 1973): 164–72.
Budgets are established and decisions in a firm are made on the basis of the sales-forecast. In the majority of firms this forecast is a single-value estimate of sales. The decisions made on the basis of the single-value estimate frequently fall short of optimal strategies because of costs that occur when actual sales differ from forecast sales. These costs, measured in terms of opportunity losses, can be minimized when considered in conjunction with a probability distribution of sales. Three methods for determining the probability distribution of sales are considered in this paper. These are regression-analysis, Schlaifer's approach for establishing a subjective distribution, and Bayesian regression. The use of the distribution in conjunction with linear and quadratic loss functions is illustrated.

446. Clarkson, Geoffrey P. E., ed. *Managerial Economics: Selected Readings.* Harmondsworth, England: Penguin, 1968. 429 p.
These readings relate to the various theories of managerial decision process whose objective is to maximize net revenue and utility. Topics covered include utility, conflict, bargaining, uncertainty, and heuristic programming. Applications include corporate diversification, brand loyalty, and capital budgeting.

447. Clough, D. J. *Decision in Public and Private Sectors: Theories, Practices and Processes.* Englewood Cliffs, NJ: Prentice-Hall, 1984. 366 p.
A comparative study of how managers make decisions in industry as well as in governmental organizations.

448. Cohan, A. B. *Financial Decision Making—Theory and Practice.* Englewood Cliffs, NJ: Prentice-Hall, 1971. 546 p.
Techniques that help management analyze financial decisions are discussed here. The topics covered include risk and rates of return, present value, investing in liquidity, cash cycle, investing in accounts receivable and inventory, source of funds and cost of capital, and leverage.

449. Cohen, Kalman J., and Cyert, Richard M. *Theory of the Firm: Resource Allocation in a Market Economy.* Englewood Cliffs, NJ: Prentice-Hall, 1965. 406 p.
This book explains in great detail the decision-making process of firms in a variety of market structures. It also explains the role of firms in the resource allocation process.

450. "Computer-Aided Managers Make Better Decisions in Marketing Wars." *Marketing News* 15 (11 Section 2) (November 27, 1981): 5.
Decision support systems can connect various business areas by linking databases, communication facilities, and software. Decision support systems should include decision models, sets of numerical procedures for processing data, and judgments to assist managerial decision making. A decision model is created by testing assumptions. The model can aid in identifying product weaknesses, competitive pressure, and marketing opportunities. Areas in which decision models are valuable include development of a market portfolio, new product development, media budget allocation and selection, and the stochastic brand choice model.

451. Cooley, Philip L., and Roenfeldt, Rodney L. "Decision Evaluation for Owner Wealth." *Business Horizons* 17 (4) (August 1974): 67–72.
This framework for evaluating managerial decisions from the owner's viewpoint uses capital market theory concepts. Each decision is viewed according to its effect on return and risk. One solution of the return-on-investment method of assessing decisions is the adoption of the wealth maximization objective. Achievement of this objective necessarily requires a trade-off between risk and return. Managers may incorporate considerations of risk and return into their thinking by making decisions which result in greatest capitalized cash flows.

452. Cooper, Cary, and Hatfield, John. "Risk-Takers of the World." *Management Today (UK)* (November 1984): 86–88, 164.
The results of a 1983 survey of management's risk-taking attitudes were analyzed by the University of Manchester Regional Computer Centre. The

data showed a more optimistic approach to risk taking, particularly in the UK, Italy, and Australia/New Zealand. The survey also revealed that the most important factor in preventing risk taking is a depressed market, but that the availability of capital and rewards for success are more important in finally taking that risk.

453. Coppinger, Richard J., and Epley, E. Stewart. "The Non-Use of Advanced Mathematical Techniques." *Managerial Planning* 20 (6) (May/June 1972): 12–15.

American businesspeople as a whole are not using the newer, more sophisticated math techniques for planning and decision making to any great extent. Results of a survey show that 83 percent of firms use discount-cash-flow (DCF), 45 percent use multiple-regression analysis, 44 percent use simulation, and 33 percent use linear-programming. Other methods are used much less.

454. Cornell, Richard D. "The Age of Entrepreneurialism—What It Means to You." *Supervisory Management* 30 (1) (January 1985): 22–24.

Entrepreneurship implies the freedom to take a calculated risk in decision making. Entrepreneurship is emerging in the corporate world under the title of "intrapreneurship," which is the creation of an entrepreneurial climate within a large, complex organization.

455. Cottle, Rex L.; Macaulay, Hugh H.; and Yandle, T. Bruce. "Codetermination: Union Style." *Journal of Labor Research* 4 (2) (Spring 1983): 125–35.

"Union codetermination" means that the right to make decisions affecting capital is shifted from capitalists to labor. Article discusses this aspect of decision making.

456. Cox, Connie A. "Gap Analysis: A New Business Planning Essential." *Business Marketing* 68 (5) (May 1983): 70, 72, 73.

Gap analysis is a simple planning approach used to search for a gap in a market that no other product or service adequately fills. It helps marketing decisions by providing the transition of a good idea into a successful business opportunity. Article discusses the technique.

457. Crain, W. Mark; Shugart, William F., II; and Tollison, Robert D. "The Convergence of Satisficing to Marginalism: An Empirical Test." *Journal of Economic Behavior & Organization (Netherlands)* 5 (3) (September/December 1984): 375–85.

Richard Day (1967) formulated a simple learning model in which the traditional profit maximization result expected from equating revenue and cost at the margin emerges from "satisficing" behavior. Article attempts to determine whether Day's rules describe actual decision making in the economy. Day's behavioral learning model is found to characterize a significant proportion of managerial decision making, but no simple link exists between adherence to such a strategy and the market for managerial services. Overall, however, Day's claim that "satisficing" and marginalism may be coincidental in actual decision making holds true in most cases.

458. Cronbach, Lee Joseph, and Gleser, Goldine C. *Psychological Tests and Personnel Decisions.* 2d ed. Urbana, IL: University of Illinois Press, 1965. 347 p.

The book deals with the following topics: types of personnel decisions, characteristics of decision problems, selection decisions with single-stage testing, placement decisions, two-stage sequential selection, efficient testing procedures, the bandwidth fidelity dilemma, classification decisions, a dollar criterion in fixed-treatment employee selection, and teaching a digital computer to assist in making decisons.

459. Curley, Douglas G. "Employee Sounding Boards: Answering the Participative Need." *Personnel Administrator* 23 (5) (May 1978): 69–73.
Enlightened management in today's firms have recognized their responsibilities to individual employees' desires to express their opinions concerning decisions affecting them on the job, under increasing nonunion modes of operation. Appropriate forms of employee participation are continually being sought by management. The two-way communication program at General Electric's Appliance Park-East was very effective in establishing management's willingness to hear employee opinions. Article describes the process.

460. Darden, William R., and Lamone, Rudolph P. *Marketing Management and the Decision Sciences: Theory and Applications.* Boston: Allyn & Bacon, 1971. 576 p.
Deals with the content and scope of the decision sciences in marketing; the management science and marketing; tools and techniques such as marketing models and simulation; Bayesian statistics; analysis of variance multiple regression analysis; discriminant analysis of audience characteristics; factor analysis; numerical taxonomy; and canonical analysis. Also covers techniques for quantitative analysis of consumers such as estimating consumer preference distributions, stochastic process models of consumer behavior, and prediction of consumer innovators by an application of multiple discriminant analysis. Other topics covered include pricing and product decisions in marketing management such as marketing mix decisions for new products, product characteristics and marketing strategy, advertising expenditure models, state of the art, and prospects and allocating advertising dollars by linear programming.

461. Davar, Ruston S., ed. *Executive Decision Making: Modern Concepts and Techniques.* Bombay, India: Progressive Corp., 1966. 319 p.
Reprints of articles previously published, grouped under the following headings: decision making—theory and process, operations research and its weapons, managerial control and analysis, and specific applications. The articles treat such topics as linear programming, queueing models, break-even analysis, PERT (project evaluation and review technique), and inventories.

462. Davies, Duncan, and McCarthy, Callum. *Introduction to Technological Economics.* New York: Wiley, 1967. 194 p.
Economics is a study of decision making. This book studies different types of decisions: decisions by plant manager dealing with cost, quality control and inventory control, and maintenance; decisions by the marketing manager in terms of sales, profitability, price policy, competition, seasonal sales, stock control, and decision making in project planning in terms of discounted cash flow and return of capital costs; raw materials, conversion, and capital costs; decisions by the innovator; and decisions in corporate planning such as company financing and accounting.

463. Davis, Wayne J., and Whitford, David T. *The Generalized Hierarchical Model: A New Approach to Resource Allocation within Multilevel Organizations.* Urbana, IL: College of Commerce and Business Administration, Bureau of Economic and Business Research, University of Illinois at Urbana-Champaign, 1981. 43 p.
The paper describes a three-level organizational model or decomposition procedure named the Generalized Hierarchical Model (GHM). The GHM algorithm focuses upon a multiple criteria approach to hierarchical decision making via mathematical programming decomposition theory. The GHM has been implemented on a DCD CYBER-175 computer and has been tested extensively. The results of this research tend to confirm that the GHM can offer a systematic approach to organizational design, multiperiod planning, and resource allocation in decentralized organizations.

464. Day, Charles R., Jr. "Management's Mindless Mistakes." *Industry Week* 197 (5) (May 29, 1978): 34–35, 38–42.
Common mistakes adversely affecting business are waste, inefficiency, and sagging morale. These combined with a failure to understand commands can have a devastating effect. Taking the time to listen, understand, question, think, and rethink before making decisions can mean the difference between poor and good management.

465. *Decision Making in Administration: Text, Critical Incidents and Cases.* Philadelphia, PA: W. B. Saunders, 1979. 289 p.
This is a book of case studies in managerial decision making. Cases cover the following topics: planning and objective setting, organization and staffing, understanding the individual, understanding the social system, leadership, the organization and its environment, and controlling.

466. *Decision Making in Hospital Construction Projects.* Madison, WI: Institute for Health Planning, 1984. 73 p.
This document describes the criteria used by hospital decision makers as they make decisions related to construction projects. The critical decisions addressed are organized into three broad phases. First, the predesign phase includes determining functional and space needs, financial feasibility, and appropriate financing options. The design phase follows and includes the selection of an architect and the development and revision of schematics, design development drawings, and construction documents. The final phase includes choosing a construction delivery method, selecting a contractor, and evaluating change orders suggested during construction. For each of these decision phases, material is drawn from participating hospitals in order to describe the criteria or factors important to the decision-making process.

467. *Decision Making in Marketing.* New York: The Conference Board, 1971. 103 p.
Business decisions come in a variety of flavors. Made under varying degrees of urgency, risk, and uncertainty, some of them establish policy of strategy in the company. Others deal with tactics or procedure; still others relate to routine operations. Big or small, all decisions in the company are interrelated. With corporate success so often synonymous with marketing success, it is understandable that management is particularly concerned with the quality of decision making in this key functional area. Fortunately, marketing decision makers now have access to important new

tools to help them in making their decisions. This report examines the use of these tools and other possibilities for improving marketing decisions.

468. Dewhurst, James. "Managerial Decisions for Small Businesses." *Management Accounting (UK)* 61 (4) (April 1983): 24–25.
The financial management of a small firm differs from that of a larger organization in that the skills must be exercised by a single person, that a person will usually not have any particular expertise or professional qualifications in the area, and if wrong financial decisions are made, the owner will suffer. Article discusses decision skills needed in the financial management of small businesses.

469. Dickson, Gordon C. A. "A Comparison of Attitudes towards Risk among Business Managers." *Journal of Occupational Psychology (UK)* 54 (3) (1981): 157–64.
An investigation was made of comparisons in attitudes toward risk between risk managers and nonrisk managers. Responses to hypothetical business decisions were measured. Half of the decisions involved the prospect of profit or breaking even, the other half the prospect of loss or no loss. There was great similarity in attitude over all subjects in those decisions involving profit, but in potential loss-producing problems, the risk managers were more averse to risk.

470. Domsch, Michel. "The Organization of Corporate R & D Planning." *Long Range Planning (UK)* 11 (3) (June 1978): 67–74.
Explains how research and development planning can be effectively conducted with the establishment of a computer information system. This information system would gather and store information relative to research and development objectives and convert the data to a form which can be used to make informed management decisions. The data should define the details of a project, the material, the human resources required, and a cost/benefit analysis.

471. Donaldson, Gordon. *Decision Making at the Top*. New York: Basic Books, 1983. 208 p.
Examines how critical decision choices affect corporate survival. It provides an inside perspective on corporate financial goals and describes how the system works by balancing the supply and demand for corporate funds. Other topics covered include the psychology of executive choice and strategic choice under managerial capitalism.

472. Drucker, Peter F. "How to Make People Decisions." *Harvard Business Review* 63 (4) (July/August 1985): 22–26.
Many executives are inept at staffing and promotion decision making. Article discusses steps in making effective staffing and promotion decisions such as evaluation of the assignment to determine what kind of person it calls for; looking at qualified candidates; thinking hard about how to evaluate the candidates and determine whether a candidate has the right strengths for the job; discussing the candidates with people who have worked with them; and ensuring that the appointee understands the job and its requirements.

473. Drucker, Peter F. "Managing for Tomorrow—Managing in Turbulent Times." *Industry Week* 205 (1) (April 14, 1980): 54–64.
In turbulent times managers must manage for change, keeping the enterprise lean and muscular and controlling assignment of its resources. The enterprise needs a systematic abandonment policy at all times, sloughing

off the past so that resources are available for tomorrow. A growth strategy is also essential, and enterprises should shift resources to specific areas of strength.

474. Duhaime, Irene M. "Investigating Strategic Divestment." *Managing* (1) (1983): 9–12.
Analyzes the factors that are assumed to be major determinants in the divestiture decision, namely financial strength of the firm, competitive and economic strength of the unit to be sold, general economic environment in which the firm and unit operate, the type of strategic relatedness sought by firms, and extent of interdependency between the unit and the firm's other businesses. Executives of diversified firms were interviewed to examine the influence of these factors in actual divestiture decisions.

475. Duhaime, Irene M., and Schwenk, Charles R. "Conjecture on Cognitive Simplification in Acquisition and Divestment Decision Making." *Academy of Management Review* 10 (2) (April 1985): 287–95.
Acquisition and divestment decisions usually involve complexity, ambiguity, and lack of structure. It is suggested that business decision makers may employ some systematic and predictable simplification processes in defining such poorly structured problems. Four major biases that explain decision-making errors are reasoning by analogy, illusion of control, escalating commitment, and single-outcome calculation.

476. Duhaime, Irene M., and Grant, John H. "Factors Influencing Divestments Decision Making: Evidence from a Field Study." *Strategic Management Journal (UK)* 5 (4) (October/December 1984): 301–18.
Examines factors that influenced the divestment decisions of large, diversified firms. The results suggest that the important divestment influences are a business unit's strength, its relationship with other units in the firm, and its parent firm's financial position relative to its competitors.

477. *DuPont Guide to Venture Analysis; A Framework for Venture Planning.* Wilmington, DE: DuPont de Nemours (E.I.) and Co., 1971. 147 p.
Venture analysis is a systematic and quantitative discipline for organizing and processing information to guide business decisions. It combines several methodologies to identify and condense, in a communicable format, the basic data required to describe and evaluate a business venture. The venture information framework is constructed by applying analytical tools to develop and link blocks of information (models) concerning markets, marketing strategy, costs, and investment. The heart of any venture plan is market analysis and the resulting picture of the environment in which a product must find its place. Information relevant to market opportunity is placed in the venture information framework through market models. This book describes how decision makers use venture analysis.

478. Eisenstadt, David, and Kennedy, Thomas E. "Control and Behavior of Nonprofit Firms: The Case of Blue Shield." *Southern Economic Journal* 48 (1) (July 1981): 26–36.
There is a large body of literature investigating the implications of managerial decisions on firm behavior. Under some circumstances, it has been predicted that managerial decisions would deviate from cost-minimizing/profit-maximizing decisions. It has also been argued that this deviation is

greater in nonprofit firms due to their attenuated property rights structures. Article examines how managerial decision making has been explored in nonprofit health insurance companies, specifically Blue Cross/Blue Shield plans.

479. Elbing, Alvar Oliver. *Behavioral Decisions in Organizations.* Glenview, IL.: Scott, Foresman & Co., 1970. 879 p.

Contains case studies providing a behavioral framework for the decision process. Examines concepts such as structured and unstructured stimuli, self-awareness, identification and acceptance of feelings, separation of feelings from situations, tendency to equate new and old experiences and to use available solutions to deal with problems at face value, the tendency to direct decisions toward a single goal, and the tendency to confuse symptoms and problems. It also stresses the importance of diagnostic process and builds behavioral models.

480. Elgers, Pieter T., and Murray, Dennis. "Financial Characteristics Related to Management's Stock Split and Stock Dividend Decisions." *Journal of Business Finance & Accounting (UK)* 12 (4) (Winter 1985): 543–51.

Several studies have surveyed corporate managers regarding the factors that influence their stock distribution decisions. Article investigates whether the factors identified in these studies are in fact associated with managers' actual stock distribution decisions. The conclusion is that management issues large stock distributions to keep the per share price in an optimal range and to signal optimistic managerial expectations to the market. Firms with relatively low per share prices tended to issue small stock distributions. The signaling motivation also played a role in this decision.

481. Elrod, Robert H., and Hubbard, Charles L. "Applying Means-End Decision Trees." *Business* 29 (1) (January/February 1979): 17–25.

A means-end decision tree is an organizing technique that professional problem solvers can use to deal with complex, ill-structured situations by systematically displaying the problem elements so that important relationships become organized by the decision maker. Chain reasoning is considered to be a hierarchical means-end process in which one moves step by step through logical relationships. Management science models operate with means-end chains and are considered to be formalizations of reflective thought. Means-end analysis can be seen as a tool to be used in the decision making process.

482. Engelberg, Stephen. "Simulating the Financial Future of an Insurance Company." *Best's Review (Life/Health)* 78 (12) (April 1978): 89–95.

Article presents a heuristic business model which focuses on the major determinants of corporate profitability and via simulation teaches young managers the futurity of current decisions.

483. English, John Morley, ed. *Cost-Effectiveness: The Economic Evaluation of Engineered Systems.* New York: Wiley, 1968. 301 p.

Produced from notes prepared for a one-week short course offered in April 1967 by the Engineering Physical Sciences Extension Division of University Extension, University of California, Los Angeles. Deals with systems engineering and decisions relating to engineering estimates and costs.

484. Ennis, F. Beaven. "Finding the Golden Ages of a Product's Life-Cycle." *Product Management* 4 (11) (November 1975): 36–41.
In spite of the difference of opinions among marketing managers, the product life cycle concept is getting more attention by top management due to its influence on basic marketing decisions. This article explores the use of the concept.

485. Fabrycky, Walter J., and Banks, Jerry. *Procurement and Inventory Systems: Theory and Analysis.* New York: Van Nostrand Reinhold, 1967. 239 p.
Discusses the theory, structure, and decision-making procedures of procurement and inventory systems. The systems presented are multi-item, single-source; single-item, multisource; single-item, single-source; and multi-item, multisource. The decision models are formulated for both deterministic and probabilistic situations. These models are based on calculus, linear programming, direct enumeration, Lagrangian multipliers, and dynamic programming.

486. Fama, Eugene F., and Jensen, Michael C. "Separation of Ownership and Control." *Journal of Law and Economics* 26 (2) (June 1983): 301–25.
Explains the survival of organizations characterized by separation of ownership and control. The separation of decision and risk-bearing functions observed in large corporations is common to other organizations, such as large professional partnerships, financial mutuals, and nonprofits. The separation of decision and risk-bearing functions survives in these organizations in part because of the benefits of specialization of management and risk bearing, but also because of an effective common approach to controlling the agency problems caused by separations.

487. Farrar, Donald Eugene. *The Investment Decision under Uncertainty.* Englewood Cliffs, NJ: Prentice-Hall, 1962. 90 p.
Explains such concepts as risk versus uncertainty, choice criteria under risk, expected return maximization, certainty equivalence, and mechanical programming. Examines the properties of models such as classical utility theory model, certainty equivalence model, mathematical programming model, and Freund's programming model.

488. Fenwick, Ian. "Advertising Experiments by Retailers." *Journal of Advertising Research* 18 (4) (August 1978): 35–40.
Explains how advertising decisions in retail industries required a high level of managerial commitment.

489. Fetter, Robert B., and Dalleck, Winston C. *Decision Models for Inventory Management.* Homewood, IL.: Richard D. Irwin, 1961. 123 p.
A guide to the theory of inventory problems which will lead to the development of ordering rules for effective inventory control. Develops graphical and mathematical models used in optimal inventory policy and the associated ordering rules. Discusses the data requirements for the inventory models and presents illustrations.

490. Fink, S. S., ed. *Turning Sense into Dollars.* New York: Harvard Management Associates, 1965. 175 p.
A creative analysis of executive and investment decision making. Corporate decision involves huge sums of money. Such decisions should be

based on rational analysis rather than intuition. This book discusses such analytical statistical techniques and explains their applications to capital investments, franchise opportunities, and business forecasting.

491. Fitzroy, Peter T. *Analytical Methods for Marketing Management.* London; New York: McGraw-Hill, 1976. 336 p.
Deals with decision in marketing, statistical methods of data analysis, consumer buying behavior, market segmentation, organizational buying behavior, and forecasting.

492. Folsom, Marion Bayard. *Executive Decision Making: Observations and Experience in Business and Government.* New York: McGraw-Hill, 1962. 137 p.
Basic text on the processes and practices of corporate decision making. Concepts analyzed include goal setting, evaluation of alternatives, information collection, and making and implementation of decisions.

493. Ford, J. L. *Choice Expectation and Uncertainty.* New York: Barnes & Noble Books, 1983. 210 p.
While dealing with time and uncertainty in economics, the book provides a perspective on the orthodox approach, specifically in the areas of portfolio selection and decision theory.

494. Forsyth, John Donald. "Capital Budgeting and the Decision Making Process in a Decentralized Business Organization." Ph.D. dissertation, University of Illinois at Urbana-Champaign, 1968. 135 p.
Deals with the utilization of mathematical programming techniques for decisions related to capital investment in decentralized organizations.

495. Freear, John. *Financing Decisions in Business.* London: Haymarket Publishing, 1973. 211 p.
Explains with examples the accounting and financial techniques which are involved in corporate decisions.

496. Fuller, Gerald W., and Beaupre, Eugene M. "Physicians and Administrators Can Work Together." *Healthcare Financial Management* 33 (10) (October 1979): 14–24.
Discusses how the Mild Maine Medical Center has successfully involved physicians in hospital management's decision-making processes. One of the initial steps was the reorganization of the management structure from that of the traditional organization to a physician input organization having three levels of decision-making authority. Some of the results included the alteration of inpatient utilization rates and outpatient surgery rates.

497. Furst, Sidney, and Sherman, Milton. *Business Decisions that Changed Our Lives.* New York: Random House, 1964. 396 p.
First-hand accounts of the inner workings of modern business corporations. Contains case histories of business decisions which changed consumer behavior and habits.

498. Fusfeld, Alan R. "How to Put Technology into Corporate Planning." *Technology Review* 80 (6) (May 1978): 51–55.
Key management decision makers have inadequate background and ability to make judgments and forecasts in the area of technology. Technological issues enter as a result of activities both inside and outside the industry. They can affect a whole range of corporate activities. To improve the

understanding of technology in a corporation, an adequate unit of analysis is needed. The analysis must be on the level of generic technologies.

499. Gaither, Norman, and Fraser, Donald R. "Setting Aggregate Inventory Levels: An Operations Management Decision?" *International Journal of Operations & Production Management (UK)* 4 (1) (1984): 18–33.
A group of 500 financial executives from North American firms were surveyed to obtain a perspective on the basis on which aggregate inventory decisions are taken. Responses revealed that more functions than might have been expected were involved in the process of determining inventory levels. It was found that production or operations, finance or accounting, and marketing or merchandising have the most influence on aggregate inventory decisions in the firms.

500. Gellerman, Saul W. *Cases and Problems for Decisions in Management.* New York: Random House, 1984. 270 p.
Casebook dealing with real world situations in corporate life. Discusses qualitative techniques applicable to different aspects of corporate decision making.

501. Gellerman, Saul W., "Gellerman Case-Book Three." *Management Today (UK)* (June 1973): 72–75, 150.
Of all managerial requirements, none is more important than knowing what information to seek for decision making. This is a case study of two executives, one a project manager, the other a newly appointed manager of sales promotion. The project manager's problem was the threat of a damaging shutdown to a newly installed machine. The manager of sales promotion wanted to make the most effective possible use of a device for encouraging salespeople's efforts.

502. Gilligan, Colin; Neale, Bill; and Murray, David. *Business Decision Making.* Birmingham, England: Philip Allan, 1983. 197 p.
Provides a comprehensive introduction to the origins of decision theory, types of decision, levels of decision making, references and further reading, and the decision-making process. It also deals with information and information systems in terms of the desirable characteristics for information, problems in information system design, and management information systems, behavioral aspects of decision making, and individual versus group decision making. Other topics discussed include decision making under risk and short-term operating control decisions; linear programming; stock control problems; periodic control decisions, such as the replacement decision; and strategic decision making, such as criteria for divestment and strategic postaudit.

503. Gillis, Floyd E. *Managerial Economics: Decision Making under Certainty for Business and Engineering.* Reading, MA: Addison-Wesley, 1969. 296 p.
This is a book on business mathematics with applications to interest rate problems, break-even analysis, inventories, replacement, demand, firm costs, and pricing under perfect and imperfect competition.

504. Goehle, Donna G. *Decision Making in Multinational Corporations.* Ann Arbor, MI: UMI Research Press, 1980. 226 p.
The central question addressed in this research is, what is the nature of the relationship between subsidiary performance and the centralization or

decentralization of decision making? The issue is viewed primarily as a question of what decision-making authority the subsidiary has in the following areas: finance, manufacturing, marketing, personnel, purchasing, and research and development. The focus is on three major areas: a description in terms of function, industry, and country; the degree of centralization of decision-making authority; an explanation of how the characteristics of the firm, the subsidiary, and the subsidiary's environment affect the degree of centralization of that authority; and an examination of the relationship between the degree of centralization and unit performance.

505. Gordon, Lawrence A., et al. "The Pricing Decision." *Management Accounting* 62 (9) (March 1981): 59–60.
The primary objective of a study cosponsored by the National Association of Accountants and the Society of Management Accountants of Canada was to determine how manufacturing companies in the U.S. and Canada are presently making pricing decisions. Generally, profits, closely followed by the ratio of return on investment, as well as market share and the measure of total sales, were the key objectives used in setting pricing policies for the firms.

506. Gordon, Lawrence A.; Miller, Danny; and Wintzberg, Henry. *Normative Models in Managerial Decision-Making: A Study Carried out on Behalf of the National Association of Accountants, New York, NY, and the Society for Industrial Accountants of Canada; Hamilton, Ontario, Canada.* New York: The National Association of Accountants, 1975. 121 p.
Provides an overview of normative decision theory in terms of decision models by functional areas, by process and level, and by output. Considers nine decision models, namely, new product decision, distribution channels decision, acquisition decision, divestment (product abandonment) decision, capital expenditure decision, lease-buy decision, make-buy decision, pricing decision, and manpower planning decision. Also provides illustrations of nonprogrammed decision processes.

507. Green, Paul E., and Wind, Yoram. *Multiattribute Decision in Marketing; A Measurement Approach.* Hinsdale, IL: Dryden Press, 1974. 396 p.
Discusses quantitative marketing research techniques dealing with decisions relating to product planning, testing, pricing, and promotion management.

508. Greene, James Harnsberger. *Production and Inventory Control; Systems and Decisions.* Rev. ed. Homewood, IL: Richard D. Irwin, 1974. 714 p.
Today's manager is more interested in understanding system design and decision making for production planning and control than in day-to-day operations of a production control office. The book presents a logical systems design approach. It discusses decision-making techniques for control such as the Gantt Chart and PERT (project evaluation and review technique) as well as linear programming. Also presents actual case studies explaining how companies have solved specific problems.

509. Greenwood, William T. *Decision Theory and Information Systems: An Introduction to Management Decision Making.* New Rochelle, NY: South-Western, 1969. 818 p.
This book is an introduction to recent decision theories and management problem solving. It deals with techniques such as heuristics, decision models using management, production, personnel, and finance and accounting. It also delves into decision environment systems, organizational decision behavior and computer information control systems.

510. Groff, Gene K., and Muth, John F. *Operations Management: Analysis for Decisions.* Homewood, IL: Richard D. Irwin, 1972. 572 p.
Deals with operations planning and control as well as with designing operations systems, including analysis for plant and equipment investment, project planning, reliability maintenance, forecasting, decision rules for inventory control, operations scheduling, statistical quality control, labor performance, and work measurement.

511. Gul, Ferdinand A. "An Empirical Study of the Usefulness of Human Resources Turnover Costs in Australian Accounting Firms." *Accounting, Organizations & Society (UK)* 9 (3–4) (1984): 233–39.
Presents a laboratory experiment designed to investigate the usefulness of applying human resources accounting to the problem of labor turnover. Discusses the relevance of the concept to management decision making.

512. Hague, Douglas Chalmers. *Managerial Economics: Analysis for Business Decisions.* New York: Wiley, 1969. 356 p.
Many of the manager's problems are decision problems all of which have one basic characteristic in common: how to get the best out of expensive resources. Since economics is basically the study of scarcity and the problems to which scarcity gives rise, business decisions are of interest to economists. This book explains how managerial economics brings managers, operation researchers, and accountants together. Explains application to business of economic concepts like demand curves, demand elasticities, flex and fix-priced markets, price theories, cost curves, and discounted cash flow. Decision techniques like linear programming and queueing theory are also discussed along with their application to transportation, inventory, pricing, and investment problems.

513. Hale, Jack A., and Ryan, Lanny J. "Decision Science and Management Accountant." *Management Accounting* 60 (7) (January 1979): 42–45.
The responsibilities of the management accountant include designing information systems needed for executive decision making. Article examines how the accountant can improve overall functioning in this advisory role through the use of decision science techniques.

514. Haley, Charles W., and Schall, Lawrence D. *The Theory of Financial Decisions.* New York: McGraw-Hill, 1973. 383 p.
Presents topics such as decisions under uncertainty, capital budgeting, probability and random variables, portfolio theory, single-period and multiperiod firm financial decision models, financing decisions in perfect markets, and firm investment in perfect and imperfect markets.

515. Hardy, John W., and Orton, Bryce R. "Decentralized Decision Making and Responsibility Accounting in a Selected Segment of Business." *Cost & Management (Canada)* 57 (1) (January/February 1983): 43–46.
The study attempts to determine the extent to which the retail drugstore industry uses decentralization and responsibility accounting. The degree of decentralization, the frequency with which management accounting reports were provided, the type of revenue and cost information in financial reports, and the extent to which the revenue and cost factors were controllable at selected management levels were investigated. This study shows that decision making in the retail drugstore industry is highly centralized.

516. Helmi, Medhat A., and Tanju, Murat N. "Budget after the Fact: An Auditing Tool for Management Evaluation." *Abacus (Australia)* 16 (2) (December 1980): 124–32.
"Budget after the fact" is a useful tool which can be incorporated in auditors' work whenever they start performing the expanded role. It is based mainly on the use of optimization models and facilitates comparison of decisions made and those that should have been made. For example, using a multiple regression mode for estimating the costs in the production department, the auditor may ask the client to explain why the company had one extra run during the year which resulted in an extra set-up cost. The reasons for the deviation of actual runs from the optimum number may shed light on the efficiency of operations.

517. Hempel, George H. "The Changing Environment for Bank Management Decisions in the 1980s." *Review of Regional Economics and Business* 6 (1) (April 1981): 9–16.
Emphasizes how important it is to anticipate the environment in which commercial banks will make their management decisions during the next few years. Although it is impossible to accurately predict all aspects of the future environment for bank management decisions, some reasonable inferences can be made about the future from economic trends, recent legislation, and developments in the banking industry.

518. Hensher, David A., and Johnson, Lester W. *Applied Discrete-Choice Modelling.* London: Croom Helm; New York: Wiley, 1981. 468 p.
Presents statistical and mathematical models in decision making relating to situations where a choice needs to be made among many competing alternatives.

519. Herman, Roger E. "Retrenching for Results." *Managing* 5 (1) (1983): 20–24.
Retrenching is the responsive strategy in a recessionary economy. The paper talks about two approaches to retrenchment decisions: realignment of present resources without reduction in personnel and systematic cost reduction, with consideration given to subsequent reorganization of the company and modified resource utilization at a later date.

520. Hernandez, Melvin, and Henderson, Glenn V., Jr. "A Generalized Approach to the Operational Audit of Management Information." *Internal Auditor* 36 (3) (June 1979): 70–76.
Operational auditing seeks to improve the development and use of management information as a basis for making decisions. The decision process

can be thought of as having three stages: formulation, forecasting, and finalization. Breaking a decision down into its component parts may enable the auditor to increase the benefits of that decision, and that is the purpose of operational auditing.

521. Hirouchi, Tetsuo, and Kosaka, Takeshi. "An Effective Database Formation for Decision Support Systems." *Information & Management (Netherlands)* 7 (4) (August 1984): 183–95.
Decision support systems (DSS) have failed to achieve widespread use for management control because they have generally lacked databases that are designed specifically to meet the information needs of managers. A database system is described that was developed to support DSS, structured according to the primary management tasks of monitoring/controlling business activities and planning for those of the future. DSS architecture is used to connect both management and planning databases.

522. Holland, F. A.; Watson, F. A.; and Wilkinson, J. K. *Introduction to Process Economics.* London; New York: Wiley, 1974. 290 p.
This is an introductory text devoted to managerial accounting considerations in decision making. It includes explanation and application of concepts such as financial accounting, cost accounting, price and cost trends, value engineering and cost-benefit analysis, marketing, and risk and insurance. Special attraction is devoted to comparative profitability based on the time value of money, uncertainties in profitability estimates, capital cost, manufacturing cost, and some numerical methods for decision makers.

523. Horowitz, Ira. *Decision Making and the Theory of the Firm.* New York: Holt, Rinehart & Winston, 1970. 468 p.
There is a growing trend among economists to proffer solutions to problems of decision making in organizations. It is also true that today's managers are reciprocating by recognizing that economists have something to contribute in that direction. This book on managerial economics explores some of the theory, extensions, and techniques which have helped bridge the gap between neoclassical price theory and managerial decision making. It develops quantitative models and techniques for decision making and the analysis of decision making in the firm.

524. Hosmer, LaRue Tone. "Managerial Ethics and Microeconomic Theory." *Journal of Business Ethics (Netherlands)* (4) (November 1984): 315–25.
Most economists believe that moral standards in business are irrelevant because profit-maximizing behavior under market and resource constraints leads unalterably to social welfare optimization. The opposing view is that modern markets are not competitive enough to be constraining. Thus profit maximization frequently leads to social harm, and welfare benefits are unequally distributed. Inappropriate assumptions about the nature and worth of human beings in economic theory necessitate the use of moral standards for business decisions and actions.

525. Houston, Samuel R.; Duff, William L.; and Lynch, Robert M. *Applications in Bayesian Decision Processes.* New York: MSS Information Corp., 1975. 79 p.
Bayesian statistical methodology and its possible uses in the behavioral sciences are discussed in relation to the solution of problems in both the use and teaching of fundamental statistical methods, including confidence

intervals, significance tests, and sampling. The Bayesian model explains these statistical methods and offers a consistent model that ties together expectation of results, design of studies, analysis, and predictions of future observations. Topics covered include Bayesian statistics in marketing, probability, statistical decision theory, and accounting, organization decision theory, Bayesian statistics in retail inventory management, a Bayesian approach to estimating decision parameters in a replacement inventory system, and Bayesian approach to advertising budgets.

526. Huegli, Jon M. "The Internal Auditor as Change Catalyst." *Internal Auditor* 37 (3) (June 1980): 53–57.

Recommendations by internal auditors often do not have their intended impact because these auditors do not recognize their role, as catalysts of change, which influences management's receptivity in decision roles. In their role as change catalysts, internal auditors give managers information and interpretations and recommend courses of action. They must make management receptive to change by anticipating resistance, implementing change tactics, and using resistance-reducing techniques.

527. Hughes, George David. *Demand Analysis for Marketing Decisions.* Homewood, IL: Richard D. Irwin, 1978. 306 p.

Marketing managers' decisions in the key areas of products, prices, channels of distribution, promotion, and public policy start from an understanding of the needs of buyers and consumers. The process for understanding these needs is known as demand analysis. This text applies the theories, models, and measures from the four behavioral disciplines used for demand analysis, namely, demography, economics, sociology, and psychology. A simple model of demand is developed and elaborated upon in the book. Variations on the model by each discipline provide the information needed for marketing decisions.

528. Hunter, Jairy C. "Managers Must Know the Mission: If It Ain't Broke, Don't Fix It." *Managerial Planning* 33 (4) (January/February 1985): 18–22.

Today's managers frequently face the dilemma of whether or not to make organizational changes. Decisions to expand, diversify, or specialize are being made constantly. In order to make sound and constructive decisions, managers must know and honor the mission of the organization because its mission determines its overall direction. Managers must understand the planning process in order to establish a mission and set goals.

529. Hylas, Robert E. "Black Magic?" *Management Focus* 30 (1) (January/February 1983): 28–31.

Computerized corporate planning models encourage organization, expedite decision making, and promote profits. The computer is especially effective in determining finance, marketing, and production areas in which the models are most helpful. This paper talks about how to use these models.

530. "Industrial Democracy: Government Seeks Wider Consultation." *Accountancy (UK)* 89 (1019) (July 1978): 23.

Examines the suggestion that all employers in companies employing more than 500 should be obligated to discuss with the employees' representatives all major proposals affecting the employees before decisions are made.

531. Jablonsky, Stephen F., and Dirsmith, Mark W. "Is Financial Reporting Influencing Internal Decision Making?" *Management Accounting* 61 (1) (July 1979): 40–44.
While the discounted cash flow technique has been suggested as an appropriate mechanism for making capital investment decisions and evaluating performance, it has not been found that a majority of companies employ an accounting return on investment criterion in evaluating divisional performance and that generally accepted accounting principles tend to influence the methods used in calculating the profit and investment base of the division. The financial reporting system does have an impact on internal decision making. Management could reduce the impact of financial reporting on internal decision making by altering the methods used to evaluate the performance of divisional managers.

532. Janger, Allen R., ed. *External Challenges to Management Decisions: A Growing International Business Problem.* New York: The Conference Board, 1981. 68 p.
The world's senior business executives are finding it increasingly necessary to respond effectively to groups and individuals who are outside the management group but have their own ideas about how and for what purposes the company should be managed. This report studies the impact of outsider activity on company decision making and examines company responses to these outside challenges. The scope of the study is worldwide.

533. Jauch, Lawrence R., and Wilson, Harold K. "A Strategic Perspective for Make or Buy Decisions." *Long Range Planning (UK)* 12 (6) (December 1979): 56–61.
Too many companies leave "make or buy" decisions up to purchasing managers who base their decisions on quantifiable cost considerations. Instead, top management needs to become involved and realize that this question is also an important strategic one. Article discusses how top management should be involved in this decision.

534. Jean, William H. *The Analytical Theory of Finance: A Study of Investment Decision Process of the Individual and the Firm.* New York: Holt, Rinehart & Winston, 1970. 206 p.
Focuses primarily on project selection and the financial structure of the firm, and the theory that is developed is based on investment decisions under risk using the investor's utility function. Topics include capital rationing models, capital structure of the firm, portfolio theory, and the theory of security markets.

535. Jerman, Roger E., and Anderson, Ronald D. "Marketing a Contingency Approach." *Quarterly Review of Marketing (UK)* 4 (1) (Autumn 1978): 9–17.
The contingency approach stresses that the marketing function is no more important that any other function. Article stresses that marketing's role is to do a good job of aiding the mixing and matching of resource input-output relationships. If this is not done, it will be achieved anyway by controlled production and/or consumption or some combination thereof. The contingency approach offers a basis for coping with the complexities of the decision-making tasks in marketing.

536. Johnson, L. Todd. "Current Replacement Costs and Potential Managerial Benefits." *Management Accounting* 59 (6) (December 1977): 31–36.

Replacement cost data can be used in the managerial decision-making and budgeting processes by using the accounting system as a value measurement system rather than a cost allocation system. Specifically, holding gains or losses can show the effect of the timing of purchases and sales of assets. Also, current operating income can show income based on the current cost of assets.

537. Kamin, Jacob Y., and Ronen, Joshua. "Effects of Budgetary Control Design on Management Decisions: Some Empirical Evidence." *Decision Sciences* 12 (3) (July 1981): 471–85.

A test is made for differences in budgetary slack allocations between management-controlled firms and firms of similar size and market power that are owner controlled. It reveals that management-controlled firms behave as if they allocate more slack resources than do owner-controlled firms. It indicates that slack behavior in the budgetary process is reflected in accounting operating-income numbers and concludes that managerial characteristics and the economic environment may contribute to the failure of budgetary control systems and that this failure may lead to inefficient resource allocation and to inferior profit performance.

538. Kaminski, Peter F., and Rink, David R. "PLC: The Missing Link Between Physical Distribution and Marketing Planning." *International Journal of Physical Distribution & Materials Management (UK)* 14 (6) (1984): 77–92.

Discusses the need for carefully conceived physical distribution decision strategies based on product portfolio analysis, market attractiveness, business position analysis, and product life cycle.

539. Kania, John J., and McKean, John R. "Decision-Making in the Extensive Firm." *Nebraska Journal of Economics & Business* 18 (1) (Winter 1979): 25–42.

Past research has proposed many models to analyze the decision-making process of management. Management has been demonstrated to make choices which will maximize sales, growth, and profits. Additionally, it has been shown that management is averse to market risk and that decisions consider risk aversion tactics. However, past research has not included the concept of extra-market risk aversion. Article formulates a model which gives consideration to this additional variable in the decision-making process.

540. Kienast, Philip, et al. "Employing Conjoint Analysis in Making Compensation Decisions." *Personnel Psychology* 36 (2) (Summer 1983): 301–13.

Explains how the conjoint decision analysis method helps determine level of satisfaction by employers regarding benefit packages.

541. Kindler, Herbert S. "Decisions, Decisions: Which Approach to Take." *Personnel* 62 (1) (January 1985): 47–51.

The four basic decision processes are unilateral decision making, collaboration, bargaining, and decision rule. Two important dimensions that underlie all four processes are the degree to which power is used by the decision maker and the degree to which the decision maker's interests and values align with those of others involved in or affected by decision implementation. In the unilateral situation, for instance, one person exercises sole judgment in choosing between alternatives. A unilateral process suggests a hierarchical relationship. Article presents a power/alignment model to help decision makers assess situations and choose a decision process that meets the power and alignment needs of the situation.

542. King, William Richard. *Quantitative Analysis for Marketing Management.* New York: McGraw-Hill, 1967. 574 p.
To become an effective marketing manager, one must combine interest with a basic knowledge of management principles and an understanding of the values and limitations of the process of analysis which can be brought to bear on marketing decision problems. This book is about the decisions with which the marketing manager is constantly faced. The topics covered include formulation of marketing models, product decisions, market analysis and test marketing, purchasing and pricing decisions, advertising and distribution, and production. The book emphasizes the role of models in marketing analysis.

543. Kniffen, Fred W. "Stagflation Pricing—Seven Ways You Might Improve Your Decisions." *Marketing News* 8 (10) (November 15, 1974): 3.
Actions that managers currently are using to gain competitive edge from pricing include improvement on feedback of pricing information concerning the market. Involvement in pricing actions should be maintained by the pricing team. Pricing formulas should be reexamined for product line pricing. Price making responsibilities should be reviewed throughout the marketing organization.

544. Kotler, Philip. "How to Milk Fading Cash Cows." *Marketing Times* 27 (3) (May/June 1980): 11–16.
Harvesting implies the final stage of a product or a business; it suggests that the product has matured, and the company is now going to extract its remaining value. It is a strategic management decision to reduce investment in hope of reducing costs and/or improving cash flow.

545. Kotler, Philip. *Marketing Decision Making: A Model Building Approach.* New York: Holt, Rinehart & Winston, 1971. 720 p.
While traditional marketing managers regarded marketing as an art form, the new breed of managers are turning more to analytical approaches in response to the increasing pressure on management to tie sales to profits. Marketing expenditures account for a large part of the company's total expenses, and hence management wants solid analysis to back up such investment. This book provides a meaningful frame of reference for the analysis of marketing processes and problems. Subjects dealt with include macromarketing decision theory like demand and cost functions, marketing mix determination, competitive strategy, market share determination, production planning, allocation of marketing budget, distribution strategy, location, logistics and management, pricing decisions, salesforce decisions, advertising, sales models for new and established products, and the role of marketing information systems.

546. Kulkarni, Deepak. "Can Exposure Draft 24 Really Give Help to Management?" *Accountancy (UK)* 90 (1030) (June 1979): 110–12.
The chief objective of internal financial reporting is to assist management in discharging their responsibilities, which include decision making, both

routine and ad hoc. Inflation accounting systems can by no means satisfy all the financial information needs of management. Consideration should be given to the particular ways in which an entity is vulnerable to inflationary effects and the cost-effectiveness of any inflation adjustments in internal reporting.

547. Lacey, Dan, and Chadwin, Mark L. "The Directive's Advocate Gives His Views/The Amended Version of the Vredeling Directive." *Personnel Administrator* 28 (9) (September 1983): 56–60.
Article discusses the impact of the European Community decision under which multinational corporations would have to consult with their employees before making decisions which would affect the workers' jobs or living conditions.

548. Lambert, Douglas M., and Sterling, Jay U. "The Product Abandonment Decision." *Management Accounting* 67 (2) (August 1985): 20, 60.
Discusses a research project on managers making the product abandonment decision, conducted jointly by the National Association of Accountants and the Society of Management Accountants of Canada, so as to develop a descriptive model of how businesses make this important decision.

549. Lang, James R.; Dittrich, John E.; and White, Sam E. "Managerial Problem Solving Models: A Review and a Proposal." *Academy of Management Review* 3 (4) (October 1978): 854–66.
Although problem-solving models have developed from learning theory, they have not reached the refinement of expectancy motivation models which were derived from the same sources. An integrative problem-solving model, which includes applicable constructs from expectancy theory, suggests that, in order to achieve improvement in problem solving, it is necessary that appropriate functional skills be acquired or learned and that necessary organizational resources be forthcoming.

550. Leslie, Mary; Magdulski, George; and Champion, Neil. "The Role of the Accountant in the Survival of Small Business." *Australian Accountant* 55 (1) (January/February 1985): 22–30.
Two neglected and possibly controversial aspects of small business failure are the way in which business advice is given and the narrowly financial nature of the advice. Nonfinancial factors have an important influence on business decision making, and often the attempt to satisfy personal goals is what leads to financial difficulties.

551. Lesser, Arthur, ed. *Decision and Risk Analysis: Powerful New Tools for Management.* Hoboken, NJ.: Engineering Economist, 1972. 198 p.
Proceedings of the Sixth Triennial Symposium sponsored by Engineering Economy Division, American Society of Engineering Education, and the American Institute of Independent Engineers. Covers topics such as decision and utility theory, decision analysis of a facility's expansion problem, the role of precognition in risk analysis, a Bayesian view of decision process and decison process dynamics, investment planning decisions under uncertainty, evaluation modeling in the context of the systems decision process, measuring multiattribute utilities, a higher order computer language for risk analysis, and group decision theory.

552. Lesser, Arthur, ed. *Decision-Making Criteria for Capital Expenditures.* Papers and discussions of the fourth summer symposium of the Engineering Economy Division, American Society for Engineering Education, June 10–20, 1965, Illinois Institute of Technology. Hoboken, NJ: The Engineering Economist, 1966. 105 p.
Covers various topics, including cost of capital theories, technological forecasting, decisions under risk and uncertainty, forecasting returns from industrial investments, capital budgeting systems for large organizations, evaluating research and development projects, and analogue computing for project evaluation.

553. Levy, Haim, and Sarnat, Marshall. *Capital Investment and Financial Decisions.* Englewood Cliffs, NJ: Prentice-Hall, 1986. 703 p.
The book is about financial policy with special emphasis on the allocation of a firm's long-term capital resources. Investment and financing decisions that decide the future course of the firm have a great deal in common: they refer to a highly uncertain future, they must be made on the basis of incomplete information, and only a few of the relevant variables are controllable. But perhaps the salient characteristic of such decisions is that they cannot be avoided. "No decision" is itself a "decision." The financial manager's objective is to spell out an operational framework for reaching the attainable financial decisions. The book provides such guidelines for practical financial management.

554. Liao, Woody M. "Effects of Learning on Resource Allocation Decisions." *Decision Sciences* 10 (1) (January 1979): 116–25.
Discusses the importance of learning curves for managerial planning and control and the effect of learning on managerial planning models for product-mix problems that can be handled by a linear programming formulation. A linear programming problem is presented as an illustration of the feasibility and superiority of the proposed approach over the traditional approach. The managerial planning model is used for production decisions and allocation of scarce resources. However, it is also useful in other problem areas such as pricing, work scheduling, standard and cost determination. In fact, concepts of learning should be considered in decision making whenever the effect of learning is significant.

555. Little, John D. C "The Marvelous Marketing Machine." *Wharton Magazine* 4 (1) (Fall 1979): 28–33.
Discusses the Market Decision Support System (MDSS) as an aid in the gathering and interpreting of relevant information and turning it into a basis for decisions of marketing intermediaries.

556. Lodish, Leonard M. "Vaguely Right Approach to Sales Force Allocations." *Harvard Business Review* 52 (1) (January/Febraury 1974): 119–24.
No longer is it enough to rely on history or rules of thumb in making salesforce allocation decisions. The precise historical data available to sales managers are just not enough for them to rationally decide on salesforce size, territory boundaries, and call frequencies for each account and prospect. If maximizing profits is the mission of the sales manager, then it is better to be vaguely right than precisely wrong. The "precisely wrong" decision-making procedures include allocating calls in proportion to sales or potential, concentrating on travel time, and defining territories by call

frequencies proportional to sales or potential. Article notes that an adoption of simple allocation procedures will improve sales force efficiency.

557. London, Manuel. "What Every Personnel Director Should Know about Management Promotion Decisions." *Personnel Journal* 57 (10) (October 1978): 550–55.
Explains how promotion decisions are made in most large organizations and how these decisions affect corporate growth in many areas.

558. MacCrimmon, Kenneth R., and Wehrung, Donald A. "The Risk In-Basket." *Journal of Business* 57 (3) (July 1984): 367–87.
A study is presented in which over 400 executives confronted four risky situations cast in an "in-basket" format. Each situation involves a decision between a risky and a sure alternative. The executives responded by writing memos to specify how each situation should be dealt with. This allows an examination of a rich variety of actions for modifying risk. Responses in the form of probability equivalencies and rating scales were also obtained. The results show that the executives have a relatively strong tendency toward risk seeking, especially when the payoffs are negative.

559. "Make-or-Buy Can Be a Make-or-Break Decision." *Small Business Report* 8 (10) (October 1983): 24–28.
The decision to make or buy parts affects production methods, working capital, borrowing costs, and a company's competitive position. Few companies have a comprehensive make-or-buy policy that is consistent with corporate goals and objectives. For top management, make-or-buy decisions should be an integral part of a corporation's activities. These decisions should be analyzed as often as objectives and conditions change.

560. Manne, Alan Sussmann. *Economic Analysis for Business Decisions.* New York: McGraw-Hill, 1961. 177 p.
Graduate-level text dealing with managerial decision problems in areas such as resource allocation, capital budgeting, product mix choices, marketing, inventory control, and cost. Explains techniques such as linear programming, transportation modeling, integer programming, scheduling, and sequencing.

561. Mantel, Samuel J. *Cases in Managerial Decisions.* Englewood Cliffs, NJ: Prentice-Hall, 1964. 201 p.
These are twenty case studies involving the application of economic theory to business and industrial decision making in the areas of marketing, production, finance, and budgeting.

562. Mao, James C. T. *Quantitative Analysis of Financial Decisions.* New York: Macmillan, 1969. 625 p.
Emphasizes the theory of financial management. Topics include profit planning, financial budgeting, investment decision, cost of capital, valuation, shares, and working capital management.

563. Marshall, G. P., and McCormick, B. J. *Economics of Managerial Decision Making.* Oxford; New York: Basil Blackwell, 1986. 364 p.
Provides a complete grounding in the essentials of economic theory and practice relevant to modern business. Contemporary management issues of financing, production, personnel management, investment, marketing, and pricing are analyzed, with an emphasis on the role of economic principles in decision making. A particular feature of the book is its treatment of strategic management and business policy issues in determining the evolu-

tion of British, German, American, and Japanese firms. Topics covered include the propensity of barter and exchange, the nature of the firm, changing patterns of marketing, consumer behavior, pricing policy and market structures, product policy, distribution policy, cost and production management, personnel management, investment and financial management, and public enterprise and the public regulation of private enterprise.

564. Masse, Pierre. *Optimal Investment Decisions Rules for Action and Criteria for Choice.* Englewood Cliffs, NJ: Prentice-Hall, 1962. 500 p.
This book provides an introduction to the search for the optimum both in quality and quantity. Discusses topics like rates of return, determination of service life, choice of equipment and linear programming, peak demand problem, and inventory management.

565. Mathews, H. L., et al. *Analysis and Decision Making.* Englewood Cliffs, NJ: Prentice-Hall, 1971. 251 p.
Collection of case studies which simulate real business decision-making situations to help the executives analyze data and also structure this analysis in a data-rich and complex problem environment. Topics of application include market analysis, product decisions, pricing, distribution channels, physical distribution, and promotion management.

566. McCosh, Andrew M., and Morton, Michael S. Scott. *Management Decision Support System.* New York: Wiley, 1978. 238 p.
Deals with data processing techniques used in corporate financial decision making. It explains the fundamental character of decision support systems and design process. Some of the applications examined include a profit planning support system, budgeting, the financial analysis of merger opportunities, the pricing decision, and their organizational implications.

567. McLagen, Donald. "Improving Cash Flow Projections with Economic Models." *Planning Review* 7 (3) (May 1979): 13–16.
Some cash flow models require a vast amount of detailed input. They cannot respond quickly to changed circumstances and are not easily simulated to test the company's risk to alternative assumptions. Article discusses a second generation of cash flow models developed to overcome these shortcomings. These models produce more aggregated pro forma corporate financial statements, require relatively simple input, and produce answers quickly. Computerized systems for linking the company's numbers to economic forecasts are readily available, and a third generation of cash flow models now provide a cost-effective way of quantifying economic uncertainty to make more informed financial decisions.

568. "Media Advice to a Brand Manager." *Media Decisions* 8 (11) (November 1973): 55–57, 126–34.
The brand manager's role is to manage media decisions, not to make them. The brand manager who gets the most effective media schedules for his or her brand is the one who knows how to get that extra effort out of his or her media support organization, both in house and at the agency. He or she continually probes basic assumptions and formula methods of decision making. Current emphasis on market segmentation can lead the brand manager into a false position of assuming that demographics and psychographics coincide. Finding the most efficient combination of media weight and sales promotion with a given copy platform continues to be a critical problem for brand management.

569. Mehr, Robert I., and Forbes, Stephen W. "The Risk Management Decision in the Total Business Setting." *Journal of Risk and Insurance* 40 (3) (September 1973): 389–401.
This paper attempts to recast risk management theory in light of the complex objectives of modern corporations and to suggest that risk management theory needs to merge with traditional financial theory in order to bring added realism to the decision-making process.

570. Michel, Allen. "The Inflation Audit." *California Management Review* 24 (2) (Winter 1981): 68–74.
Article provides a systematic analysis of the effect of inflation on a company and its industry. Calls for an inflation audit which will help the financial manager decide important issues, including the proper degree of leverage for the company, the amount and timing of capital expenditures, and the advisability of adding or dropping product lines.

571. Mikkelson, Wayne H. "Convertible Calls and Stock Price Declines." *Financial Analysts Journal* 41 (1) (January/February 1985): 63–69.
A company's decision to force conversion of convertible securities generally results in a stock price decline. Possible causes of this negative response include the change in interest expense tax which shields the potential redistribution of wealth from common stockholders to holders of preferred stock and debt claims, the increase in shares outstanding, and the change in earnings per share.

572. Mitroff, Ian, and Kilmann, Ralph H. "Teaching Managers to Do Policy Analysis—The Case of Corporate Bribery." *California Management Review* 20 (1) (Fall 1977): 47–54.
Managers lack formal training for ill-structured problems, or those which are hard to define, produce conflict, or that do not fit easily into standard solution techniques. A new method of solving these problems is needed that allows managers to be aware of each other's styles of problem solving, to appreciate diverse styles, and to look at important problems from the point of view of different styles. Too often, the solution is developed for the wrong problem. A dialectic approach should be implemented to solve ill-structured problems. An experiment in the application of the dialectic approach was conducted on the issue of corporate bribery. It led managers to deciding what the policy implications of a decision were.

573. Moore, Peter Gerald, and Thomas, H. *The Anatomy of Decisions.* Harmondsworth, England: Penguin, 1978. 239 p.
Mathematics has come to play an important part in business decisions. Although nothing can eliminate uncertainty, a reasoned appreciation of risks, and a rigorous application of the rules of probability theory can mean that at least the most dangerous options can be discarded and a proper ranking made of those that remain. This book sets out the principles with which skillful managers will approach their difficulties. Examples from business and industry, both private and public, as well as from government, are used to illustrate the complexity of the problems which can be solved by intelligent decision analysis, ranging from a manufacturer's concern over the best way of producing a new product to the infinitely more complicated matter of choosing the most effective modes of publicity in launching a new product.

574. Moore, Peter Gerald, and Hodges, Stewart Dimont, eds. *Programming for Optimal Decisions: Selected Readings in Mathematical Programming Techniques for Management Problems.* Baltimore, MD: Penguin, 1970. 360 p.

This book is a collection of papers previously published in journals and elsewhere grouped under the following headings: applications of linear programming, applications of other programming techniques, and theoretical developments. Some of the topics include applications in linear programming in forest management, transistor production, agricultural production, iron foundries, portfolio selection, separable programming applied to ore purchasing, open-pit mining, models for hospital menu planning, job scheduling, and warehouse location. The theoretical developments include nonlinear programming, linear programming under uncertainty, integer programming, and optimum seeking with branch and bound techniques.

575. Moriguchi, Chikashi. *Business Cycles and Manufacturers' Short Term Production Decisions.* New York: American Elsevier, 1967. 152 p.

Analyzes nonlinear relationships between sales fluctuations and production decisions via standard least squares regression techniques with extensive dummy variables. The empirical applications are in the cement, paper, and lumber industries for the postwar period and the nature of autocorrelation bias is stressed.

576. Morris, William Thomas. *The Analysis of Management Decisions.* Rev. ed. Homewood, IL: Richard D. Irwin, 1964. 551 p.

Attempts to use the decision process as a conceptual structure for organizing a variety of examples of scientific staff assistance to management decision makers. Explains the dynamics of the decision process in terms of data gathering, prediction and judgment, and evaluating outcomes. Also discusses applications such as replacement policy, decisions under risk, the recognition of risk vs. assumed certainty, inventory policy, bidding policy, purchasing policy, diversification, and decisions under pressure.

577. Morris, William Thomas. *Decision Analysis.* Columbus, OH: Grid, 1977. 290 p.

Decision analysis is the study of human decision making. It involves the development of models or structures and the experimental study of the models. The book's purpose is to give structure to or model a variety of business decision-making situations in the real world and to apply concepts of preference and uncertainty analyses. Topics covered in these applications include insurance decisions, inventory policies, bidding policies, purchasing policies, competition, and conflict using game theory and multiple criterion decision analysis.

578. Muldrow, Tressie, and Bayton, James A. "Men and Women Executives and Processes Related to Decision Accuracy." *Journal of Applied Psychology* 64 (2) (April 1979): 99–106.

A study of managerial decision making was undertaken using 200 male and female executives in federal agencies in Washington as subjects. They were given a personnel decision task, a dogmatism scale to complete, a questionnaire on risk taking, and instruments that measured sex role perceptions. There were no significant differences between male and female executives on any of the decision task variables. However, female executives appeared less prone to risk taking than their male counterparts, and they demonstrated a tendency toward androgyny.

579. Murray, Thomas J. "More Power for the Middle Manager." *Dun's Review* 111 (6) (June 1978): 60–62.
Several companies have begun involving lower-echelon managers in the corporate decision-making process. This involvement takes the form of a junior board of directors that is free to investigate any aspect of corporate business except wages and salaries. Specific courses of action are recommended to the corporate board of directors.

580. Naylor, Thomas H., and Vernon, John M. *Microeconomics and Decision Models of the Firm.* New York: Harcourt Brace and World, 1969. 482 p.
Presents a decision-oriented approach to microeconomic theory and managerial economics. Includes topics like dynamic and probabilistic models, mathematical programming models, computer simulation, investment models, risk, uncertainty, and marginal analysis models of the firm.

581. Needles, Belverd, Jr. "Pollution Control—A Framework for Decision Making and Cost Control." *Management Advisor* 9 (3) (May/June 1972): 24–31.
Article presents a pollution-control information system that identifies the internal and external constraints and critical decision points in handling the problem of pollution abatement.

582. Nees, Danielle. "Increase Your Divestment Effectiveness." *Strategic Management Journal* 2 (2) (April/June 1981): 119–30.
In many large diversified corporations, it is prevalent to consider divestment decisions as classified and secret information. Information about potential divestitures is restricted to top management and only a small number of senior managers are involved in the decision-making process. Article examines the reasons for this and suggests that the most successful divestments are those where line management's cooperation has been elicited at very early stages and that such a participative management mode is probably going to produce better results. An examination of fourteen divestments in the U.S. and Europe indicates that the division manager is a key person in the divestment process and accomplishes varied missions.

583. Neuhauser, John N., and Viscione, Jerry A. "How Managers Feel about Advanced Capital Budgeting Methods." *Management Review* 62 (11) (November 1973): 16–22.
Article discusses new models for sound capital investment decisions. However, nonacceptance is still substantial. This nonacceptance indicates a lack of trust for academicians. It is felt that exact predictions of models do not take into account the "feel" of the situation.

584. Newman, Joseph W. *Management Applications of Decision Theory.* New York: Harper & Row, 1971. 210 p.
Contains an introduction to and the applications of the Bayesian approach. Discusses decision making under uncertainty, the cost and value of information, evaluating research proposals, planning the development and marketing of a major product innovation, identifying and screening alternatives and structuring the analysis, developing a model for the analysis of

one-and two-brand alternatives, evaluating one-and two-brand alternatives using the computer, and prior analysis output and management decision.

585. Niskanen, William, et al., eds. *Benefit-Cost and Policy Decisions, 1972.* Chicago: Aldine, 1973. 535 p.
Presents analyses of public allocation decisions grouped under the following headings: challenge and response, general theoretical contributions, the discount rate issue, evaluation of benefit and cost estimates, investments in people, and investment in physical resources.

586. Noble, Carl E. "Solving Ill-Structured Management Problems." *Business* 29 (1) (January/February 1979): 26–33.
The low success rate in solving management problems is due to a lack of intuitive decision scientists. Decision science can contribute to solving ill-structured problems through the use of the idea-generation method and the strong inference method. Solutions to ill-structured problems can be discovered by using a system that incorporates people, decision science models, and computers.

587. Oakford, Robert V. *Capital Budgeting: A Quantitative Evaluation of Investment Alternatives.* New York: Ronald Press, 1970. 276 p.
Presents topics such as decisions based on complete and incomplete information, borrowing and investment decisions, sensitivity analysis, and probability and treatment of uncertainty.

588. Oxenfeldt, Alfred Richard. *Cost-Benefit Analysis for Executive Decision Making.* New York: AMACOM, 1979. 432 p.
Before the go-ahead decision can be given to any new corporate project, it has to be analyzed in terms of what it would cost the firm and what benefits would occur. This text discusses the technique of cost-benefit analysis and its applications.

589. Oxenfeldt, Alfred Richard., et al. *Insights into Pricing from Operations Research and Behavioral Science.* Belmont, CA: Wadsworth, 1961. 124 p.
Presents the use of operations research and behavioral science concepts in the field of business. Topics included are decision theory, game theory, pricing in competitive bidding, perception and pricing, attitudes and pricing, and group membership and pricing.

590. Parsons, Leonard J., and Price, W. Bailey. "Adaptive Pricing by a Retailer." *Journal of Marketing Research* 9 (2) (May 1972): 127–33.
Retailers operating in an environment in which competitors are the price leaders must determine how to adapt their prices to those of their competitors. A discount store does not need to post low prices on every item in order to achieve a low-priced image. Selected products are given low prices by the manager to convey this image. Managers must be highly sensitive to the effect of the local environment on their small subset of products priced at their discretion. This article describes a method that helped one chain store manager deal with this problem, by using a Markov process with rewards to meet the sequential decision problem facing the manager.

591. Partington, Graham H. "Dividend Policy and Its Relationship to Investment and Financing Policies: Empirical Evidence." *Journal of Business Finance & Accounting (UK)* 12 (4) (Winter 1985): 531–42.

An empirical study of the relationship between dividend, investment, and financing decisions. It shows that managers had definite motives for adopting other than a residual dividend policy. Analysis also suggests that independent dividend and investment policies were usual and that this was because external financing was determined on a residual basis.

592. Pastin, Mark. "Ethics as an Integrating Force in Management." *Journal of Business Ethics (Netherlands)* 3 (4) (November 1984): 293–304.
Ethics will not be incorporated into the management decision-making process until it is no longer regarded as an "add-on" to decisions. The concepts of good and valuable must be incorporated into an ethically and economically effective decision process. These concepts uncover a key fault in strategic thinking and generate questions central to any complex decision. The concept of the valuable is employed to distinguish goals and purposes.

593. Permut, Steven Eli. "Decision-Making of the Multi-National Marketing Executive: A Quantitative Approach." Master's thesis, University of Illinois at Urbana-Champaign, 1970. 103 p.
Deals with mathematical techniques in marketing available for use by marketing executives in multinational corporations.

594. Petrof, John V.; Carusone, Peter S.; and McDavid, John E. *Small Business Management: Concepts and Techniques for Improving Decisions.* New York: McGraw-Hill, 1972. 410 p.
Deals with topics such as marketing strategy planning, external and internal sources of information, improving information management, ratio analysis budgeting and break-even analysis, pricing, use of credit, improving production performance, improving personnel performance, planning for and improving sales performance, and advertising.

595. Piercy, Nigel. "Analysing Corporate Mission—Improving Retail Strategy." *Retail & Distribution Management (UK)* 11 (2) (March/April 1983): 31–35.
In recent years, considerable attention has been given to improving strategic planning in business because it identifies the long-term future direction for a company. At the heart of strategic planning is the difficult concept of corporate mission. The analysis of corporate mission offers insight concerning the strategic options faced and the ability to make more creative, aggressive strategic decisions.

596. Piper, J. A. "Classifying Capital Projects for Top Management Decision Making." *Long Range Planning* 13 (3) (June 1980): 45–56.
There is an imbalance in the research and literature of capital project analysis. Much work on the quantitative aspects of project analysis exists, yet empirical surveys show limited use of such techniques. There is some work on the organizational processes of project choice, but there seems to be almost no research on formal organizational systems for project selection. Article discusses the classification systems for capital projects.

597. Puglisi, Donald J., and Schillereff, Ronald L. "Goal Orientation: The Basis for Managerial Decision Making." *Federal Home Loan Bank Board Journal* 15 (10) (October 1982): 2–7.
Due to the recent period in which high interest rates have exceeded the

average gross yield on their fixed-rate asset portfolios, savings and loan associations (S&Ls) have experienced losses and survival struggles. S&L managers now have financing and investment decisions to be made. Discusses how critical it is that managers be goal-oriented in order to develop effective decision strategies. The proper goal is the attainment of maximum value of the organization for residual owners whose capital is at risk.

598. Rados, David L. "Selection and Evaluation of Alternatives in Repetitive Decision-Making." *Administrative Science Quarterly* 17 (2) (June 1972): 196–206.
Article describes a two-step structure and generation and selection of alternatives in repetitive decision making. In the first, decision makers generate and maintain a large, stable set of alternatives generally acceptable in the repetitive decision. In the second, they choose their action from this stable set. Evidence tending to support this hypothesis is presented. Further hypotheses on repetitive decisions from the Cyert-March theory of the firm are also evaluated.

599. Rappaport, Alfred. "Executive Incentives vs. Corporate Growth." *Harvard Business Review* 56 (4) (July-August 1978): 81–88.
Article examines that restructuring management incentives would be beneficial in that it would reintroduce the risk-taking spirit of earlier history without doing away with the cost-benefit approach to decision making.

600. Rice, G., and Mahmoud, E. "Forecasting and Data Bases in International Business." *Management International Review* 24 (4) (1984): 59–71.
Before studying the data pattern in a forecasting method, it is essential to evaluate the available databases to verify the reliability of the data. The characteristics of international databases and their possible forecasting applications are examined.

601. Rice, L. W. "Control Problems in Fight against Inflation." *Management Accounting* 50 (2) (February 1972): 41–44.
Accountants have an important part to play in management decision making. They must appreciate that the data which they handle each day have considerable inherent value. This article concentrates on one area, improving capital investment decisions, and the information involved in optimizing decision making. It presents the discounted-cash flow method of investment analysis and some ways of showing effects of inflation in the accounts.

602. Robinson, R. A. "An Approach to Human-Resource Accounting." *Cost & Management* 48 (3) (May/June 1974): 26–32.
Executives view that firms cannot afford to neglect human resources accounting (HRA) in their decision making. The development of adequate HRA methods will be a long and difficult task facing business firms in the future. The best approach to take is to make an immediate start in expanding the knowledge of the firm about its human resources that would permit immediate application of the results in more profitable managerial decision making.

603. Rosenberg, Philip. "Zero-Base Budgeting." *Local Finance (Netherlands)* 7 (1) (February 1978): 29–32.
Zero-base budgeting is a method of management analysis. It sets a minimum level below the previous year's base and provides the opportunity to present a series of levels or increments leading to or beyond the prior

year's base. It is flexible and must be adapted to each environment, but certain steps are common: identification in terms of the decision unit(s) for each decision unit, formulation of decision packages, and evaluation and ranking of decision packages.

604. Roseman, Ed. "Emotional Managers Need Guidance/Support." *Product Marketing* 6 (11) (November 1977): 42–43.
Any manager who is an emotional problem solver violates the basic tenets of problem solving and often creates major problems in trying to solve minor ones. Unsolved and partially solved problems accumulate, and old problems lead to a rash of new difficulties. Fortunately this person can be helped. Article has some advice for the emotional product manager.

605. Roussel, Philip A. "Cutting down the Guesswork in R&D." *Harvard Business Review* 61 (5) (September/October 1983): 154–60.
Because they find it difficult to communicate with research and development (R&D) staff, managers find it hard to choose worthwhile R&D projects. The primary problem is how to arrive at an understanding of the technical uncertainty of R&D planning and how to transform the uncertainty into an estimate of risk. Article discusses a suitable technique for taking the guesswork out of R&D.

606. Royce, William S. "The Problems with Planning." *Managerial Planning* 27 (3) (November/December 1978): 1–5, 40.
Planning is a system of analyses and decisions that directs the purpose of an organization, prepares it for change, and guides ongoing operations. Strategic planning involves setting corporate direction and determining the allocation of resources to meet those objectives. Article discusses the planning function and concludes that successful planning is done continuously and that a good plan recognizes uncertainty and provides warning mechanisms.

607. Rudolph, Barbara. "The Stupidness Was Mine." *Forbes* 129 (9) (April 26, 1982): 43–44.
Case study of how bad management decision contributed to a company's troubles.

608. Sarrazin, Jacques. "Decentralized Planning in a Large French Company: An Interpretive Study." *International Studies of Management and Organization* 7 (3–4) (Fall/Winter 1977–78): 37–59.
Examines the main factors that seem to make it difficult for large French companies to apply the classic planning models. Planning as a decision-making process covering all future activities of the organization must face up to the complexity of the environment. The proliferation of strategic studies gives rise to a multiplicity of real decision-making centers. Planning cannot be neutral vis-à-vis the social structure of the organization that adopts it; the classic planning model does not lend itself to genuine integration into the general management system of the organization.

609. Schiff, Michael. "A Note on Transfer Pricing and Industry Segment Reporting." *Journal of Accounting Auditing & Finance* 2 (3) (Spring 1979): 224–31.
Research was conducted to ascertain the effect of external influences on the transfer pricing policies of firms. Generally, transfer pricing is viewed as a function of the management accountant and internal management decision making. A review of currently issued financial statements suggests

some interference on the part of government and the Financial Accounting Standards Board (FASB) in this management decision.

610. Schlacter, John L. "Impact of Improved Information on Performance in the Distributive Trades." *Arizona Business* 22 (4) (April 1975): 17–26.

To survive, the distributive trades of retailing and wholesaling must focus on profits which, in turn, depend on the ability to get timely and accurate information as a basis for management decisions. To obtain this, retailers may use a modified return-on-investment model. Its objectives are to generate a favorable return-on-assets-investment and return-on-net worth. Article discusses the model.

611. Schlaifer, Robert. *Analysis of Decisions under Uncertainty.* New York: McGraw-Hill, 1969. 729 p.

Introduction to logical analysis of the problems of business decisions under uncertainty. Topics covered include assessment of preferences and probabilities, sampling, and simulation. Applications include cash-flow analysis, cost estimates, forecasting, income analysis, and value measurement.

612. Schmalensee, Richard. *Applied Microeconomics: Problems in Estimation, Forecasting and Decision-Making.* San Francisco, CA: Holden Day, 1973. 118 p.

Assuming a knowledge of calculus and access to a computer program for multiple regression analysis, the text presents a sequence of computer-based exercises in applied microeconomics. Topics include statistical estimation and pricing in competition, monopoly, and oligopoly markets.

613. Schultz, Randall L., ed. *Applications of Management Science.* Vol. 1. Greenwich, CT: JAI Press, 1981.

Annual series based on the view that the principal goal of management science is the improvement of decision making by managers in organizations. While not presuming to provide solutions to problems faced by decision makers, the papers provide a good balance between decision theory and practice. Recent volumes in the series contain articles on descriptive decision making, application of a general decision support system to project management, and mathematical models designed to improve decision making to functional areas such as marketing, finance and operations, and human resource management.

614. Sengupta, S. Sankar. *Operations Research in Sellers' Competition: A Stochastic Microtheory.* New York: Wiley, 1967. 228 p.

Analyzes the structure of optimal decision rules with respect to pricing, selling costs, management of production, and inventories and capital investment. Emphasis on integrating probability theory with the classical theory of the firm, with extensions to renewal and Markov models.

615. Sheridan, John H. "Do More, Work Less." *Industry Week* 197 (2) (April 17, 1978): 58–62.

G. Economus, director of the Graduate School of Business, DePaul University, Chicago, has discovered that by analyzing a job it is possible to work less and accomplish more. Suggests that management should have priorities, make decisions, and not linger over them. Managers tend toward two classic categories: achievement-motivated and power-motivated. For both types, setting priorities and getting others to do the job will free the executive for other more important activities.

616. Siegel, S., and Fouraker, L. E. *Bargaining and Group Decision Making.* New York: Greenwood Press, 1977. 132 p.
The situation in which a single buyer of a specific commodity is confronted by a single seller of that commodity is called either isolated exchange or bilateral monopoly. Decisions made under these conditions are examined in this book.

617. Simmons, Martin. "Planning and Optimising Investment in Stores." *Journal of the Market Research Society (UK)* 15 (4) (October 1973): 207–23.
This paper examines the contribution of market research to the location development and appraisal of individual stores. The trend toward fewer but larger stores, offering a wider range of merchandise, an extension of self-service, and longer opening hours, has increased the capital investment in building a new outlet. Market research, at a fractional cost of the total investment, can provide guidance to retailers on their management decisions.

618. Simon, Herbert Alexander. *Administrative Behavior: A Study of Decision Making Processes in Administrative Organization.* New York: Free Press, 1976. 364 p.
This is one of the major works on administrative decision making. Although more applicable to public institutions like the government, its analysis may have relevance to corporations and other profit-making organizations.

619. Stafford, John, and Fahey, Noel. "Do-It-Yourself Simulation Is Cheap and Easy." *Savings & Loan News* 99 (10) (October 1978): 122–25.
Article explains how models are currently being adopted specifically for use in banking. Widespread use of the models will free up executive time to analyze and estimate the effects of alternative courses of action on the profitability of operations.

620. Stambaugh, David M. "Imputed Opportunity Costs." *Management Accounting* 56 (6) (December 1974): 39–40.
An accountant's responsibility is to cover all considerations when weighing the merits of various proposals. Two important elements, often ignored by the accounting profession, are "imputed" costs and "opportunity" costs. They can be used in judging the value of alternative courses of action.

621. Starr, Martin Kenneth. *Production Design and Decision Theory.* Englewood Cliffs; NJ: Prentice-Hall, 1963. 120 p.
Designing industrial products is a difficult problem. This book explains how decision theory and analysis can help.

622. Sudit, Ephraim F. "The Role of Comparative Productivity Accounting in Export Decisions." *Journal of International Business Studies* 15 (1) (Spring/Summer 1984): 105–18.
The importance of comparative productivity accounting and productivity-based analysis in export decisions at the firm level under diverse market conditions is discussed. The structure of the relationships between productivity ratios, input prices, scale effects, demand patterns, and exchange rates is developed within the context of a simple macroeconomic framework.

623. Szego, Giorgia P., and Shell, Karl, eds. *Mathematical Methods in Investment and Finance.* New York: American Elsevier, 1972. 665 p.
Contains papers of symposium held at University of Venice in September 1971. They cover decision making under the following headings: mathematical theories of portfolio allocation, mathematical models of finance, applied portfolio theories, optimal bank portfolio selection, forecasting models, and application of stochastic models.

624. Tanju, Murat N., and Powers, Ollie S. "Managerial Decision Making under Changing Prices." *Cost & Management (Canada)* 57 (4) (July/August 1983): 26–29.
Many large, publicly held corporations have recently been required by accounting standard-setting bodies to disclose the effects of inflation on their results of operations and financial position. Accountants have traditionally been reluctant to depart from historical cost, but these requirements are causing accountants, managers, and other interested parties to take a hard look at corporate operating results in real-dollar terms. Article examines the impact of these rules on corporate price level decisions.

625. Taylor, George A. *Managerial and Engineering Economy: Economic Decision Making.* 2d ed. New York: Van Nostrand Reinhold, 1975. 534 p.
Economic decision making establishes a guide for every course of action in an industrial enterprise. It includes both generating and evaluating alternatives. The book develops this concept and its application to decision situations. Topics covered include rate-of-return analysis, comparison of annual worth vs. annual cost, equivalence, present worth analysis, cost of capital, replacement economy, analysis of risk, and uncertainty and forecasting.

626. Theil, H. *Optimal Decision Rules for Government and Industry.* Amsterdam, Holland: North-Holland; Chicago: Rand McNally, 1964. 363 p.
Explains the static theory of quadratic preferences and linear constraints, applications of the static theory, dynamic theory of linear decision rules, dynamics of production and employment scheduling, macrodynamic decision rules, and multiperson problems.

627. Tibbits, G. E. "Small Business Management: A Normative Approach." *MSU Business Topics* 27 (4) (Autumn 1979): 5–12.
The restricted resources of a small business make many classical theories irrelevant. The orderly theory of decision making that works for big business gives way to intuitive decision making in small businesses. Small businesses generally have informal organizations with the top executives performing those tasks they do best. The small business people must stay in touch with changes in the environment and the market.

628. Tietz, Reinhard, ed. *Aspiration Levels in Bargaining and Economic Decision Making.* New York; Tokyo: Springer-Verlag, 1983. 406 p.
Proceedings of the Third Conference on Experimental Economics, Winzenhol, Germany, August 29–September 3, 1982. The conference included the following papers: aspiration-oriented decision making; aspiration/competitive effects on the mediation of bargaining; balancing of aspiration levels as fairness principle in negotiations; information-processing in bargaining reactions to an opponent's shift in concession strategy;

international speculation with random demand in experimental market; and game-theoretic expectations, interest groups, and salient majorities in committees.

629. "Time Is Money." *CPA Journal* 49 (1) (January 1979): 79–80.
Formal time control procedures have been developed in connection with the production of goods and services, but in other areas of economic effort controls tend to be informal. In any work situation in which time must be measured, the prime requisite is the good faith of the person working. Overreporting of time applicable to any particular task will result in overstatement of labor costs and distortion of information for management planning and decision making.

630. Tummala, V. M. Rao, and Henshaw, Richard C. *Concepts and Applications of Decision Models.* Lansing, MI: Division of Research, Graduate School of Business Administration, Michigan State University, 1976. 476 p.
Collection of papers devoted to mathematical models used to analyze business decision situations. Includes topics such as simulation, forecasting, and testing.

631. Verespej, Michael A. "Personnel 'Undecisions': A Manager's Undoing." *Industry Week* 199 (6) (December 11, 1978): 58–61.
One of the most difficult problems that managers face is how to handle the underperforming worker. Some workers spend years in a company without producing at normal capacity. The problem is further compounded by the manager's reluctance to deal with underperformers. As a result, personnel decisions are not made, and the problem mushrooms. Article suggests regular performance reviews to help identify problems and discuss ways to deal with them.

632. Weber, C. E., and Peters, G., eds. *Management Action: Models of Administration Decisions.* Scranton, PA: Int. Textbook, 1969. 324 p.
Focuses on model building and brings together empirical studies in several institutional settings including retail department stores and basic metal industry. Field-based models are used as an aid to decision making. Applications include sales planning, purchasing, vendor selection, administrative budgeting, and program budgeting.

633. Weihrich, Heinz, and Krajewski, Lorraine. "Is There a Difference between Managerial Systems in Business and Education?" *Industrial Management* 20 (6) (November/December 1978): 21–26.
Examines decision-making processes and procedures in business organizations and educational organizations. If businesses and schools realized how much their managerial systems have in common, they could learn from each other and share knowledge, research, and practical applications.

634. "What's the Product Manager's Role in Media Decision-Making?" *Media Decisions* 10 (11) (November 1975): 67–69.
Media responsibilities of all brand managers start at the point where they decide how to allocate all marketing dollars. They are concerned primarily with advertising, promotional activity, and all other brand management pursuits. The corporate philosophy is that if we provide the consumer with a quality product the consumer will appreciate and recognize its value and respond with a high degree of loyalty.

635. White, Peter N. "Setting Customer Service Levels." *Quarterly Review of Marketing (UK)* 5 (2) (Winter 1979/1980): 16–19.
Decisions regarding customer service should take into account the following: order fill (the number of times on the average that it is possible to fill an individual order for specific stock), the type of delivery service, the speed of delivery service, and minimum order size. A nonlinear relationship exists in the increasing percentage of order fills one may attempt. To achieve a 99 percent fill rate would cost 50 percent more in inventory than an 80 percent fill rate. Flexible delivery schedules will permit a higher level of customer service than will fixed delivery schedules. Customer service levels must be given periodic reviews to maximize the possibility that the preferred level is in step with current conditions.

636. Wild, Ray. "Organization Design, Technology and the Influence of Operations Management." *Personnel Review (UK)* 8 (3) (Summer 1979): 5–11.
Operations managers' decisions influence the entire organization, the jobs within it, and the manner in which the whole is managed. This study explores their influence with particular reference to two major operations management decisions: choice of operating system structure and the selection of operations management strategies.

637. Wilhelm, Jochen. *Objectives and Multi-Objective Decision Making under Uncertainty.* Berlin, Germany; New York: Springer-Verlag, 1975. 111 p.
Explains the concepts of objectives under both certainty and uncertainty. Shows the techniques of qualitative analysis of multiobjective situations and their applications to business problems like product planning, factor procurement, raw material inventory, product management, sales, and financing.

638. Wills, J. R., Jr., and Ryans, J. K., Jr. "An Analysis of Headquarters Executive Involvement in International Advertising." *European Journal of Marketing (UK)* 11 (8) (1977): 577–84.
Examines the role of headquarters management in international advertising from a decision-making viewpoint. Conclusions drawn from the findings are the following: the international advertising decision process is complex; it is not subject to simplistic analysis; significant variation exists in headquarters management participation levels in different decision areas. The management tends to be less involved in creative strategy and media decisions, although it sometimes give final approval to such decisions.

639. Woodruff, R. L., Jr. "Measuring Staff Turnover." *Canadian Chartered Accountant (Canada)* 102 (2) (February 1973): 37–39.
Acquiring, training, familiarizing, and developing employees are regarded as investments and capitalized. By providing human resource information to managers in dollar terms, the impact of major decisions affecting human resources could be reflected directly in the profit and loss statement for the unit. As specific applications of the human resource accounting information are developed and refined, this tool will strengthen the everyday decision making of managers.

640. Wright, Charles R. "Decision Trees: Computer Modeling Facilitates Their Use to Improve Managerial Planning." *Managerial Planning* 31 (2) (September/October 1982): 30–34.

Although decision tree theory has been criticized by many as being too theoretical and impractical for business planning, the rapid development of computer-based financial planning models and the successful use of decision tree analysis in the public sector make the time ripe for the private sector to adopt the decision tree. A decision tree lays out schematically the alternative decisions, events, and outcomes that face the decision maker. Although decision trees provide useful schematics, their primary role is to assist in the quantification of the relevant factors for risk-neutral decision makers. Some hypothetical examples of the practical use of decision tree analysis are presented.

641. Wright, Robert Wood. *Investment Decision in Industry.* London: Chapman, 1964. 170 p.

Deals with capital budgeting, project appraisal, portfolio analysis and investment selection.

642. Yanahan, Patrick. "Marketing Decision Models: Why and How They're Used or Ignored." *Industrial Marketing* 67 (3) (March 1982): 84–87.

Marketing decision models have gained widespread acceptance. Nevertheless, it is clear that modeling must overcome management resistance, a lack of management sophistication, and interdepartmental communication problems if it is going to be used effectively. Article discusses a survey of companies using marketing decision models.

Decision Aids

643. Abdel-Khalik, Ahmed Rashad. "The Effect of Linear Aggregation of Accounting Data on the Quality of Decisions." Ph.D. dissertation, University of Illinois at Urbana-Champaign, 1973. 221 p.
The dissertation discusses the several ways to present analytic accounting information for corporate decision making.

644. Akoka, Jacob. "A Framework for Decision Support Systems Evaluation." *Information & Management (Netherlands)* 4 (3) (July 1981): 133–41.
Decision support systems (DSS) constitute a category of information systems used in organizations to assist managers in semistructured decision processes to improve effectiveness of decision making. DSS development involves design, implementation, and evaluation. Article presents a framework for the DSS evaluation problem. The framework determines the optimal methods of evaluation suitable to the characteristics of the DSS concerned.

645. Alwan, Jabbar. "The Role of a Forecaster in the Decision-Making Process." *Industrial Management* 25 (2) (March/April 1983): 20–21.
Forecasting techniques are emerging as practical tools in managerial decision making, although forecasting itself is not an exact science. Forecasting has become significant for current operational processes because of increased computer expertise and the use of interactive systems in business. The problem of forecasting should be viewed in totality. Article recommends the characteristics of a suitable forecasting system.

646. Amey, Lloyd R. *Readings in Management Decision.* London: Longman, 1973. 272 p.
The book is a collection of papers at a symposium sponsored by the Association of University Teachers in Accounting in 1973 in England. Deals with application of management accounting concepts to decision making. Topics concerned include cost of decision and external effects; utilities, attitudes, and choices; organizational goal; cost of capital and structure of the firm; information value; and theory of replacement.

647. Baker, Jerome D. "Rational Computerization." *Business Horizons* 15 (2) (April 1972): 36–40.
Article presents some logical guidelines for proper data management approaches. Top management should make the computerization decision. A list of questions are included as a test of data processing needs.

648. Baltz, Howard B., and Baltz, Richard B. *Fundamentals of Business Analysis.* Englewood Cliffs, NJ: Prentice-Hall, 1970. 546 p.
Examines the economic, social, and legal dimensions of business decision; the fundamentals of the decision process; and the mathematical and statistical aids to decision making.

649. Banbury, John. "The Vital Information Resource: Top Decision Making and the Computer/The Problem of Programming Your Hunch." *Management Today (UK)* (February 1980): 84–88.
Managers will need to have access to what is already known and to be aware of those areas of uncertainty in which judgment rather than expertise must be relied upon. Currently the analyst undertakes a disproportionately large part of processing corporate information, which results from default on the part of management. Ideally, the process by which information needs are made explicit should be based upon a combination of user judgment and insight, analyst's rational analysis and presentations, and organizational policies aimed at management control.

650. Bartholomew, John J. "Implementing a Change in the Accounting MIS of a Bank." *Cost & Management (Canada)* 55 (2) (March/April 1981): 14–20.
In implementing an accounting decision aid, it must be decided whether the decision aid will benefit the organization as a whole. Consideration must be given to the participants whom the decision aid will affect. Application of this principle to the management information system of one bank and its impact are discussed.

651. Bennett, John L. *Building Decision Support Systems.* Reading, MA: Addison-Wesley, 1983. 227 p.
The book focuses on building decision support systems and its development. Explains how to evolve complex systems out of simple components and how to use prototypes as the base for joint user-designed learning. The book draws on artificial intelligence in order to meet its goals of helping managers improve their effectiveness.

652. Bently, Trevor J. *Making Information Systems Work.* London: Macmillan, 1981. 229 p.
Explains how information is a vital resource for decision making. Also deals with developing effective systems and making them work.

653. Boer, Germain. "A Decision-Oriented Information-System." *Journal of Systems Management* 23 (10) (October 1972): 36–39.
The quality of a manager's decision varies directly with the quality of the information on which these decisions are based, and the quality of the information flowing to the decision makers is directly related to the effectiveness of the formal information system. Analysts, in evaluating a system, can access the value of the data in that system only if they know something about the kinds of decisions that will use the data. A procedure to make and also to increase the involvement of managers in the design of the information system is presented here. Variations of this procedure have been used successfully in the several companies to define the information requirements of an information system.

654. Bomzer, Herbert Wallace. "Stochastic Programming Mode Models." Ph.D. dissertation, University of Illinois at Urbana-Champaign, 1974. 70 p.
Discusses mathematical models in decision making.

655. Bonczek, R. H.; Holsapple, Clyde W.; and Whinston, Andrew B. *Foundations of Decision Support Systems.* New York: Academic Press, 1981. 393 p.
Provides an introduction to information processing, decision making, and decision support; frameworks for organizational information processing and decision making; representative decision support systems; new ideas in decision support; formalizations of purposive systems; conceptual and operational constructs for building a database knowledge system; building a database knowledge system; language systems for database knowledge systems; and problem-processing systems for database knowledge systems.

656. Bonini, Charles P. *Computer Models for Decision Analysis.* Palo Alto, CA: Scientific Press, 1980. 140 p.
This volume is a collection of interactive computer models. Since the introduction of time-share computers some years ago, the use of such models has grown immensely. The cases included have been developed over many years, but they all were developed with the same conviction that students could benefit greatly by building simple models themselves, translating these models into computer programs (or at least seeing how they could be so translated), and exercising the computer models and thus gaining insight about the decision problem involved. Many of the cases have (A) and (B) parts. The (A) case gives a general description, which allows defining the model at least in general terms. The (B) case gives specifics that allows creating a specific computer model and doing analysis with the model. There are computer programs to accompany each case. Simple instructions are included at the end of the appropriate case. Detailed program listings and documentation are available in the instructor's manual.

657. Bonini, Charles P. "Computers, Modeling, and Management Education." *California Management Review* 21 (2) (Winter 1978): 47–55.
The focus on computers in organizations has shifted from their use as merely a data processing tool to a new place as part of a management information system (MIS) designed to support management decisions. At the same time, the operations research/management science (OR/MS) profession has expanded into the area of strategic management decisions and away from merely routine and structured decisions. The reasons for failure of computer models for top management are lack of communication, lack of management incentive, and difference in cognitive styles. In order for managers to successfully use computer modeling they must know OR/MS and MIS technology involved.

658. Bonini, Charles P. *Simulation of Information and Decision Systems in the Firm.* Englewood Cliffs, NJ: Prentice-Hall, 1963. 160 p.
Presents a simulation model of a hypothetical firm. The model is a synthesis of theories from several disciplines of economics, accounting, organization theory, and behavioral science; and its purpose is to study the effects of informational, organizational, and environmental factors upon

the decisions of a business firm. The analysis is accomplished by making alterations in the model and by observing the effects of these alterations upon the firm's behavior.

659. Boone, Louis E., and Hackleman, Edwin C. *Marketing Strategy: A Marketing Decision Game.* 2d ed. Columbus, OH: Charles E. Merrill Publishing Co., 1975. 156 p.

This is a book of management games which can be used in training managers to acquire and perfect their decision analysis techniques. Games relate to topics such as sales planning forecasting, product strategies, and promotion.

660. Boot, Johannes Cornelius Gerardus. *Mathematical Reasoning in Economics and Management Science: Twelve Topics.* Englewood Cliffs, NJ: Prentice-Hall, 1967. 178 p.

Discusses mathematical models in decision making in industrial management.

661. Brightman, Richard W.; Luskin, Bernard J.; and Tilton, Theodore. *Data Processing for Decision Making: An Introduction to Third-Generation Information Systems.* 2d ed. New York: Macmillan, 1971. 480 p.

This text supplies a general understanding of the role and techniques of data processing within business and other organizations. Never before has the quality of decision making been so much under the influence of those not responsible for making the decision—the data processing staff members. To an important extent, this book is an effort to protect decision makers from the vagaries of their information system and to prepare them to make better use of its potential.

662. Brilliant, Roslyn. *Decision Support Systems.* New York: New York Institute of Technology, 1984. 77 p.

Thesis presented as part of a requirement for a master's of business administration degree. It discusses the impact of decision support systems on managerial decision makers.

663. Brooks, LeRoy D. *The Financial Management Decision Game: Participant's Manual.* Homewood, IL: Richard D. Irwin, 1975. 101 p.

Designed for use in finance, managerial economics, and executive training programs, this book outlines a comprehensive multiperiod finance case designed to provide an environment where skills are developed in both finance and general decision making. A multiperiod decision-making setting that is not duplicated with standard cases or problems is provided. Feedback on the results of previous decisions is received with each iteration of play, thereby providing repeated reinforcement in learning financial definitions, analytical tools, and solution techniques. Furthermore, an iterative decision-making environment forces the participants to recognize the importance of maintaining flexibility by maintaining a large set of feasible future options for their company. The game was developed at the University of Delaware.

664. Broom, Halsey N. *Business Policy and Strategic Action: Text, Cases and Management Game.* Englewood Cliffs, NJ: Prentice-Hall, 1969. 580 p.

A collection of case studies on managerial decision making in terms of company goals, policies, and strategy. Covers decision-making fundamentals, long-range planning, company resources, organization structure and business operation, operations and facilitation systems, management information system, operating results and operating controls, going concern operations and reformulation of policies, and strategy and business ethics.

665. Buckley, John Wiler; Buckley, Marlene H.; and Chiang, Hung-Fu. *Research Methodology and Business Decisions.* New York: National Association of Accountants, 1976. 89 p.
This is the third release from the project on Business Decision Models, which is cosponsored by the Society of Industrial Accountants of Canada. The purpose is to explore the potential for developing a management accounting system consistent with the decision processes and managerial uses of accounting information in decision making. The release presents the results of the first phase in the empirical investigation, which is concerned with the methodology to be used in the empirical studies within the project.

666. Burke, Richard C. *Decision Making in Complex Times: The Contribution of a Social Accounting Information System.* Hamilton, Ontario, Canada: The Society of Management Accountants of Canada, 1984. 185 p.
Explains the Society of Management Accountants of Canada's project on the development of an integrated social accounting information system. The study is made up of three parts: Part I describes the environmental and conceptual background for a social accounting information system; Part II sets out the benefits and the framework of such a system; and Part III is a case study implementing the system in a particular firm. It is important that management accountants understand how to implement and operate a social accounting information system and interpret its output. This system is the means by which management accountants are able to provide input to management to ensure that the social impact of their decisions is appropriately considered.

667. Burns, Thomas J., ed. *Behavioral Experiments in Accounting; Papers, Critiques and Proceedings.* Columbus, OH: College of Administrative Science, Ohio State University, 1972. 533 p.
Proceedings of Accounting Symposium, Ohio State University, 1971. Examines the method of using selected human performance variables to examine behavior with accounting information systems. Also discusses the impact of erroneous standards and varying environmental conditions on the setting of decision criteria. Analyzes the processing of accounting information perceptual bases. Investigates the use of accounting reports by middle managers and evaluates performance measures and incentive alternatives in a multivariable setting.

668. Burns, Thomas J., ed. *Behavioral Experiments in Accounting II: Papers, Critiques, and Proceedings.* Columbus, OH: College of Administrative Science, Ohio State University, 1979. 439 p.
Proceedings of Accounting Symposium, Ohio State University, 1978. Papers presented cover a wide range of topics including the following: accuracy of subjective probabilities for a financial variable; an empirical investigation of the information process underlying four models of choice behavior; procedures for the communication of uncertainty in auditor's working papers; behavioral assumptions of normative decision theory; an

experimental test of the independence axiom in an accounting business concept; empirical evidence about the effects of an accounting change of information processing; and human cognition in accounting.

669. Burns, Thomas J., ed. *The Use of Accounting Data in Decision Making: Papers, Critiques, and Proceedings.* Columbus, OH: College of Administrative Science, Ohio State University, 1967. 250 p.
Proceedings of Accounting Symposium, Ohio State University, 1966. The purpose of management accounting is to provide necessary financial and cost information to managers so as to enable them to make qualitative decisions. This is a collection of papers dealing with types of accounting information available and their likely uses in decision-making situations.

670. Bursk, Edward C., and Chapman, John F. *New Decision Making Tools for Managers.* Cambridge, MA: Harvard University Press, 1963. 413 p.
Deals with mathematical programming as an aid in the solving of business problems. Topics dealt with include PERT (project evaluation and review technique), econometrics, evaluation of new capital investments, mathematical models in capital budgeting, simulation as a tool for distribution, tests for test marketing, less risk in industry estimates, strategies for diversification, selecting profitable products, production scheduling, and quality control.

671. Business International Corp., New York. *100 Checklists: Decision Making in International Operations.* New York, 1970. 112 p.
Guidebook for international business enterprises, which provides step-by-step outline of the processes and procedures for decision making.

672. Butterworth, John Edmund. "Accounting Systems and Management Decision." Ph.D. dissertation, University of California, Berkeley, 1967. 272 p.
Deals with an analysis of the role of accounting information in the management decision process.

673. Byrd, Jack, and Moore, Ted. *Decision Models for Management.* New York: McGraw-Hill, 1982. 407 p.
Explains the techniques for the construction and use of mathematical models for computer decision making.

674. Carlson, John G. H., and Misshauk, Michael J. *Introduction to Gaming: Management Decision Simulations.* New York: Wiley, 1972. 184 p.
A textbook dealing with simulation and gaming; management decision gaming techniques; models design and decision processing; and management laboratories. Other topics include concepts in games design, how to design business games, behavior in gaming situations, and briefing material.

675. Carroll, T. Owen. *Decision Power with Supersheets.* Homewood, IL: Dow Jones-Irwin, 1985. 269 p.
Introduces the use of popular spreadsheets such as LOTUS, Symphony, and Framework as powerful decision analysis tools. These "supersheets" allow executives to perform decision analysis using a familiar spreadsheet format. Demonstrates the versatility, capability, and adaptability of the supersheets in various business settings including project planning and scheduling, linear programming, forecasting, statistics, and networks. Also

provides detailed guidelines for preparing the supersheets so that they enable managers and executives to maximize the utility of their software programs in all areas of the decision-making process.

676. Carson, Iain. "Taking Decisions by the Book." *International Management (UK)* 27 (9) (September 1972): 50–54.
A new decision-making technique devised by two U.S. behavioral scientists, Charles Kepner and Benjamin Tregoe, is discussed. It lays down seven rules for tracing the underlying cause of any problem. It also provides a scoring system for comparing alternative decision options. New managers are given a book about the Kepner-Tregoe method and then are run through exercises to train them in its use. Basically the approach consists of fourteen steps to prevent managers from jumping to conclusions about the cause of a problem or the best alternative to choose when making a decision. It works on the assumption that a decision is made up of small subjective judgments. A scoring system helps keep track of these judgments, to weigh one alternative against another. Essential objectives are noted along with desirable objectives, and each is weighed according to importance.

677. Causey, D. Y. *Accounting for Decision Making.* Columbus, OH: Grid, 1978. 557 p.
Emphasises the use of accounting for decision making. Covers essentials of financial accounting and analysis, cost-volume-profit and accounting for manufacturing firms, realization, matching, the cash basis vs. the accrual basis, and present value measurement of leases and long-term obligations.

678. Chacko, George Kuttickal. *Applied Operations Research: System Analysis in Hierarchical Decision-Making.* Amsterdam, Holland: North-Holland; New York: American Elsevier, 1976. 2 vols.
A volume in the Studies in Management Science and Systems series, this book explains how techniques of operations research and systems analysis are basic to rational decision making.

679. Chakraborty, Manash. "Decision Support Systems." Master's thesis, Florida Institute of Technology, Melbourne, FL, 1982. 63 p.
Discusses the concepts, controversies, and successes of the leading decision support systems.

680. Chandler, John S.; Trone, Thomas; and Weiland, Michael. "Decision Support Systems Are for Small Businesses." *Management Accounting* 64 (10) (April 1983): 34–39.
Decision support systems (DSS) are needed by small businesses as much as they are needed by larger firms. A DSS can be built cost-effectively for the small business. The goals of a DSS are to facilitate decision making, to support but not automate decision making, and to be able to adapt to the changing needs of decision making. The small business person needs to know what decisions should be made and what data are required to make them. DSSs can be an effective mechanism for these purposes.

681. Charko, Phil, and Harvey, Dan. "Building an Effective Modeling Capability: A Practical Guide for Managers." *Optimum (Canada)* 13 (4) (1982): 5–21.
The use of computer modeling systems as an integral part of organizational planning and decision making is increasing. To use computer modeling successfully, an organization should develop a computer modeling capabil-

ity that matches its particular needs. An analysis is conducted of the major challenges that managers face in building an effective modeling capability in their organization.

682. Claret, Jake. "Computers for Efficient Utilization of Resources." *Management Accounting (UK)* 63 (2) (February 1985): 24–27.
The management of resources requires information for the entire cycle of planning, deciding, and operating. The development of computer systems will extend the characteristics of accounting into all the functions of business. Article describes accounting system involvement in decision levels.

683. Corbett, P. *Accounting and Decision Making.* London: Longman, 1977. 207 p.
Management accounting deals with concepts of financial analysis needed for decision making. This text discusses these concepts. Included are cost and value analysis, financial reporting, pricing strategies, and other essential accounting techniques.

684. Cotter, Richard V. *The Business Policy Game: Player's Manual.* New York: Appleton-Century-Crofts, 1973. 111 p.
A general management simulation that provides a challenging decision-making exercise. Games relate to actual problems such as pricing, sales planning, research and development expenditures, new model production, employee compensation, capital investments, bank financing, sale or redemption of bonds, dividends, marketing and distribution, advertising strategy, forecasting sales, production scheduling, plant expansion, and evaluation of alternatives.

685. Cox, Keith Kohn, and Enis, Ben M. *The Marketing Research Process: A Managerial Approach to Purchasing Relevant Information for Decision Making.* Pacific Palisades, CA: Goodyear Publishing Co., 1972. 622 p.
Sound marketing techniques involve collection and analysis of information. Without accurate data, marketing plans produce suboptimal results. Book discusses what is involved in marketing research.

686. Cox, Keith Kohn, and Enis, Ben M. *Readings in the Marketing Research Process.* Pacific Palisades, CA: Goodyear Publishing Co., 1973. 400 p.
Companion volume to the compilers' *The Marketing Research Process.* It is a collection of readings on marketing research devoted to decision-making techniques.

687. Darden, William R., and Lucas, William H. *The Decision Making Game: An Integrated Operations Management Simulation.* New York: Appleton-Century-Crofts, 1969. 165 p.
Deals with management games relating to simulation methods and corporate decision-making techniques.

688. Dearden, John. "Will the Computer Change the Job of Top Management?" *Sloan Management Review* 25 (1) (Fall 1983): 57–60.
The developments that have taken place in computing and information technology over the past twenty-five years have led many to predict that the computer will significantly alter the role of top management in the future. However, despite claims of the coming information revolution, it

appears that computers will be used in the future much as they are used currently—for data storage and analysis. Computers are making a data revolution possible, but the available data do not contain the information needed by top management for decision making. Top management will continue to rely upon staff personnel for important information.

689. "Decision Making through Time-Sharing." *Best's Review (Prop/ Casualty)* 75 (5) (September 1974): 98.
For the first time in the insurance industry, the power of time-shared computing is available to decision makers at all management levels. Article discusses the approach at Aetna Insurance, which has an online planning model for regional offices called SOLAR (Simultaneous On-line Accessibility of Region). SOLAR may be likened to an independent management simulation system for Aetna's regional offices. The database for the system is developed on Aetna's in-house computer system at company headquarters, with the information structured into a modeling environment as set forth within the original programming.

690. Decoster, Don T., and Schafer, Eldon L. *Management Accounting: A Decision Emphasis.* Santa Barbara, CA: Wiley, 1976. 751 p.
Accounting provides a database for both types of economic decision making—interfirm and intrafirm. This book deals with the types of accounting data needed and available for decision making, use of the data and planning, and control systems for decision implementation. The concepts covered included costing, revenue and pricing decisions, investment analysis, product decisions, and budgeting.

691. DePrabuddha, Sen-Arun. "Logical Data Base Design in Decision Support Systems." *Journal of Systems Management* 32 (5) (May 1981): 28–33.
The decision support system (DSS) concept views the role of the computer in management decision-making processes as one of supporting, rather than replacing, managerial judgment. The computer improves effectiveness of decision making rather than its efficiency. DSSs are being designed for a variety of applications from product promotion to portfolio management. Article discusses the common requirements of any DSS.

692. Dhalla, N. K. "Regressional Analysis Means Better Forecasts." *Canadian Business (Canada)* 46 (11) (November 1973): 38, 42, 45.
Article attempts to provide guidelines for using regression analysis to persons responsible for preparing budget decisions.

693. Diebold, John. *Business Decisions and Technological Change.* New York: Praeger, 1970. 268 p.
Contains case studies in management decision making. Covers impact of technological innovations, management of electronic data processing, corporate planning and management information systems.

694. Dock, V. Thomas. "Executive Computer Use Is Doomed without Five Key Properties." *Data Management* 23 (12) (December 1985): 27–30.
A study of the sources of and the extent to which internal and external environmental information is used for decision making by managers with access to management information systems (MIS). It was found that managers rarely used a terminal as an information source medium for obtaining routinely generated information. Computer printouts are used most of the time to obtain routine and personally initiated requests for

internal information. The managers said that the computer-supplied information lacked accuracy, timeliness, completeness, conciseness, and relevance.

695. "Does Management Science Influence Management Action?" *Columbia Journal of World Business* 12 (3) (Fall 1977): 105–12.
Management science affects management action by its pervasiveness on executive decisions. It consists of many hypotheses and models such as inventory control models, project management models, and linear production planning models. As these techniques are communicated to managers, they initiate particular actions. Another consequence of management science is the development of management information systems. Depending on the objectives and design of these systems, certain types of information, on which they will base decisions, will be channeled to the managers.

696. Dreze, Jacques H., et al., eds. *Allocation under Uncertainty: Equilibrium and Optimality*. New York: Wiley, 1974. 256 p.
Workshop papers presented in Bergen, Norway, August 1971. Topics include axiomatic theories of choice, decisions under uncertainty, optimum accumulation under uncertainty, stochastic preferences and general equilibrium, competitive equilibrium of the stock exchange and Pareto efficiency, discount rates of public investments under uncertainty, and continuity of the expected utility.

697. Ebert, Ronald J. "Time Horizon—A Concept for Management." *California Management Review* 15 (4) (Summer 1973): 35–41.
Time horizon may be defined as that distance into the future to which a decision maker looks when evaluating the consequences of a proposed action. Time horizon is an intuitively appealing concept, because every manager is conscious of time as one of the important variables in almost every business decision. Time horizon can be used as a tool of management, for selection and assignment of personnel and projects, and as a tool for research in organizational behavior.

698. Edds, J. A. "We Still Don't Use Computers Properly." *Canadian Business (Canada)* 48 (12) (December 1975): 30–31.
Electronic data processing (EDP) is an expensive resource that can be frittered away when it is used unimaginatively. EDP, properly used, provides information by which managers can improve their decision making. Only a top executive has all the knowledge of enterprise operations to establish priorities for tackling EDP projects. To get the most from EDP, the manager must determine business problems and then provide the specifications for the systems that will furnish information to resolve those problems.

699. Edwards, James B. "Modeling—The State of the Art." *Managerial Planning* 2 (6) (May/June 1972): 8–11.
At the very heart of scientific decision making lies the concept of model-building. Models operate as guides and should be validated so that users can be confident that it does what it is supposed to do. In an economic world of limited resources and unlimited demands, all decisions are a matter of compromise. By constructing models, one can simulate complex situations, observe potential results, inject judgment, and make choices based on reality.

700. Elmore, Robert. "Mastering the Micro Makes Business Sense." *ComputerData (Canada)* 8 (3) (March 1983): 4–5.
Explains how computers aid goals in today's business climate. The capacity for executing financial modeling is becoming increasingly important.

701. *Executive Decision Making through Simulation.* 2d ed. Columbus, OH: Charles E. Merrill Publishing Co., 1971. 264 p.
Contains case studies and simulation in management strategy design and implementation.

702. Fairhead, J. N. *Exercises in Business Decisions.* London: English Universities Press, 1965. 218 p.
This is a manual for management education meant for training decision makers in a simulated environment.

703. Firholm, Gilbert W. "A Reality Basis Management Information System Decisions." *Public Administration Review* 39 (2) (March/April 1979): 176–79.
Managers who use technology in dealing with information come to think in terms of these systems. Still, successful executives are measured by their decision making, and computers are not of actual benefit in terms of judgment and initiative.

704. Feigo, Joseph Anthony. "Parameter Estimation by Management Judgment—An Experiment." *Mississippi Valley Journal of Business and Economics* 9 (3) (Spring 1974): 40–48.
Most heuristic programming simulations have shown that actual management decision making is based upon a variety of intangible factors not easily incorporated in the traditional demand function. However, it may be possible to incorporate these factors in another way, by way of the market response parameters from management judgment. In this way, the intangible factors inherent in this management judgment may be used with formal theory to develop decision rules which use all available information.

705. Felsen, Jerry. *Decision Making under Uncertainty: An Artificial Intelligence Approach.* New York: CDS Publishing Co., 1976. 134 p.
Objective in this monograph is to develop applications of artificial intelligence techniques to computer-based automation of judgmental decision making in complex real-life situations. Specifically, it reports the results of research into programming decision making by weighing evidence under conditions of uncertainty. Examples of such decision processes include analysis and control of economic processes, investment decision making, and many other problem-solving tasks in the real world. Recent advances in cybernetic disciplines (computer sciences, operations research, control engineering, etc.) make it now possible to automate some of those judgmental problem-solving tasks that have been considered the exclusive domain of the human mind. This work emphasizes the applications of artificial intelligence techniques to solving practical problems.

706. Field, Anne R. "Programs that Make Managers Face the Facts." *Business Week* 2889 (Industrial/Technology Edition) (April 8, 1985): 74.
A computer program called "Trigger" is an example of the new group of decision-making programs that are being used to help executives develop

business strategies and make qualitative decisions. Many smaller businesses, which cannot afford to hire consultants, have been particularly receptive to these programs.

707. Fisher, Robert A. "Decision Support Systems: Don't Look Back." *Computerworld* 13 (44) (October 29, 1979): Special Report/16.
Processing systems have been traditionally geared toward the needs of operational and middle managers. However, there is increased pressure for systems to meet the forecasting, decision making, and planning needs of top management. Most of the problems of top management are unstructured, which makes traditional structured systems unsuited to the task of providing support for decision making. Relational database management systems have been developed to help with this problem, requiring only that the end user tell what is needed and in what format.

708. "4 Factors Determine If Research Can Deliver Benefits or Technology." *Marketing News* 9 (18) (March 26, 1976): 9.
Capability, cost, credibility, and control will determine if marketing research will deliver the benefits made possible by technological advances. With correct use of these factors, the researcher can now predict the effects of certain decisions. Yet in order to be successful, the researcher must know the limitations of modern techniques as well as the advantages. Article expands on this view.

709. Fox, Harold W. "Managerial Motivations and the Pricing Mystique." *RIA Cost and Management (Canada)* 46 (5) (September/October 1972): 16–20.
Pricing decisions are not always made rationally but are often the result of a somewhat mysterious subjective process. The biases of the executives involved play a large part in this process and are worthy of further research. If we had a better understanding of what motivates executives in different jobs to price high or low, then we would have a sound basis for improving the process.

710. Freyenfeld, W. A. *Decision Support Systems.* Manchester, England: NCC, 1984. 72 p.
This is an executive review of interactive computer-assisted decision making in the UK. Includes a discussion of data processing support systems.

711. Frost, Michael John. *How to Use Cost Benefit Analysis Project Appraisal.* 2d ed. New York: Wiley, 1975. 202 p.
Corporate executives make decisions on new projects based on analysis of costs vs. benefits to the firm. This is a how-to book on appraising the worth of a project by using this technique.

712. Gallagher, Michael J. "Software that Helps You Manage." *Systems/3X World* 13 (9) (September 1985): 26–30.
Management software, designed to help the manager in decision making, generally fall into one of three categories: business-oriented diagnostic and learning systems, problem-oriented advisors, and problem-oriented decision-making tools. Article reviews three management software packages.

713. Garlick, Richard. "Decision, Decisions—Can Your Skills Be Improved?" *Chief Executive (UK)* (January 1983): 22–24.
Some managers are better at making decisions than others. There are many consultants that have a variety of approaches to better decision

making. Article discusses the approach of one firm designing information systems for better decision making.

714. Gibbs, George. *Accounting for Management Decisions.* Scranton, PA: International Textbook Co., 1969. 110 p.
Accountants have become part of the management team that makes decisions. This book discusses accountants' role in decision making. It discusses important concepts such as classification and measurement of income, present and future values, interpretation of financial reports, sources and uses of funds, and comparative position statements.

715. Gibson, James L., and Haynes, W. Warren. *Accounting in Small Business Decisions.* Lexington, KY: University of Kentucky Press, 1963. 133 p.
This is an empirical study of how small firms actually use accounting data in making operating decision. It investigates the role accounting can play seeking to establish norms of reasonable behavior. It also determines actual practices. The small businesses included in the survey ranged from printing firms, nurseries, retail stores, to manufacturing firms. Topics covered include merchandising budgets, product diversification, investment, and pricing decisions.

716. Ginzberg, Michael J., et al., eds. *Decision Support Systems.* New York: North-Holland, 1982. 174 p.
Contains the proceedings of a Symposium on Decision Support Systems held at New York University during May 21–22, 1981. Topics include the following: the integration of business information systems for Decision Support Systems in APL; the evolution from management information systems to decision support systems, optimization for interactive planning systems, and applying artificial intelligence to decision support.

717. Glimell, Hans. "Designing Interactive Systems for Organizational Change." Ph.D. dissertation, Göteborg University, Foretagsekonomiska Institute, Göteborg, Sweden, 1975. 184 p.
Constructs a management information system designed for decision making for organizational change.

718. Gochin, Roger. "The Chips Debate." *Industrial & Commercial Training (UK)* 11 (12) (December 1979): 502–03.
Expresses the view that in the near future computers will become important parts of decision making, and hierarchical division within the organization will become less obvious. As microelectronic technology becomes more sophisticated, organizational structures and individuals will show few similarities to current organizations. The challenge of the future will have to be met by two types of management: those who will facilitate the introduction of the new organizations and those who understand the behavioral aspects of management and relate this knowledge to the changing environment.

719. Goldman, Thomas A., ed. *Cost-Effectiveness: New Approaches in Decision Making.* New York: Praeger, 1967. 231 p.
Papers presented at the Symposium on Cost Effectiveness sponsored by the Washington Operations Research Council in 1966. Analyzes the military applications of cost-effectiveness. The nonmilitary applications are in the areas of poverty, such as job training programs, metropolitan transportation systems, and incentive contracting problems.

720. Gordon, Robert Mark. "Decision Support Systems." Master's thesis, San Diego State University, San Diego, CA, 1983. 114 p.
Discusses the implementation process for "data processing systems" for collecting and analyzing information for managerial decision making.

721. Graham, Robert J. "The First Step to Successful Implementation of Management Science." *Columbia Journal of World Business* 12 (3) (Fall 1977): 66–72.
Management science models can prove much more useful in decision making if managers and management scientists first work together to define the problem and then build the appropriate model. Problems must first be defined, management must participate, problem sources must be identified, and all groups with a share in the organization's future must be analyzed. As many managers as possible should interact to isolate problems, rather than debating possible solutions. The combination of people and events leading to a problem situation should be identified to find the source of the problem. Groups affecting or affected by the larger system should be examined to determine the consequences of their actions on the system. A checklist integrating all of the important variables should be made for every problem defined.

722. Greenstein, Joel Sandor. "Models of Human Decision Making in Multi-Task Situations." Ph.D. dissertation, University of Illinois at Urbana-Champaign, 1979. 113 p.
Covers topics such as event detection, attention allocation, and their implications for computer aiding.

723. Grofman, Bernard, ed. *Information Pooling and Group Decision Making.* Proceedings of a Conference on Political Economy, University of California, Irvine. Greenwich, CT: JAI Press, 1986. 279 p.
This book is based on the premise that the study of optimal group decision-making process could benefit from bringing together scholars from a number of different disciplines. Provides an overview of the nascent field of "information pooling and group judgmental accuracy." Topics are organized around five review essays: one on information pooling from the perspective of models of individual judgment (Batchelder); group probability and group utility from a Bayesian perspective (Bordley); information pooling and group judgment (Grofman and Owen); group judgment in applied settings (Hastie); and organizational design (Radner).

724. Gruber, Josef. *Econometric Decision Models.* Berlin, Germany: Springer-Verlag, 1983. 364 p.
Deals with econometric decision models in theory and practice and examines experiences and problems in large-scale applications. Discusses methods for obtaining the weights and target value in the scalar valued objective function of the linear quadratic econometric decision model.

725. Harvey, Sterling. "Computers and Management Decisions." *Canadian Manager (Canada)* 8 (3) (September 1983): 21–22.
Computers can be used as tools to aid in decision making, but they must not be treated as the decision makers themselves. The computer has a specific role to play in each stage of the decision-making process. Its ability to store and manipulate large amounts of data makes it an excellent tool for collecting and manipulating information. However, the data must be arranged and presented in a particular format in order for it to be

meaningful to the decision maker. The computer also plays an important role in developing and assessing alternatives. The decision maker can feed new data into the computer, use data already in the computer, or combine both to explore alternatives. Once the decision is made, the computer can be used to track the results and determine how well the results must meet expectations. The computer can also indicate whether further decision will be required.

726. Hastings, N. A. J., and Mello, J. M. C. *Decision Networks.* New York: Wiley, 1978. 196 p.

Computer networking is a major advance in the decision-making process. Its contribution includes communication and analysis of information needed to arrive at a decision. This book explains the impact of networks for this important corporate function.

727. Heap, John. "Management Information Systems and Their Impact on Productivity." *Management Services (UK)* 29 (3) (March 1985): 14–17.

It is the job of an information system to process data in such a way that it becomes relevant to future planning and decision making. The management information system (MIS) is an effort to accomplish this on a broad basis for managerial planning with the perception of MIS.

728. Hoard, Bruce. "Best DSS Save Managers' Time, Assist Their Judgment, Exec Says." *Computerworld* 16 (43) (October 25, 1982): 30.

Explains how a good decision support system (DSS) assists managerial judgment and increases the amount of time managers have to apply toward areas where they excel. There is more need than ever before on the part of managers for complex analytical online tools. When these tools are in the form of a DSS, managers will have more time for analytical thoughts.

729. Hoard, Bruce. "Execs Surveyed Say DP Operations Inefficient." *Computerworld* 15 (48) (November 30, 1981): 13.

A recent telephone survey conducted by Dennison National Co. (Holyoke, MA) has found more than 70 percent of data processing managers and 50 percent of operating managers feel their companies are not using computers as efficiently as possible. Discusses the results of a survey that found that computer-generated information is being used primarily in tactical rather than strategic decision making. Furthermore, doubt was expressed that even with the right kind of information, strategic decision making will always be cost-effective. A major roadblock to the use of computers in strategic decision making is the format used to present the information; it should be in summary form, and executives should be able to ask ad hoc questions.

730. Hoffman, Gerald M. "The Contribution of Management Science to Management Information." *Interfaces* 9 (1) (November 1978): 34–39.

Management science is the application of all sciences to management problems. Management information systems focus on managerial decisions. Their function is to capture data, and process it into a form useful to the manager, transmitting in a timely and useful way. Management science is not a set of techniques but a process of changing the management decision process.

731. Horwitz, Bertrand, and Kolodny, Richard. *Financial Reporting Rules and Corporate Decision.* Greenwich, CT: JAI Press, 1982. 195 p.
Discusses how rules relating to corporate financial reporting have the potential to affect behavior of firms. Specific rules examined include disclosure and management, segment reporting, and research and development expenditures.

732. House, William C. *Decision Support Systems.* New York: PBI, 1983. 468 p.
Data processing systems as aids to managerial decision making are of comparatively recent origin. This basic text discusses this databased, model-oriented and user-developed discipline.

733. House, William C., ed. *Interactive Decision Oriented Data Base Systems.* New York: Petrocelli/Charter, 1977. 372 p.
Deals with the components, characteristics, limitations, and languages of database management systems. Also deals with decision analysis which is an extension of decision-oriented information systems. Areas analyzed include decision trees, Bayesian approach, an interactive graphics system for analysis of business decisions, management and marketing decision models, and risk analysis. The book also contains a useful list and description of Harvard case studies on database systems and database management and a list and description of Harvard case studies on decision and simulation models.

734. International Data Corp. *Decision Support Systems.* Framingham, MA, 1984. 144 p.
A joint publication of IDC, Execucom Systems Corporation, and Evaluation and Planning Systems Corporation, this publication explains the electronic data processing systems that go into the setting up of a management information network.

735. Jackson, Barbara Bund. *The Value of Information.* Boston: Division of Research, Graduate School of Business Administration, Harvard University; distributed by Intercollegiate Case Clearing House, 1979. 55 p.
Uncertainty is a pervasive element in decision problems. We generally must make decisions today that are best, or at least acceptable, in the face of an uncertain future. Most people are made distinctly uncomfortable by uncertainty. As a result, for many people in many decision situations involving uncertainty, the first automatic reaction is to say "I need more information." They suggest collecting data to help learn more about the uncertainties in their problem. Unfortunately, it usually takes time and money to collect additional information. Further, in many problems there are numerous ways to proceed in collecting additional information. Methods are needed to evaluate potential sources of additional information to decide which, if any, possible choices for data collection seem worth the effort. This course module covers concepts useful for that purpose.

736. Janulaitis, M. Victor. "Are the Risks Worth Taking?" *Computerworld* 18 (33) (August 13, 1984): 13–22.
Integrating information services technology involves the risks of jeopardizing the resources of the company. The level of risk that should be taken in order to gain a competitive advantage should be consistent with the level of risk that the business executive can successfully manage.

737. Jarzebowski, Mark. "Forecast for Success: Practical Applications of Decision Support Systems." *ICP Administrative & Accounting Software* 9 (1) (Spring 1984): 18–23, 32.
In the past, computer systems were implemented in business to reduce the cost of handling basic business transactions. These systems were essential in reducing costs and improving efficiency, but they were largely restricted to the lower management levels within an organization. Managers can now construct their own modeling and information systems. Business modeling involves the modeling of business situations or possibilities before they occur so as to decide which course of action to adopt.

738. Jensen, Ronald Lee, and Cherrington, David J. *The Business Management Laboratory: A Computer Simulation.* Dallas, TX: Business Publications, 1977. Vol. 1 (various pagings).
This is a simulated game designed to improve analytical decision-making capabilities of corporate executives.

739. Jones, David A. "The Impact of Price Controls on Financial Decision Making." *Marquette Business Review* 18 (2) (Summer 1974): 98–98.
Institutionalized inflation is always subject in institutional controls, and threats of controls supposedly serve to cool inflationary psychology. It is doubtful that such threats seriously influence financial decision making. The actual enactment of such wage-price controls, however, definitely adds a new level of complexity to the financial decision-making process. Article discusses how certain firms, from a financial standpoint, should benefit more from controls than other firms.

740. Jones, Gilbert Thomas. *Simulation and Business Decisions.* Harmondsworth, England: Penguin, 1972. 172 p.
While incomplete information leads to uncertainty in corporate decision situations, the real world can be replicated in lay use of simulation techniques, which help managers understand the impact of alternative decisions and choose the one which would produce optimum results from the firm's point of view. This book discusses simulation techniques and their applications.

741. Jones, Jack William. "Making Your Decision Support System Pay Off." *Computer Decisions* 11 (6) (June 1979): 46–47.
Management decision support systems (DSS) offer huge potential payoffs, but to be successful they must be matched to the thinking style of the manager at the design stage. Otherwise, the manager using the system will be quickly discouraged and give it up. The purpose of DSS is to use the opportunity provided by time-sharing and computer graphics to support a manager's decision-making process in solving nonprogrammed strategic problems.

742. Kaimann, Richard A., and Erickson, Elliott E. "From EDP to MIS to DSS: Is DSS Anything New?" *Mid-South Business Journal* 2 (1) (January 1982): 20–23.
Article discusses the decision support system (DSS) which is essentially a variation of the management information system (MIS). Both systems are headed in the same direction, but the MIS is directed toward clerical efficiency, while the DSS is directed toward managerial effectiveness. MISs have achieved much success in helping managers control and direct functions but have not been as successful in the budgeting and planning areas.

743. Karson, Marvin J., and Wrobleski, William J. "A Manager's Guide to Probability Modeling." *Michigan Business Review* 24 (3) (May 1972): 23–30.
The theory of probability as the mathematics of chance provides an executive with a significant analytical tool for understanding the kinds of uncertainty with which we must cope and deal with effectively in a given managerial decision problem. Article discusses three axioms from which all managerial decision applications can be obtained.

744. Katch, David. "What Is Management Information System?" *Infosystems* 25 (6, part 1) (June 1978): 94, 96, 98.
Management information system can be defined as a system designed to provide management useful information in the necessary time frame to make decisions and to take effective action in various areas. The article discusses its applications.

745. Katz, Lawrence B. *Studies in Decision Making.* New York: Walter de Gruyter, 1982. 917 p.
Collection of papers related to decision making and information processing, theory and application of utility and decision analysis, ideation in individual and group settings, group influences on judgments concerning the future, and social and psychological aspects of future orientation.

746. Keen, Peter, G. W. "Decision Support Systems: Translating Analytic Techniques into Useful Tools." *Sloan Management Review* 21(3) (Spring 1980): 33–44.
Decision support systems (DSS) put computer power directly in the hands of managers to help them in their decision-making planning, problem solving, etc. Decentralization, differentiation, and diffusion of technical expertise have been the technological building blocks of a DSS. These new technological developments are being exploited to improve the effectiveness of decision making through a flexible, adaptive interactive system under the user's control. Article examines the factors for decision support system's success, namely, an implementer who understands the application and works with the manager and software interface to handle user-system dialogue.

747. Khorshid, Wafa M. "Decision Support Systems." Master's thesis, Eastern Michigan University, Ypsilanti, MI, 1983. 99 p.
The dissertation gives an overview of data processing systems for management information. Contains an application to marketing plan management.

748. Kievulff, Herbert E. *The Economics of Decision: A Practical Decision System for Business and Government.* New York: Kennikatt, 1976. 118 p.
This is a practical guide to application of cost-benefit analysis to everyday business decision making. It also deals with related concepts of incrementalism and implications of time as applied to areas like capital budgeting, cost of capital, and cash flow. The book also contains cases in which the application of cost-benefit analysis helped companies to achieve optimum business decisions.

749. King, William R. "Developing Useful Management Decision Support Systems." *Management Decision (UK)* 16 (4) (1978): 262–73.
Examines the element for a framework for a management decision support system (MDSS); an optimality criterion for system design; a participative

decision-oriented general systems design process; and a participative decision-oriented detailed design process.

750. King, William R. "Strategies for Success in Management Information Systems." *Management Decision (UK)* 17 (6) (1979): 417–28.
Several strategies have been associated with the successful creation of management information systems (MIS), particularly those that support managerial decisions. The system should be designed to meet user needs and user acceptance. Article discusses how to design a successful MIS for decision-making purposes.

751. Klempa, Mathew Joseph. "Decision Support Systems." Ph.D. dissertation, University of Southern California, Los Angeles, CA, 1983. 317 p.
Provides the results of a field investigation integrating cognitive style, incongruity adaption level, defense mechanism, and organizational characteristics of decision support systems.

752. Korez, George J. M. "LRC—Modern Technique for Functional Organizational Analysis." *Academy of Management Journal* 16 (3) (August 1973): 184–89.
Article discusses a relatively new managerial technique particularly valuable in clarifying and refining functional organizational structures and problems that seem to defy decision making where organizational requirements and interrelationships are especially complex.

753. Korn, S. Winton, and Boyd, Thomas. *Accounting for Management Planning and Decision Making.* New York: Wiley, 1969. 745 p.
Discusses the measuring and reporting of accounting data for decision making. Topics covered include income measurement, accumulating and adjusting accounting data for financial reporting, financial statement analysis, ratio analysis, fund flow, the flow of cash, accounting as a tool for planning and control, fixed and variable cost analysis, cost systems, fixed and flexible budgeting, cost control, distribution costing, long-term corporate financing, methods of evaluating alternative capital projects, data processing for management planning and control, and tax planning.

754. Kunstman, Albert. *Truncation of Long-Term Decision Models.* Rotterdam, Holland: Rotterdam University Press, 1971. 135 p.
Explains how medium- and long-term decisions influence first-period decision and how these influences can be corrected. Because optimization over long periods gives more information than needed, it would be better to truncate the decision model in such a way that only a limited number of periods would be needed, while approximating the same first-period optimal policy. Topics include mathematical formulation of the problem, formulation of the model, an experiment with a truncated target function, and the influence of separate link variables.

755. Laine, George P. "The Ordeal of Decision-Making." *Credit & Financial Management* 80 (5) (May 1955): 12–13, 27, 36.
Although aided by electronic computation and the correlation of statistical data, the final choice remains the executive's own. There is a vast difference between the prompt adequate decision based on facts and judgment and the impulsive, driven decision. Indecision may result from fear of making a mistake or of making a wrong decision. Wavering may stem also from perfectionism, the desire to make a decision without risks and

without disadvantages. Decision is a power process in which statistical analysis, fact finding, logic, creativity, and intuition are combined.

756. Lambin, Jean Jacques. "A Computer On-Line Marketing-Mix Model." *Journal of Marketing Research* 9 (2) (May 1972): 119–26.
The ultimate objective of an analytical marketing-mix model is to assist management in predicting the likely effects of alternative marketing strategies by a description of the marketing system, empirical estimation of response, and validation and prediction. Management is primarily concerned with the last step. This article reviews these steps as an introduction to description of a dynamic, competitive marketing-mix model, estimated by the ordinary least square method for a major oil company.

757. Lee, Sang M. *Goal Programming for Decision Analysis.* Philadelphia, PA: Auerbach Publishers, 1972. 387 p.
In today's complex organizational environment, the decision makers attempt to attain a set of goals to the fullest possible extent in an environment of conflicting interest, incomplete information, limited resources, and limited analytical ability. The primary difficulty in modern decision analysis is the treatment of multiple conflicting objectives. The question becomes one of value trades in the social structure of conflicting interests. Goal programming offers a powerful solution. This book introduces the underlying concepts and applications including the following: the graphic method and simplex methods of goal programming, postoptimal sensitivity analysis, parametric goal programming, financial planning, portfolio selection, marketing decisions, and corporate planning like sales optimization and media selection.

758. Levin, Richard I., and Lamone, Rudolph P. *Linear Programming for Management Decisions.* Homewood, IL: Richard D. Irwin, 1969. 308 p.
Presents linear programming for students and managers. Numerous examples are provided. Appendix consists of a simplex algorithm written in FORTRAN for solving linear programming problems.

759. Lin, W. Thomas, and Scheiner, James H. "Management Decision Activities and Information Requirements for Health Care Institutions." *Cost & Management (Canada)* 56 (5) (September/October 1982): 37–39.
Health care institutions are facing an interesting challenge from management information systems. The institutions have increased their use of computer-based management information systems substantially because of the pressure for cost reduction and the demands for information. Users have felt frustrated after the implementation of these systems because they have been unable to receive expected information. Article develops a framework for an effective decision information system.

760. Lindgren, B. W. *Elements of Decision Theory.* New York: Macmillan, 1971. 278 p.
Explains the use of data in making decisions, testing and estimation, normal distributions, the Bernoulli model, rectangular games, and sequential procedures.

761. Lindgren, Richard K. "Justifying a Decision Support System." *Data Management* 19 (5) (May 1981): 30–32.

A decision support systems (DSS) is easiest to justify when concerned with specific company goals, such as quantifying monetary risk of a given decision; whereas such problems as position by position justification of personnel, another DSS function, is more difficult to quantify. The central premise of DSS design is the description of normative and existing decision processes from various aspects of the decision-making process. DSS can be justified from financial bases but most often should be stressed as a means to improve organizational operation outside of the traditional cost/benefit overview.

762. Little, John D. C.; Mohan, Lakshmi; and Hatoun, Antoine. "Yanking Knowledge from the Numbers—How Marketing Decision Support System Can Work for You." *Industrial Marketing* 67 (3) (March 1982): 46–56.

A decision support system (DSS) is a coordinated collection of data, systems, tools, and techniques combined with requisite software and hardware, through which an organization gathers and interprets relevant information from the business and environment and uses it as a basis for action. DSS has significant contributions to make in problem finding and in marketing. To be useful, the marketing DSS should possess three important capabilities: customized reports tailored to managers' individual needs, analysis, and response to users' ad hoc requests in "real time." Article presents an example to illustrate the use of DSS.

763. Lopez, Felix M. *Evaluating Executive Decision Making: The In-Basket Technique.* New York: American Management Association, 1966. 159 p.

The idea that the actual job is the best predictor of future performance is the basis of this study, which simulates the job for which the executive is being named or for which a selection must be made. Assuming that a realistic job situation can be set up, that performance can be described accurately and evaluated consistently. The report presents detailed evidence for the development and use of a technique called in-basket exercise. This approach involves the representation of a manager's administrative workload on a typical day. How a person handles the sequence of problems posed in a situation is a basis for judging the person's potential.

764. Lucas, Henry C., Jr. "An Experimental Investigation of the Use of Computer-Based Graphics in Decision Making." *Management Science* 27 (7) (July 1981): 757–68.

An experiment is presented that investigates the impact of computer-based graphics on decision making. Subjects were persons taking part in an executive program for managers. Their task was to select quarterly reorder quantities under uncertain demand conditions. Trial simulations were performed using past demand data and ordering decisions based on the demand distribution. The results of the experiment showed that the graphics had a dramatic effect on the decision-making process. The system reduced the time needed for problem solving and gave users a better understanding of the decision problem.

765. Mackenzie, Eileen. "Operations Room for Fast Decisions." *International Management (UK)* 27 (1) (January 1972): 34–38.
An international company developed a decision room using space-age tactics backed up by electronic and television equipment spread throughout the companies on three continents. Article explains how decisions and retrieval of information are enhanced by the system.

766. Major, Michael J. "Plugging into the Computer-Decision Support for Managers." *Modern Office Technology* 28 (11) (November 1983): 62–72.
A decision support system (DSS) refers to the use of computer-generated information to help business executives make better, faster decisions. The DSS's ability to model is the key component that distinguishes it from other computer products. Discusses a modeling language known as the interactive financial planning system (IFPS). This system is capable of sensitivity processing, goal seeking, "what if" analysis, and "Monte Carlo" simulations.

767. Martino, J. P. *Technological Forecasting for Decision Making.* 2d ed. New York: Elsevier Science Publishing Co., 1983. 285 p.
Significant changes in the state of the art of technological forecasting include refinements and improvements on older techniques, as well as some completely new techniques. In addition, there has been a change in emphasis among techniques; for instance, a decade ago computer models were hardly used, whereas their use is now widespread. This book brings together the new techniques and the changed emphasis and integrates them with the older techniques. Also discusses a variety of applications.

768. McCosh, Andrew M., and Morton, Michael S. Scott. *Management Decision Support Systems.* New York: Wiley, 1978, 238 p.
Presents the philosophy of management decision support systems, along with examples of computer-supported decision making, especially financial and accounting decision making. Applicability to other fields of management are also examined. The book is primarily concerned with the ways in which multiple access or low-cost dedicated machinery can provide "conventional" support to solve certain types of managerial decision problems. It focuses on interactive financial systems such as budgeting. It discusses systems that support the decision processes of managers with flexible access to models and relevant information. Specific topics include profit planning, financial analysis of merger opportunities, and the pricing decisions. Also dwells upon the organizational implications of such decision support systems.

769. McDaniel, Charles. "Which Way?" *Interface: Insurance Industry* 7 (2) (Summer 1982): 8–12.
Prior to the development of decision support software (DSS), it was necessary for managers to obtain information manually. DSS is often used in narrow applications but has a far wider application than was originally envisioned. An important factor in effective use of DSS is the creative ability of management. Explains how to obtain the greatest benefit from DSS.

770. McIntosh, Henry E. "The Executive Information System: A New Dimension in Effective Decision Making." *Public Utilities Fortnightly* 109 (3) (February 4, 1982): 63–66, 68.
Explains how the executive or management information system (EIS or MIS) puts a large database containing variables that affect utility management within direct and easy reach of the executive. Advantages of EIS are

better time management for executives, direct access to information rather than depending upon staff presentation, and faster answers to questions.

771. McMillan, Claude, and Gonzalez, Richard F. *Systems Analysis: A Computer Approach to Decision Models.* 3d ed. Homewood, IL: Richard D. Irwin, 1973. 610 p.
Computer simulation permits managers to build and process systems models which produce useful information about the behavior of those systems. Simulation offers a means to understanding complex systems and requires the use of computer models and programming languages. This book deals with these topics.

772. Meddaugh, E. James "Report Frequency and Management Decisions." *Decision Sciences* 7 (4) (October 1976): 813–28.
No theory exists to prescribe how often accounting reports should be issued for management decisions. But accounting reports are discrete aggregations from continuous processes, and their frequency affects information content of reports. Therefore, if frequency affects information, then it must be a variable in the decision process. This research investigates the question of whether the report frequency has any effect on evaluations made from accounting reports issued on different intervals.

773. Mehra, Basant K. "Improvement of MIS Credibility." *Journal of Systems Management* 30 (9) (September 1979): 37–41.
It is important for the decisions made by different functional groups and departments to achieve the main objective of the organization which is to use the resources in order to maintain or increase the current levels of profitability. By trying to understand the decision-making process and developing their operating style to achieve the overall company goals and objectives, management information systems (MIS) departments can enhance their credibility. The major role of the MIS department is to provide management with information that can be used effectively.

774. Mintzberg, Henry. "The Myths of MIS." *California Management Review* 15 (1) (Fall 1972): 92–97.
A total information system is unattainable because the manager it is designed for does not exist. Research suggests that the real manager deals in current, speculative, and verbal information. Formal systems tend to provide aggregated, precise historical information which does not apply to the complex, instructed environment of the real manager. The management information system serves those who perform the routine programmed work not the manager whose work is largely unprogrammed. The manager, not the computer, is the real data bank of organizational information, and informal channels established by the manager constitute the real management information system.

775. Modigliani, Franco, and Cohen, Kalman J. *The Role of Anticipation and Plans in Economic Behavior and Their Use in Economic Analysis and Forecasting.* Urbana, IL: University of Illinois at Urbana-Champaign, 1961. 166 p.
Discusses the uses of statistical data bearing on anticipation, and plans of firms regarding decision making; the role of anticipation, plans in entrepreneurial decision making, and the nature of the "relevant" horizon; and the role of anticipatory data in economic analysis and forecasting.

776. Moody, Paul E. *Decision Making.* New York: McGraw-Hill, 1983. 192 p.
Provides a good introduction to decision makers, group decisions, human relations, nonmathematical decision-making techniques, PERT (project evaluation and review technique) analysis, force field analysis, Moody's precedence chart, decision trees, the value of information, utility theory, and probability and statistics.

777. Morgan, Bruce W. *An Introduction to Bayesian Statistical Decision Process.* Englewood Cliffs, NJ: Prentice-Hall, 1968. 115 p.
Provides an introduction to the conceptual basis of decision problems. Emphasizes the structure of the inference and decision process as opposed to the precise techniques by which particular types of problems may be solved. Concepts analyzed include Bayes' theory, the decision process in terms of the payoff matrix, the loss matrix, the expected value of perfect information and decision rules and utility, rectangular and normal probability functions, decisions on acquiring additional information including single-sample procedures, and sequential decision procedures.

778. Morton, Michael S. Scott. *Management Decision Systems: Computer-Based Support for Decision-Making.* Cambridge, MA: Harvard University Press, 1971. 261 p.
Presents a research project called a management decision system aimed at improving managerial decisions. Discusses the kinds of problems, the types of technology, and types of analyses that form the basis for the system, and it uses interactive terminals in the decision-making process.

779. Most, Kenneth S. "Wanted—A Planning Model of the Firm." *Managerial Planning* 22 (1) (July–August 1973): 1–6.
The development of a management information system must proceed from an image of the firm which represents clearly the underlying realities in respect of which managerial decisions are to be taken. This image may be called a planning model of the firm. The accounting model of the firm might be opportune to consider, particularly where the profit-maximization assumption is untenable and no other motivational assumption is wholly acceptable. Of all the theoretical structures presently available and in use, only accounting appears to be sufficiently extensive and free from restrictive behavioral assumptions. The task of developing the interface between the accounting model of the firm and similarly abstract models depicting markets and government agencies is probably simpler than it appears to be at the present time.

780. Neumann, Deev, and Hadass, Michael. "DSS and Strategic Decision. *California Management Review* 22 (3) (Spring 1980): 77–84.
Article discusses the implementation of an organizational unit which specializes in the development and maintenance of the computer decision support system. This unit must be distinct from the others that develop the transaction processing systems. Consistent and deliberate top management commitment and guidance are essential. An effective management information system (MIS) has two logical components: structured decision systems (SDS), which make structured decisions, and decision support systems (DSS), which act to support semistructured and unstructured decisions.

781. "A New Information Force Arrives at the Top." *Small Business Report* 9 (1) (January 1984): 72.
An increasing number of senior executives are using computers to enhance their analytical and decision-making capabilities. According to a recent survey by the National Association of Accountants (NAA), 60 percent of the respondents use computers in their daily activities. Computers also help executives feel more confident in their decision making.

782. Newman, David T., ed. *Decision Support Systems.* Santa Monica, CA: National Institute of Management Research, 1983. 1 vol. (Loose-leaf).
Contains the proceedings of a conference held in San Francisco, CA on November 30–December 2, 1983, sponsored by Management Education Corporation. Papers discuss the design and implementation of appropriate data processing systems for management information.

783. O'Connor, Martin E., and Probst, Lawrence E. *Analytical Techniques for Decisionmaking.* Washington, DC: Department of Defense, National Defense University, 1979. 336 p.
While most of the techniques explained in this book have military applications, they can also be used for effective decision making in industrial organizations.

784. Oglesby, Norman G. "Controlling Your Department—It's up to You." *Supervisory Management* 18 (5) (May 1973): 8–14.
Managerial control process involves the establishment of standards and the correction of deviational. The control process is both managerial and operational. In this age of computerization, comprehensive accounting systems and programmed decision making can help in the control process.

785. Phillips, Larry. "The Third Ingredient in Decision-Making-Preference Technology." *Modern Office (Australia)* 23 (7) (August 1984): 14–15.
Decision technology comprises people, information technology, and preference technology. The latter is a computer-based technique that helps to clarify subjective judgments made when evaluating possible consequences of different courses of action, the time and risks involved, and the trade-offs between different objectives. Preference technology as a decision support system for senior management differs from the traditional support system of middle management. Decision conferencing is one way to provide first-rate support for top management.

786. Piron, Stephen F. "Management Information Systems." *Management Accounting* 63 (7) (January 1982): 10, 13.
Article explains how the measuring of MIS costs on the basis of percent-to-sales is deficient in that the company is achieving benefits in productivity and decision making, which ought to be reflected as a factor. Also explains how management information systems help decision-making functions.

787. *Processes and Tools for Decision Support.* Joint IFIP WG. 8.3IIASA Working Conference of Processes and Tools for Decision Support, Schloss Laxenburg, Austria, 1982. New York: North-Holland; distributed by Elsevier Science Publishing Co., 1983. 259 p.
The developing computer technology has produced stable and acceptable decision support systems. This book discusses the processes involved in such a system and its state of the art.

788. Radford, K. J. *Information Systems for Strategic Decision.* Reston, VA: Reston Publishing Co., 1978. 181 p.
No comprehensive decision-making systems, whether related to operations management or strategic planning, can be done in the absence of complete financial, accounting, and other type of information. Book discusses the various systems available and their advantages and disadvantages.

789. Rappaport, Alfred. *Information for Decision Making; Quantitative and Behavioral Dimension.* 2d ed. Englewood Cliffs, NJ: Prentice-Hall, 1975. 398 p.
Deals with the informational aspects of management systems. Information is essential to the survival of all goal-oriented organizations. Recent developments in information technology, quantitative methods, and the behavioral sciences have greatly expanded the potential of information for organizational decision making. Where once the financial accounting model served as the formal information system, we are now witnessing the emergence of management information systems emphasizing mathematical models, systems philosophy, ex ante measures, and nonfinancial as well as financial measures. This book relates these advances in the management sciences, including the behavioral sciences, to the task of effectively designing and using decision-oriented information systems. The readings include cost, price, and output decisions; analysis of variance; budgeting; risk; and inflation.

790. Reddish, John J. "Data for Decision-Making: A Comprehensive Director Information Program." *Management Quarterly* 24 (2) (Spring 1983): 14–18.
Discusses the need for a comprehensive information system for effective management decisions. A rural electric cooperative is used as a case in point.

791. Redman, Louis N. "Effective Information: A Business Essential." *Managerial Planning* 30 (4) (January/February 1982): 21–24.
Emphasizes that a complete, integrated management information system is needed to provide decision-making information to support strategic planning, management control, and operational control. Such a system would measure performance against expectations. Article explains how to develop such a system.

792. Research Institute of America. *Decision Support Systems.* New York, 1984. 120 p.
Subtitled "Better Management through Computers," this monograph discusses business data processing systems designed to provide information and support for managerial decision making.

793. Ricciardi, Franc M., et al. *Top Management Decision Simulation.* New York: American Management Association, 1970. 126 p.
Decision making at top levels must be experienced to be truly understood, yet it is extremely difficult to simulate. This book presents the association's top management game which uses computers and problem-solving techniques to provide conditions under which a few hours of concentrated decision making under pressure will equal years of experience. In the course of the play, teams of executives make the basic decisions encountered in day-to-day operations, competing directly with one another. The game is expected to increase executive skill in decision making.

794. Ridington, Richard W. "Software Evaluations: Trigger." *Business Computer Systems* 4 (8) (August 1985): 91–95.
Review of TRIGGER, from Thoughtware, Inc. (Coconut Grove, FL), and of an automated managing by exception (MBE) package that assists with the implementation of decisions.

795. Rigley, Paul H. *Models in Business Analysis.* Columbus, OH: Charles E. Merrill Publishing Co., 1969. 102 p.
A presentation of some conceptual problems of decisions model building in business. Topics include models and decision making; the role of models in scientific inquiry; problems of model building; and the relationship among static, dynamic, deterministic, and stochastic models.

796. Riggs, James L. *Economic Decision Models for Engineers and Managers.* New York: McGraw-Hill, 1968. 401 p.
Discusses break-even analysis, inventory models, linear programming, networks, interest calculations, depreciation and replacement problems, investments, queues, and games.

797. Rivett, Patrick. *Model Building for Decision Analysis.* New York: Wiley, 1980. 172 p.
Explores the stages by which decision models may be constructed. Topics covered include influences on the decision maker, classification of models, sequenced decision, utility theory, competitive problems, forecasting, and simulation.

798. Rivett, Patrick. *Principles of Model Building: The Construction of Model for Decision Analysis.* London; New York: Wiley, 1972. 141 p.
Model building is a basic operations research technique every manager needs to master to be an effective decision maker. This book explains the process of constructing models.

799. Rockhold, Alan. "Computer Graphics as a Business Tool." *Infosystems* 28 (11) (November 1981): 68–71.
Computer graphics are being used today not only for presentations but also as a cost-effective aid to top management in high-level decision making. Managers have for many years had an abundance of data available to them. The creation of specialized databases suited to management needs has helped to convert the mass of data into pertinent information. Article discusses the role of computer graphics.

800. Romney, Marshall B. "Should Management Jump on the Data Base Wagon?" *Financial Executive* 47 (5) (May 1979): 24–30.
A database is a collection of data to be used by different application programs and is the repository of information needed for running certain functions in many organizations, including decision making. Most databases today serve a varied, but limited, set of applications, and one company may have several different databases. The most significant advantage of the database is the storage of data in a common pool. The database does not, however, solve all problems.

801. Roof, Bradley M. "A Personal Information System Check Up." *Management Accounting* 63 (7) (January 1982): 29–35.
The personal information system (PERIS) helps assure managers quality of information in their decision-making process. Article discusses a general paradigm within which a manager functions for decision making, consist-

ing of planning, organization, implementation, and evaluation in which both internal and external environmental needs exist and from which information is drawn.

802. Rue, Leslie W., and Clark, Thomas B. "Inventory and the Business Cycle—A Management Viewpoint." *Business and Economics Dimension* 9 (1) (January/February 1973): 22–24.
Presents an argument for the theory that management largely bases its decisions concerning future activity on its present inventory position as measured by the inventory sales ratio. This theory reflects the basic conservatism with which many businesspeople operate.

803. Schlaifer, Robert. *Computer Programs for Elementary Decision Making.* Cambridge, MA: Harvard University Press, 1971. 247 p.
Presents the MANECON collection of computer programs on the analysis of decision problems under uncertainty of the order of complexity. Most of the programs are used in the interactive modes and many subroutines and functions are available.

804. Schwartz, Maurice Henry. *Computers, Information, and Business Decision Making.* Austin, TX: Bureau of Business Research, University of Texas, 1965. 14 p.
Explains how computer technology has made possible the collection and analysis of information formerly not available for decision makers.

805. Semilof, Margie. "Grasping for Network Control." *On Communications* 2 (4) (April 1985): 21–24.
Communications network management system components depend on the complexity of the network. Article discusses potential of network for corporate decision making.

806. Sharif, M. N., and Aggarwal, R. L. "Solving Multicriterion Integer Programming Problems." *Industrial Management* 18 (1) (January/February 1976): 17–23.
A systematic procedure can be used for obtaining integer-valued solutions to the multidimensional conflicting objectives in management decision-making problems. Combining the techniques of goal programming and integer programming, the algorithm uses a modified simplex procedure and the cutting plane approach. Also considers the priorities associated with different goals' ordinal ranking.

807. Silhan, Peter A. "Electronic Data Processing and the Management Accountant." *Survey of Business* 17 (2) (Fall 1981): 18–23.
Explains how computers have revolutionized the role of management accountants (MA) and the decision-making activities of business. Computers and management accountants both supply information relevant to the management process. The types and amounts of information needed will depend on the various decisions and decision makers involved. Article also discusses advantages of decision support systems.

808. Singel, John B. "Computer Data-Base Systems (DBMS)—Who Needs Them?" *Price Waterhouse Review* 20 (2) (1975): 18–27.
The decision to adopt a DBMS must be based on management's judgment regarding the directions and amount of system change and development needed by the organization over the long term. This decision must be based on several key issues, including the recognition that a database facilitates the development of flexible applications, improves the respon-

siveness of systems to change, offers reduced applications maintenance expenditures, and facilitates the development of flexible inquiry applications.

809. Smartt, Philip C. "Ingredients for a Successful Decision Support System." *Data Management* 21 (1) (January 1983): 26–33.
The key to the success of any decision support system is its ability to be used effectively in the decision-making process. Discusses the characteristics of an effective decision support system, including an ability to examine and validate data, ability to provide the user with a wide range of reporting alternatives, and capability of examining all alternatives for selecting the best solution.

810. Southworth, Alan. "EFD—A Model Building Approach." *Accountancy (UK)* 87 (996) (August 1976): 104–07.
The model building approach is useful in aiding management decisions. Once the framework has been established, relevant figures may be plugged in so that information for routine business decisions is immediately available. After the basic model is established, the decisions to which it leads will be consistent. Article explains the pitfalls and benefits of this approach.

811. Spencer, William L. "What Do Upper Executives Want from MIS?" *Administrative Management* 39 (7) (July 1978): 26–27, 66–68.
All executives really want from a management information system is enough relevant information at the right time and at the best possible cost. Article explains what it takes to accomplish this purpose.

812. Spooner, Peter. "Computers—Dream Machines or a Corporate Nightmare?" *Chief Executive (UK)* 18 (3) (March 1985): 48–49.
Management often has been so overwhelmed by computer technology that it has left decisions to consultants and to data processing specialists, who may understand computers better than they understand what the company needs to grow. A manager who can decide what computing should be done and how it should be done will fit comfortably into a corporate strategy that includes a total vision of both current and future business objectives.

813. Spooner, Peter. "Intelligent Computers Can Play a Hunch." *Chief Executive (UK)* 14 (10) (October 1981): 29–30.
According to some "futurologists," the impact of computer technology on top management decision making is going to be enormous. Some predict that computers even will be able to make top management decisions. Article discusses the trend toward human and computer partnerships, with computer-aided decision making.

814. Spooner, Peter. "Who'll Decide: You or Smart Machine?" *Chief Executive (UK)* 13 (10) (October 1980): 27, 29–30.
Sperry Univac recently held a symposium on information processing technology focused primarily on macrodecisions. The concepts can be easily related to microdecisions. According to the article, two problems are apparent: the processing power of computers now exceeds the interface between man and machine, and even good decisions can be blocked by a vocal nonrepresentative minority. Article stresses that the goal of information processing specialists is a proactive management system based on intelligent forecasting. Executives are often inhibited by the sheer weight

and complexity of data. A good decision maker filters significant information from the mass of data.

815. Sprague, R. H. *Building Effective Decision Support Systems.* Englewood Cliffs, NJ: Prentice-Hall, 1982. 329 p.
Explains the impact of computer technology on the information availability for managerial decision making. There are many systems available. This book explains how to choose or construct the right one for particular situations so as to get optimum input.

816. Sprague, R. H., and Watson, Hugh J. "Bit by Bit: Toward Decision Support Systems." *California Management Review* 22 (1) (Fall 1979): 60–68.
Decision support systems, sometimes referred to as strategic planning systems, are computer systems that allow managers to analyze historical data and simulate alternative courses of action. Specifically these are integrated information systems composed of a database and decision models. The system is set up so the manager has easy access and rapid feedback, which is in contrast to typical report generation and information retrieval systems. Article discusses the components of the system.

817. Summers, E. L. *An Introduction to Accounting for Decision Making and Control.* Homewood, IL: Richard D. Irwin, 1974. 565 p.
Text dealing with management accounting which supplies financial data useful for decision makers at all levels in planning and administering an enterprise. Includes topics such as cost accounting, systems and procedures, budgeting, internal auditing, and financial analysis.

818. Surden, Esther. "Thesis Explores Motivations for Going to DDP." *Computerworld* 12 (10) (March 6, 1978): S/45, S/46.
Strong psychological, functional, and economic forces are behind management decisions to decentralize data processing (DDP) operations. A drop in hardware costs allows decentralization to occur at the initiative of lower-level managers. Decisions by lower-level managers may overlook the technological constraints of decentralization, especially the problems of networking loosely coupled computers.

819. Tersine, Richard J. "Systems Theory in Modern Organizations." *Managerial Planning* 22 (3) (November/December 1973): 32–40.
Notes that there are certain drawbacks to systems theory. It cannot improve managerial judgment, identify objectives of the managers or their organizations, nor can it aid in the prediction of future conditions and consequences of decisions. It does not indicate in what business to be, whether to diversify or consolidate, how to divisionalize, or whether to centralize or decentralize operations.

820. Thierauf, Robert J. *Decision Support Systems for Effective Planning and Control.* Englewood Cliffs, NJ: Prentice-Hall, 1982. 305 p.
This book provides a case study approach to a complete decision support system. Presents a complete decision support system for a progressive manufacturing company. Systems are analyzed, designed, and evaluated for corporate planning, finance, marketing, research and development, engineering personnel, manufacturing, purchasing, inventory, physical distribution, and accounting. Similarly quantitative and statistical models are identified and related to each functional area where deemed appropriate.

821. Tull, Donald S., and Albaum, Gerald S. *Survey Research: A Decisional Approach.* New York: Intext Educational Publishers, 1973. 244 p.

Surveys are conducted to provide information for making a decision. This book deals with topics such as methods of inquiry and survey design, sampling, research design, measurement and scaling, and techniques of analysis. The book is recommended as a text for areas in which decisional research is conducted.

822. Vazsonyi, Andrew. "Information Systems in Management Science-Decision Support Systems: The New Technology of Decision Making?" *Interfaces* 9 (1) (November 1978): 72–77.

Many managerial decisions require quick responses from decision support systems (DSS). Article discusses the major limitation of operations research/management science and suggests a solution in terms of (DSS), which relies on the decision maker's insights and judgment from problem formulation to evaluating the solutions presented.

823. Von Der Embse, Thomas J. "Choosing a Management Development Program—A Decision Model." *Personnel Journal* 52 (10) (October 1973): 707–12.

Article develops a useful framework for choosing a type of training and development program that meets the needs of the organization. The model attempts to provide the decision maker with a rationale for making a critical choice, i.e., how to optimize the development effort with limited financial and personnel resources.

824. Wagner, Gerald R. "Decision Support Systems: Computerized Mind Support for Executive Problems." *Managerial Planning* 30 (2) (September/October 1981): 9–16.

A typical support system is described, namely a computerized model of a company's field sales force. Article discusses the advantages of such a system.

825. Wagner, Gerald R. "Decision Support Systems: The Real Substance." *Interfaces* 11(2) (April 1981): 77–86.

A number of computer-based models and information systems have proven directly useful to executives. These systems actually seem to enhance manager's thinking processes. Article discusses the evolution and use of decision support systems.

826. Wagner, Gerald R. "Decision Support in the Office of the Future." *Managerial Planning* 28 (6) (May/June 1980): 3–5.

The office of the future is likely to contain many advanced communication aids: computerized scheduling calendars, access to data storage and retrieval systems, electronic communication links with superiors and subordinates, and computerized tickler files. The basic function of a manager is to make decisions, and future office technology will aid managers in this function. Article discusses decision support systems (DSS) and new planning and modeling languages. Models can be set up to deal with continuing planning questions or can be developed on an ad hoc basis to deal with specific problems or decisions. When integrated with communications advances, DSS can be a tool for enhancing and amplifying the inherent mental powers of managers and stimulating their creativity.

827. Watkins, Paul R. "Perceived Information Structure Implications for Decision Support System Design." *Decision Sciences* 13 (1) (January 1982): 38–59.
Top-level decision making in business organizations is often characterized by high degrees of uncertainty, incomplete information, and conflicting objectives. Decision support systems (DSS) have been proposed to support top-level decision making effectively. Information supplied by a DSS is selective because not all possible information sets may be feasibly or economically represented in the database. The purpose of this study is to evaluate one aspect of human information processing and its potential impact on decision making.

828. "'What If' Help for Management." *Business Week* 2620 (Industrial Edition) (January 21, 1980): 73–74.
Article discusses the so-called management support or decision support computer system. With a decision support system, executives in a matter of minutes can sift through the trade-offs among a number of operating plans to find the optimum, or least expensive, solutions to manufacturing, distribution, and marketing dilemmas. The principal use is in operational planning. Some firms are using the system for strategic planning, guiding such decisions as whether to enter a new market. At the core of any management support system is a computer model in software that describes the process to be managed. The computer can then sort through extensive "what if" scenarios. Such a system is not automatically installed. It requires time, money, an accurate model, and accurate operating data. However, the payback period on a management support system can be very short.

829. Whiteside, David. "Computers Invade the Executive Suite." *International Management (UK)* 38 (8) (August 1983): 12–18.
Computers are becoming increasingly popular with senior executives who use them to enhance their analytical abilities and help them reach management decisions faster and with greater confidence. Article discusses whether this will have an impact on managers' interpersonal skills.

830. Whiting, Marcella Denise. *A Conceptual Analysis of Decision Support Systems.* Austin, TX: University of Texas, 1983. 97 p.
Presented toward an MBA degree, this paper discusses the basic concepts in the design and implementation of a management information system for decision making.

831. Wight, Oliver. "Why People Come First in Computer-Based Systems." *Modern Materials Handling* 36 (6) (May 6, 1981): 58–62.
Computers can process information, but people make decisions. Article talks about four important systems. Principles arising from these facts are accountability, transparency, data integrity, and validity of simulation. A computer cannot be held accountable, only the people using the computer are accountable for the decisions made.

832. Willings, David Richard. *How to Use the Case Study in Training for Decision Making.* London: Business Publications, 1968. 274 p.
While some decison-making abilities are intuitive, it is also true that these abilities can be learned by managers. This book uses a case study approach for training managers in this function.

833. Willis, R. E., and Chervany, N. L. *Statistical Analysis and Modelling for Management Decision-Making.* Belmont, CA: Wadsworth, 1974. 558 p.

Deals with mathematical models that aid decision makers. Includes simulation techniques.

834. Worthington, James S. "Fire EDP as Manager, Rehire EDP as Management's Helper!" *Data Management* 18 (3) (March 1980): 48–49.

An electronic data processing (EDP) system cannot replace people in management positions. It can only assist management by providing faster, more accurate, and more reliable information. Firms should not justify hiring or expanding EDP merely because a firm is growing and successful. Managerial decisions must be reduced, or managerial results are less than satisfactory. EDP can never deviate from a prescribed pattern nor can it ever make a subjective decision. Human managers are needed to make decisions requiring intelligence reasoning and subjectivity.

835. Winberg, William B. "Information for Decision-Making." *Best's Review (Life/Health)* 73 (8) (December 1972): 60–66.

Article states that every company has a management information system, MIS, which is used to help managers make decisions. Goals for the MIS are not explored fully or achieved in a way so that the members benefit to the fullest. Changes are necessary if the system is to function and maintain its timeliness, accuracy, economy, relevance, and usefulness. The quality of the decisions cannot rise above the quality of the information as a basis for decision making.

836. Yaverbaum, Gayle J., and Sherr, David M. "Experimental Results toward the Customization of Information Systems." *Human Relations* 38 (2) (February 1986): 117–34.

Assesses the information-seeking and decision-making processes of a sample of college students participating in a management game. The game was designed to reflect stages of information gathering/decision making including subjective decision making based on the use of informal observations or advice from others, subjective/analytical decision making involving the informal analysis of data, and analytical decision making using statistical data. The experiment implied that information systems must be designed in accordance with user decision-making patterns.

837. Zuckerman, Irv. "Use a Journal to Nip that Next Crisis in the Bud." *Product Marketing* 6 (11) (November 1977): 44–45.

A good journal of past proceedings and events can often be a great asset in forecasting future events accurately and in making decisions in advance. If a problem arose in the past and nothing was done to prevent it from coming up again, it will come up again. Without a good journal to refer to, what was done in the past (the omission that probably precipitated the reoccurrence of the problem) will probably not be realized, and what was done about it last time will not be done again.

Quantitative Techniques

838. Ackoff, Russell L., ed. *Progress in Operations Research.* New York: Wiley, 1961. 505 p.
Includes topics like linear and dynamic programming, sequencing theory, replacement theory, simulation, and gaming. Also deals with foundations of operations research and decision and value theory.

839. Aigner, Dennis J. *Principles of Statistical Decision Making.* New York: Macmillan, 1968. 145 p.
Enumerates the principles of statistical decision-making process or inference. Topics include elements of the calculus of probabilities, probability distribution, moments of single variable distribution, sampling and estimation, hypothesis testing, cost of decision errors, and the optimum decision rule.

840. Aitchison, John. *Choice against Chance; An Introduction to Statistical Decision Theory.* Reading, MA: Addison-Wesley, 1970. 284 p.
Most decisions are made in situations full of uncertainties. Right decisions may really be a matter of chance. However there are some statistical techniques that help remove most of the uncertainties in decisions. This book discusses these techniques.

841. Alan, A. J., and Parisi, D. G. *Quantitative Methods for Decision Making.* St. Paul, MN: General Learning Press, 1974. 542 p.
Textbook for an introductory course in mathematical and statistical methods available for use by decision makers. Covers statistics, probability, modeling, simulation and linear programming techniques.

842. Anderson, David R., et al. *An Introduction to Management Science: Quantitative Approaches to Decision Making.* St. Paul, MN: West Publishing Co., 1976. 631 p.
Discusses linear programming and the simplex method; assignment and transportation problems; decision theory; deterministic and probablistic inventory models; PERT (project evaluation and review technique) and CPM (critical path method) models; waiting line models; simulation and dynamic programming; and Markov chains.

843. Anderson, David Ray; Sweeney, Dennis J.; and Williams, Thomas A. *Linear Programming for Decision Making: An Applications Approach.* St. Paul, MN: West Publishing Co., 1974. 378 p.
Provides students, primarily in the fields of administration or economics, with an introduction to linear programming and its applications. Theoretical topics are followed immediately by an illustration of how they can be

applied. Covers the functional areas of business and implementation procedures for large-scale linear programming models.

844. Anderson, M. Q. *Quantitative Management Decision Making.* San Francisco, CA: Brooks/Cole, 1982. 623 p.

Textbook for undergraduate courses on mathematical and statistical aids to decision making. Covers sampling, linear programming, simulation, queueing theory, Markov methods, and Bayesian analysis.

845. Anson, Cyril Joseph. *Profit from Figures: A Manager's Guide to Statistical Methods.* London; New York: McGraw-Hill, 1971. 272 p.

Sound managerial decisions are based on facts which in many instances are expressed in the form of figures. Unfortunately the measurements used in management produce figures which are subject to fluctuations. Hence, statistical methods are needed to extract the implications from these figures. The book is devoted to an examination of the statistical methods needed by managerial decision makers such as sampling, monitoring, forecasting and planning, and simulation. It is slanted toward manufacturing industries, although applications to banking and transportation industries are also discussed.

846. Armore, Sidney J. *Elementary Statistics and Decision Making.* Columbus, OH: Charles E. Merrill Publishing Co., 1973. 431 p.

Basic introductory text on the statistical basis for decision making. Covers concepts such as probability, random sampling, population and sampling models, confidence intervals, tests of hypotheses, tests relating to frequencies, analysis of variance, and nonparametric tests.

847. Baird, B. F. *Introduction to Decision Analysis.* North Scintate, MA: Duxbury Press, 1978. 440 p.

Provides a basic introduction to some fundamental concepts of decision making. The analytical techniques covered include random variables and probability distributions, probability, decision theory and inference, Bayesian concepts, construction of decision diagrams, the theory and application of utility, and sensitivity analysis.

848. Barclay, Scott, et al. *Handbook for Decision Analysis.* McLean, VA: Decisions and Designs, Inc., 1977. 276 p.

Deals with diagraming and solving decision problems, value and evaluation, measuring uncertainty, probability diagrams and hierarchical inference, the value of information, and application of decision-analytic methods.

849. Barnett, Vic. *Comparative Statistical Inferences.* New York: Wiley, 1973. 287 p.

Provides a good introduction to statistical inference and decision making. Specific topics covered include batch quality, component lifetimes, probability, utility and decision making, estimation and hypothesis testing, point estimation, region and internal estimates, Bayesian inference, decision theory, fiducial inference, likelihood inference, and structural inference.

850. Bellman, Richard E. *Dynamic Programming.* Princeton, NJ: Princeton University Press, 1957. 340 p.

Introduces the mathematical theory of deterministic and stochastic discrete and continuous, multistage decision processes for mathematicians, economists, statisticians, engineers, and operations research analysts. The processes are treated by both dynamic programming and the calculus of variations. Topics include existence optimal inventory equation, bottlenecks, multistage games, and Markovian decision processes.

851. Bierman, Harold; Bonini, Charles P.; and Haussman, Warren H. *Quantitative Analysis for Business Decisions.* 6th ed. Homewood, IL: Richard D. Irwin; 1981. 615 p.
Provides a basic introduction to quantitative analysis for business decisions. Covers basic probability concepts, expected values and decision trees, decision theory, the normal probability distribution and the value of information, game theory, mathematical programming, deterministic and probabilistic models, inventory control, queueing theory, simulation, PERT (project evaluation and review technique), Markov processes, and dynamic programming.

852. Blackwell, D., and Girschik, M. A. *Theory of Games and Statistical Decisions.* New York: Dover, 1979. 355 p.
Game theory is one of the most used techniques employed in solving difficult decision problems in today's corporate world. This book explains the basic concepts in this area. It also covers statistical decision-making techniques and their applications.

853. Blakeslee, David W., and Chinn, William G. *Introductory Statistics and Probability: A Basis for Decision Making.* Boston: Houghton Mifflin, 1975. 358 p.
Undergraduate textbook dealing with quantitative decision-making techniques such as sampling, regression analysis, Markov methods, simulation, and forecasting.

854. Boot, Johannes Cornelius Gerardus, and Cox, Edwin B. *Statistical Analysis for Managerial Decisions.* New York: McGraw-Hill, 1970. 641 p.
This textbook covers probability, combinatorial analysis, distribution, sampling and estimation, hypothesis testing, time series analysis, and statistical quality assurance.

855. Brabb, George Jacob. *Introduction to Quantitative Management.* New York: Holt, Rinehart & Winston, 1968. 576 p.
Discusses quantitative decision making concepts such as probability, statistics, sampling, linear programming, and simulation.

856. Bradley, James Vandiver. *Probability, Decision, Statistics.* Englewood Cliffs, NJ: Prentice-Hall, 1976. 586 p.
Probability, decision theory, and statistical methods all present mathematical models for the solution of real-world problems. In order to use these models properly, the practitioner must understand both the mathematical and the empirical conditions qualifying their application. This book introduces the reader to basic concepts such as statistical tests and estimates based on the binomial distribution, distribution free tests based on ranks, moments and the distribution of the sample mean, and methods related to the sample mean.

857. Braverman, Jerome D. *Probability, Logic, and Management Decisions.* New York: McGraw-Hill, 1972. 474 p.
Approaches the complex management decision situation as a problem requiring the application of various techniques for solution and the in-

tegration of all these techniques into an orderly system for decision making. Techniques covered include logical network, probability, sampling, decision theory, decision trees, and sequential analysis.

858. Bross, Irwin D. J. *Design for Decision.* New York: Free Press, 1965. 276 p.
Decision making is the process of selecting one action from a number of alternative courses of action. This book deals with statistical decision-making techniques such as prediction, probability, values, rules for action, sequential decision, models, sampling, measurement, and statistical inference.

859. Brown, Kenneth, and Revelle, Jack B. *Quantitative Methods for Management Decisions.* Reading, MA: Addison-Wesley, 1978. 569 p.
Undergraduate text to provide an introduction to quantitative methods and their applications to practical business problems, like decision making under uncertainty, pay-off tables and decision trees, production and inventory control systems, queueing, Markov processes, and network models.

860. Bunn, D. W. *Applied Decision Analysis.* New York: McGraw-Hill, 1984. 251 p.
Basic text dealing with statistical decision techniques including linear programming, scheduling, Monte Carlo method, and simulation.

861. Burger, Ewald. *Introduction to the Theory of Games.* Englewood Cliffs, NJ: Prentice-Hall, 1963. 202 p.
Translation of *Einführung in die Theorie der Spiele,* dealing with game theory, which is a well-used statistical decision-making technique.

862. Carlson, Phillip G. *Quantitative Methods for Managers.* New York: Harper & Row, 1967. 181 p.
Deals with mathematical techniques that provide a means for studying alternative actions and the consequence of implementing the various alternatives in particular situations. These techniques are applied to specific problem situations such as purchasing, trainee allocation, product mix, allocation of advertising expenditures, job sequencing, contract lot, and preventive maintenance situations.

863. Carr, Charles R., and Howe, Charles W. *Introduction to Quantitative Decision Procedures in Management and Economics.* New York: McGraw-Hill, 1964. 383 p.
Introduction to a mathematical approach for discovering operationally significant solutions to management decision problems. The text outlines theoretical material in terms of single-stage multivariate analysis and multistage analysis. Applications include resource allocation and manufacturing.

864. Cetron, Marvin J.; Davidson, Harold; and Rubenstein, Albert H. *Quantitative Decision Aiding Techniques for Research and Development Management.* New York: Gordon and Breach, 1972. 205 p.
Abstracts of selected papers which were presented at three separate sessions of the Military Operations Research Society, Working Group on Research Management. Deals with decisions relating to management of industrial research.

865. Chacko, George Kuttickal. *Applied Statistics in Decision Making.* New York: American Elsevier, 1971. 491 p.
Advanced undergraduate textbook dealing with quantitative techniques available for use by decision makers.

866. Chance, William A. *Statistical Methods for Decision Making.* Homewood, IL: Richard D. Irwin, 1969. 442 p.
Provides an introduction to the wide range of statistical methods available to the decision maker. Special attention is given to the category of statistical inference commonly called nonparametric statistics. The major emphasis is on application. Areas covered include probability and uncertainty, hypothesis tests, sampling and estimation procedures, simulation and Monte Carlo methods, and statistical decision theory.

867. Chao, L. L. *Statistics for Management.* San Francisco, CA: Brooks/ Cole, 1980. 738 p.
A basic text dealing with qualitative decision-making method. Covers data collection and presentation, data description, events and probabilities, probability rules and functions, expected value and population, discrete probability, the normal probability distribution, statistical estimation, hypothesis testing, chi-square tests, analyses of variance, decision theory, simple and multiple regression and correlation, time series, nonparametric methods, and statistical quality control.

868. Childress, Robert L. *Mathematics for Managerial Decision.* Englewood Cliffs, NJ: Prentice-Hall, 1974. 689 p.
Introduces the quantitative tools of sets, matrices, linear programming, calculus, and probability and provides numerous examples of the applicability of quantitative techniques in the administration of an enterprise. Topics include systems of equations; matrix representation of systems of equations with applications to input-output analysis; simplex method for solving linear programs; duality and sensitivity analysis; transportation and assignment problems; optimization using calculus, multivariate and exponential business models, including inventory models and the method of least squares; Bayes' theorem; random variable and the commonly used discrete and continuous probability distributions; and growth rate functions.

869. Chou, Ya Lun. *Probability and Statistics for Decision Making.* New York: Holt, Rinehart & Winston, 1972. 623 p.
Basic undergraduate textbook which discusses concepts such as sampling, regression analysis, Markov techniques, simulation, and forecasting.

870. Chu, King. *Quantitative Methods for Business and Economic Analysis.* Scranton, PA: International Textbook Co., 1969. 373 p.
Textbook which deals with deterministic or mathematical programming models and probabilistic or statistical models in which information concerning the problem is not completely known but can be specified by probabilities. The analysis is to search for the decision strategy which will optimize the expected value of the outcomes. Also covers use of computers in quantitative analysis, including the simulation method.

871. Clark, Charles T., and Schkade, Lawrence L. *Statistical Methods for Business Decisions.* Cincinnati, OH: South-Western, 1969. 750 p.
Reviews descriptive statistics with topics dealing with the computer and

statistical analysis, probability and probability distribution, sampling, inference, regression and correlation, time series, and index numbers.

872. Clough, Donald J. *Concepts in Management Science.* Englewood Cliffs, NJ: Prentice-Hall, 1963. 425 p.
Presents mathematical models in decision making. Various organizational situations are covered.

873. Costis, Harry G. *Statistics for Business.* Columbus, OH: Charles E. Merrill Publishing Co, 1973. 749 p.
The book deals with descriptive statistics and the descriptive tools that are of value in empirical studies, setting up tables, presenting data on graphs, computing averages and measures of variability, and frequency distribution. Also covers some important descriptive methods of time series, such as index numbers, trends, and seasonal variations which are nonprobabilistic, sampling theory and design, estimation, significance tests, regression analysis, nonparametric methods, analysis of variance, and Bayesian decision theory.

874. Coyle, R. G. *Mathematics for Business Decisions.* London: Thomas Nelson, 1971. 309 p.
Provides a practical approach to managers who have little formal mathematics background. Topics include advanced optimization by calculus, linear programming, basic situations, regression analysis, decision theory, and Markov processes. Also includes three case studies in manufacturing and mining.

875. Dantzig, George B., and Veinott, Arthur F., eds. *Mathematics of Decision Sciences.* Providence, RI: American Mathematical Society, 1968. 443 p.
Papers presented at the fifth summer seminar on the mathematics of the decision processes sponsored by the American Mathematical Society and held at Stanford University, July 10 to August 11, 1967. Topics covered include control theory, mathematical economics, dynamic programming, applied probability and statistics, mathematical psychology, and linguistics and computer sciences.

876. Davidson, Donald; Suppes, Patrick; and Siegel, Sidney. *Decision Making: An Experimental Approach.* Stanford, CA: Stanford University Press, 1957. 121 p.
Discusses statistical decision theories. Concentrates on the problem of choice and evaluation of alternative decisions.

877. DeGroot, Morris H. *Optimal Statistical Decision.* New York: McGraw-Hill, 1979. 489 p.
Discusses statistical decision concepts such as linear programming, activity analysis, programming under uncertainty, dynamic programming, and analysis of risk.

878. Derman, Cyrus. *Finite State Markovian Decision Processes.* New York: Academic Press, 1970. 159 p.
This book is concerned with the optical sequential control of certain types of dynamic systems. The authors assume such a system is observed periodically. After each observation, the system is classified into one of a possible number of states; after each classification one of a possible number of decisions is implemented. The sequence of implemented decisions interacts with the chance environment to effect the evolution of the

system. This process is called a Markovian decision process or discrete dynamic programming. Just as linear programming provides a general framework for formulating and solving certain optimization problems, so does the Markovian decision process, a structure within which optimal control of dynamic systems can be formulated and solved.

879. Deverell, Cyril S. *Management Techniques in Administration and Finance.* London: Gee & Co., 1976. 328 p.
Basic text that explains the various analytical techniques that are aids to decision making in areas such as budgeting, resource allocation, investment, and personnel.

880. Dyckman, Thomas R.; Smidt, S.; and McAdams, Alan Kellog. *Management Decision Making under Uncertainty: An Introduction to Probability and Statistical Decision Theory.* New York: Macmillan, 1969. 602 p.
An introductory text for students interested in the solution of managerial problems. The work is an explanation of probability and statistical decision theory and managerial applications. It will also help students become familiar with probabilistic and statistical reasoning and recognize probabilistic and statistical elements in problem situations.

881. Easton, Allan. *Complex Managerial Decisions Involving Multiple Objectives.* New York: Wiley, 1973. 421 p.
Most decisions affect multiple interests. Hence important decisions must be defensible. This book examines the decision environment for complex decisions by looking at decision-making costs, the time factor in complex decisions, and creativity in decision making. Also examines initiating the decision process, choice and evaluation, decision alternatives, measurement scales, and estimating outcomes. Case study method is used to analyze applications.

882. Ewart, Park J. *Applied Managerial Statistics.* Englewood Cliffs, NJ: Prentice-Hall, 1982. 622 p.
Advanced textbook on quantitative decision-making techniques. Includes modeling, simulation, linear programming, sampling, Bayesian analysis, and Markov chains.

883. Ewart, Park J., et al. *Probability for Statistical Decision Making.* Englewood Cliffs, NJ: Prentice-Hall, 1974. 381 p.
Text dealing with doubt in decision making. It covers mathematical techniques that minimize these doubts. Concepts covered include probability, sets and sample spaces, random variables, probability functions, commonly used discrete and continuous probability models, the value of information in decision making, and utility in decision making.

884. Fishburn, Peter C. *Mathematics of Decision Theory.* The Hague, Netherlands; Paris: Mouton, 1972. 104 p.
Examines concepts like sets and functions, binary relations, choice functions, finite linear systems, Zorn's lemma, real-valued order preserving functions, topology, mixture sets, and ordered groupoids.

885. Fishburn, Peter C. *Utility Theory for Decision Making.* New York: Wiley, 1970. 234 p.
Discusses statistical techniques relating to utility theory and their applications to corporate decision making.

886. Fleming, Frank J., and Luke, Roy. *Mathematics for Decision Making: An Introduction.* Columbus, OH: Charles E. Merrill Publishing Co., 1974. 321 p.
Basic undergraduate text introducing the reader to quantitative decision-making techniques such as probability and statistics, regression analysis, forecasting, linear programming, simplex and Monte Carlo methods.

887. Forester, John. *Statistical Selection of Business Strategies.* Homewood, IL: Richard D. Irwin, 1968. 220 p.
Management is judged on its ability to make and implement correct decisions because the profitability of the firm is dependent upon the cumulative results of many previous decisions. Problems involving costs, time, profits, rates of returns, strength of materials, and other qualified variables are amendable to rational analysis, even under uncertain conditions. This book explains the quantitative techniques that could help decision makers deal with the variables. Topics discussed include graphic analysis, Bayesian strategies, value of information, utility, a priori estimates, sampling, and linear modeling.

888. Gallagher, Charles A., and Watson, Hugh J. *Quantitative Methods for Business Decisions.* New York: McGraw-Hill, 1980. 604 p.
Undergraduate text covering probability and statistical linear programming, time series analysis, queueing theory, and forecasting.

889. Giffin, Walter C. *Introduction to Operations Engineering.* Homewood, IL: Richard D. Irwin, 1971. 632 p.
Topics covered include transform techniques in systems analysis and probability modeling, forecasting and stochastic processes, economics of decision making, statistical quality control, deterministic inventory models, probabilistic inventory models, waiting-line analysis, mathematical programming, scheduling techniques, and simulation.

890. Gordon, Gilbert, and Pressman, Israel. *Quantitative Decision Making for Business.* 2d ed. Englewood Cliffs, NJ: Prentice-Hall, 1983. 596 p.
Introductory text to concepts in quantitative decision making. Covers elements of probability and statistics, decision trees and survey information, utility research, and linear programming. The applications considered include portfolio selection, equipment purchases, remote utilization, and advertising selections.

891. Grawoig, Dennis E. *Decision Mathematics.* New York: McGraw-Hill, 1967. 370 p.
Presents mathematical models related to decision making. Topics covered include probability, sampling, forecasting, linear programming, and scheduling.

892. Gupta, Shanti S., and Berger, James O. *Statistical Decision Theory and Related Topics.* New York: Academic Press, 1982. 2 vols.
Discusses topics such as the Bayesian analysis and its applications, linear regression and correlation, Markov processes, and hypothesis testing.

893. Gupta, Shanti S., and Panchapakesan, S. *Multiple Decision Procedures: Theory and Methodology of Selecting and Ranking Populations.* New York: Wiley, 1979. 573 p.
This book is an introduction to statistical inference, which provides the methodology to build a theoretical model to help sift and analyze evidence

before making a business decision. Areas covered include indifference zone formulation; ranking and selection problems for discrete distribution selection from univariate populations; optimum sampling and estimation of probability of current selection; sequential and nonparametric selection procedures; Bayesian selection and ranking; subset selection formulation and comparison with a control; estimation; and related topics.

894. Hadley, George F. *Introduction to Probability and Statistical Decisions.* San Francisco, CA: Holden Day, 1967. 580 p.
Concepts of statistical decision theory are discussed, including probability, sampling, and distribution.

895. Hamburg, M. *Statistical Analysis for Decision Making.* 3d ed. New York: Harcourt Brace Jovanovich, 1983. 829 p.
Deals with concepts such as probability, statistics, sampling, queueing, Monte Carlo methods, linear programming, and forecasting.

896. Hamburg, Morris. *Basic Statistics: A Modern Approach.* New York: Harcourt Brace Jovanovich, 1979. 451 p.
Discusses the mathematical techniques of decision making such as hypothesis testing, chi-square tests and analysis of variance, regression and correlation analysis, nonparametric statistics, decision making under uncertainty, time series, and index numbers.

897. Harris, Roy Duane, and Maggard, Michael J. *Computer Models in Operations Management.* 2d ed. New York: Harper & Row, 1977. 230 p.
Contains twelve computer models for use in management analysis and decision making. The purpose of these models is to teach the use of the computer as a tool of the manager, including LINPRO, which will solve linear programming problems via the simplex algorithms, and material requirements planning (MRP), which will compute net requirements and compute order quantities with lead time offsetting.

898. Hein, Leonard W. *The Quantitative Approach to Managerial Decisions.* Engelwood Cliffs, NJ: Prentice-Hall, 1967. 386 p.
Explains managerial vs. nonmanagerial decisions and decisions in the face of certainty, risk, uncertainty and competitive action. Analyzes the impact of computers on managerial decisions. Other topics include graphical approach to linear programming; the simplex method; the learning curve; probability and probability distributions—the Poisson, the Gamma, and the normal distributions; the Monte Carlo method; waiting lines; quality control charts; work sampling; and performance and cost evaluation.

899. Heinze, David Charles. *Management Science.* Cincinnati, OH: South-Western, 1978. 430 p.
This book provides a basic introduction to management science, particularly decision making. Topics explained include algebra and probability; decision theory models; Monte Carlo simulation; inventory models; linear programming; special graphic applications; simplex method; assignment models, queueing models, bidding, purchasing; and replacement models; forecasting; CPM (critical path method) and PERT (project evaluation and review technique); game theory; and Markov process.

900. Heinze, David Charles. *Statistical Decision Analysis for Management.* Columbus, OH: Grid, 1973. 220 p.
The book provides an introduction to sampling, the revision of probability distributions with discrete priors, optimal sampling, utility and decision diagrams, inventory analysis, game theory, and replacement policy.

901. Holloway, Charles A. *Decision Making under Uncertainty.* Englewood Cliffs, NJ: Prentice-Hall, 1979. 522 p.
Covers introductory quantitative decision-making concepts such as modeling, probability, discrete and continuous random variables, probability distributing, Bayesian state, Monte Carlo method, choices, preferences, and raise sharing and incentives.

902. Horowitz, Ira. *An Introduction to Quantitative Business Analysis.* 2d ed. New York: McGraw-Hill, 1972. 310 p.
Basic undergraduate text covering concepts like probability, expected value, utility, value of information, linear programming, integer programming, inventory models, queueing theory, and simulation.

903. Howard, Ronald A. *Dynamic Probabilistic Systems.* New York: Wiley, 1971. 2 vols.
Deals with decision and control in organizations. Covers Markov models, Semimarkov, and decision processes. Also discusses topics relating to system analysis.

904. Howell, James Edwin, and Teichroew, Daniel. *Mathematical Analysis for Business Decisions.* Rev. ed. Homewood, IL: Richard D. Irwin, 1971. 424 p.
Devoted to a preservation of mathematical models in decision making and their application to business situations. The analysis includes, in addition to basic algebra, transcendental and multivariate functions, linear systems matrices, linear programming, concepts of discrete mathematics, and rates of change. The application relates to such management problems as break-even analysis, advertising and pricing, and investment analysis.

905. Hughes, Ann J., and Grawoig, Dennis E. *Linear Programming: An Emphasis on Decision Making.* Reading, MA: Addison-Wesley, 1973. 414 p.
Linear programming models are increasing in use in decision-making situations. This book explains its analytical techniques and its applications.

906. Humphreys, R. G. *Analysing Uncertainty: An Introductory Workbook for Decision-Making.* London: The Institute of Cost and Management Accountants, 1980. 52 p.
This workbook includes text and exercises relating to the uncertainty problem, uncertainty curves, making choices, optimization, approximation methods, and simulation.

907. Hymans, Saul H. *Probability Theory with Applications to Econometrics and Decision-Making.* Englewood Cliffs, NJ: Prentice-Hall, 1967. 333 p.
Basic text which deals with probability and statistics, forecasting, queueing theory, linear and integer programming, and other qualitative techniques for decision making.

908. Ignizio, James P.; Gupta, Jatinder N. D.; and McNichols, Gerald R. *Operations Research in Decision Making.* New York: Crane Russak & Co., 1975. 343 p.
Discusses the goals of decision making and operations research, their definition, history, and applications. Topics include decision theory, linear programming, network analysis, probability models and simulation, inventory systems, queueing and sequencing, and scheduling problems.

909. Jedamus, Paul, and Frame, Robert. *Business Decision Theory.* New York: McGraw-Hill, 1969. 290 p.
Provides an elementary treatment of statistical inference and decision theory. Covers topics such as the economics of decision rules and sampling, decision making under uncertainty without sampling, hypothesis testing for continuous distribution, and problems of estimations.

910. Jedamus, Paul, et al. *Statistical Analysis for Business Decisions.* New York: McGraw-Hill, 1977. 622 p.
Textbook for an introductory course in quantitative techniques for managerial decision making. Covers probability, sampling, distribution, linear programming, Markov methods, and Bayesian analysis.

911. Johnson, Rodney D., and Siskin, Bernard R. *Quantitative Techniques for Business Decisions.* Englewood Cliffs, NJ: Prentice-Hall, 1976. 485 p.
Undergraduate text dealing with concepts like probability, decision strategies, utility and game theory, decision and dynamic programming, linear optimization models, measurement and analysis of risk, Markov process, queueing theory, and simulation and forecasting.

912. Jolson, Marvin A., and Hise, Richard T. *Quantitative Techniques for Marketing Decisions.* New York: Macmillan, 1973. 238 p.
This book provides a number of case studies that can be used as a framework for marketing decisions. It covers the construction of marketing models, certainty and marketing decision, risk and the marketing decision, decision tree analysis, and utility and attitudes toward risk. It also includes the application of Bayesian decision theory, Delphi process, Bernoulli process, and the binomial distribution. Other chapters cover simulation as a marketing tool and linear programming for marketing decisions.

913. Jones, J. Morgan. *Introduction to Decision Theory.* Homewood, IL: Richard D. Irwin, 1977. 368 p.
Introduction to statistical concepts of decision theory, including probability, analyzing problems without sampling, an extended analysis of the expected value criterion, simple and binomial sampling, and continuous probability distributions.

914. Joshi, Madhukar V. *Management Science: A Survey of Quantitative Decision-Making Techniques.* North Scituate, MA: Duxbury Press, 1980. 561 p.
Undergraduate text dealing with probability, decision theory, scheduling, models, formal models of waiting lines, Monte Carlo simulation techniques, linear optimization models, assignment and traveling salesman models, transportation (distribution) models, network models, graphical method, and duality and integer solutions.

915. Kaufmann, Arnold. *The Science of Decision-Making.* New York: McGraw-Hill, 1968. 253 p.
Develops a science of action based on combinatorial methods rather than on continuous functions. Considers topics encountered in decision making, including games, dynamic programming, cybernetics, simulation, sensitivity analysis, and linear programming.

916. Keeney, Ralph L., and Raiffa, Howard. *Decisions with Multiple Objectives: Preferences and Value Tradeoffs.* New York: Wiley, 1976 569 p.
Deals with the structuring of uncertainty, trade-offs under uncertainty, unidimensional utility theory, multiattribute preferences with two or more attributes, preferences over time, and aggregation of individual preferences.

917. King, William Richard. *Probability for Management Decisions.* New York: Wiley, 1968. 372 p.
Most, if not all, managerial decisions are made in an environment of uncertainty. The connection between probability and the analysis of organizational decisions is an intrinsic one. The only scientific way of dealing with uncertainty is through probability. It helps managers organize their thinking and analyze problems in a general scientific framework without resorting to sophisticated mathematics. This is an introductory book to probability concepts such as expectations and variability, Bayesian analysis, and stochastic processes analysis and their basic applications.

918. Kovacic, Michael L. *Mathematics: Fundamentals for Managerial Decision Making.* Boston: Prindle, Weber & Schmidt, 1971. 464 p.
Undergraduate textbook which introduces mathematical concepts in decision making to business students. These concepts include properties of real numbers, analytic and graphic aids for decision making, optimum allocation of capital, analysis of market equilibrium, systematizing numbers for optimum results, linear programming, decision making under uncertainty, role of derivative in decision making, and integral calculus, which is a practical tool for decision makers.

919. Kwak, N. K., and DeLurgio, Stephen A. *Quantitative Models for Business Decisions.* Belmont, CA: Wadsworth, 1980. 769 p.
Intended as a text for courses in quantitative analysis, management science, and operations research. Places primary emphasis upon the use of business-oriented examples and problems and the avoidance of excessive formalization and abstract terminology.

920. Lange, Oskar Richard. *Optimal Decisions: Principles of Programming.* New York: Pergamon Press, 1971. 292 p.
Discusses the theory of linear programming with solutions by the simplex method, mostly under conditions of uncertainty. Topics include linear and marginal programming, activity analysis, programming under uncertainty, dynamic programming of purchases under certainty and uncertainty, and dynamic programming of production under certainty and uncertainty.

921. Lapin, Lawrence L. *Statistics for Modern Business Decisions.* 3d ed. New York: Harcourt Brace Jovanovich, 1982. 877 p.
Undergraduate text covering statistical concepts relevant to managerial decision making. Topics include probability, sampling, normal distribution, statistical estimation, hypothesis testing, regression and correlation analysis, time series analysis and forecasting, chi-square applications analysis of

variance, nonparametric statistics, decision theory, and Bayesian analysis of decision using experimental information.

922. Lapin, Lawrence L. *Quantitative Methods for Business Decisions.* New York: Harcourt Brace Jovanovich, 1981. 774 p.
Standard text describing probability and statistical methods for decision making. Includes topics such as linear programming, distribution, and regression analysis.

923. Levin, Richard I., and Lamone, Rudolph P. *Quantitative Disciplines in Management Decision.* Belmont, CA: Dickenson Publishing Co., 1969. 209 p.
Decision making is at the core of a manager's job. Quantitative disciplines add a new dimension to this function. This book contains a collection of articles on managerial decision making and quantitative approaches to it. Topics include operations research, management information systems, structure of decision theory, system simulation and analysis, and planning models.

924. Martin, Edley Wainwright, Jr. *Mathematics for Decision Making: A Programmed Basic Text.* Homewood, IL: Richard D. Irwin, 1969. 2 vols.
Textbook for business mathematics courses. Volume 1, consisting of five parts, focuses on matrices and linear programming and volume 2, consisting of four parts, primarily focuses on differential and integral calculus.

925. Martin, James John. *Bayesian Decision Problems and Markov Chains.* New York: Wiley, 1967. 202 p.
Presents solution of decision problems in Markov chain with uncertain transition probabilities based on both sequential sampling and fixed sample size problems. The idea of a family distribution closed under sampling is introduced and then applied to the study of adaptive control problems.

926. McAdams, Alan Kellog, and Janssen, Christian T. *Mathematical Analysis for Management Decisions: Introduction to Calculus and Linear Algebra.* New York: Macmillan, 1970. 354 p.
Basic undergraduate text which covers concepts in probability and statistics including linear programming and simulation techniques.

927. McLaughlin, Frank S., and Pickhardt, Robert C. *Quantitative Techniques for Management Decisions.* Boston: Houghton Mifflin, 1979. 478 p.
Provides a basic introduction to quantitative managerial analysis, including decision theory, probabilities and decision analysis, inventory models, linear programming, goal and integer programming, network models PERT (project evaluation and review technique) and CPM (critical path method), queueing models, simulation, and Markov analysis.

928. McMillan, Claude. *Mathematical Programming: An Introduction to the Design and Application of Optimal Decision Machines.* New York: Wiley, 1970. 496 p.
A textbook for a course in mathematical programming with emphasis on nonlinear and discrete aspects of management science, operations research, and economics. Topics include classical optimization of functions of one and of many variables with and without constraints; gradient methods of optimization; simplex method and branch metric, dynamic, linear, integer, binary (zero-one); discrete (integer nonlinear); and heuristics.

929. Mine, Hisashi, and Osaki, Shunju. *Markovian Decision Processes.* New York: American Elsevier, 1970. 142 p.
Presents the mathematical theory and algorithms of some of the most important types of Markovian decision processes, including semi-Markovian and general sequential decision processes and stochastic games.

930. Moore, Peter Gerald. *Risk in Business Decision.* New York: Wiley, 1973. 365 p.
Develops an analytical approach to the consideration of risk in business decisions by using a statistical decision analysis approach. Other concepts that are introduced in the process include probability, discrete and continuous random variables, single-stage decision problems, decision trees, economics of binomial sampling, utility functions, and testing and estimation.

931. Namias, J., ed. *Applications of Quantitative Methods for Business Decisions.* New York: St. John's University Press, 1974. 511 p.
Textbook which illustrates the application of statistical concepts to actual business decisions. These concepts include personal media probabilities, decision model on marketing research expenditures, Bayesian analysis in auditing, application of sampling to business operations, procedure for audit of accounts receivable, statistical technique for product acceptance, multivariate analysis in marketing, cluster analysis in test market selection, discriminate analysis of audience characteristic, quality control in research, factory location, profit planning, and business forecasts.

932. Newson, E. F. Peter, ed. *Management Science and the Manager: A Casebook.* Englewood Cliffs, NJ: Prentice-Hall, 1980. 237 p.
Contains case studies intended to reveal the role of elementary quantitative methods in managerial decision making. Demonstrates what quantitative analysis can do for the manager as opposed to how it works. Topics include defining and modeling uncertainty, resource allocation decisions, uncertainty, risk, decision making, model formulation, and evaluation.

933. Paik, C. M. *Quantitative Methods for Managerial Decisions.* New York: McGraw-Hill, 1973. 403 p.
Undergraduate text dealing with concepts such as probability, statistics, sampling, queueing theory, Markov models, linear programming, and forecasting.

934. Palmer, C. F. *Quantitative Aids for Management Decision Making.* London: Saxon House, 1980. 202 p.
Undergraduate text dealing with statistics and probability, linear programming, distributions, time series analysis, Markov processes, and queueing theory.

935. Paranka, Stephen. *Business Applications of Decision Sciences.* New York: Petrocelli/Charter, 1975. 156 p.
Purpose of the book is twofold: to provide a fundamental understanding of computer operations and quantitative techniques useful in the decision-making process and to present examples of how these techniques are applied in real-life business situations. The techniques discussed include Bayesian decision making, Markov chains and regression, and correlation analysis.

936. Parket, L. R. *Statistics for Business Decision Making.* New York: Random House, 1974. 434 p.
Introduction to quantitative decision-making techniques including modeling, sampling, simulation, regression analysis, linear programming, and forecasting.

937. Parsons, R. *Statistics for Decision Makers.* New York: Harper & Row, 1974. 638 p.
Elementary treatment of quantitative decision-making techniques including sampling, distribution, time series analysis, regression analysis, and forecasting.

938. Peters, W. S., and Summers, G. W. *Statistical Analysis for Business Decisions.* Englewood Cliffs, NJ: Prentice-Hall, 1968. 540 p.
Basic text dealing with quantitative decision-making techniques such as probability, sampling, regression analysis, Markov methods, and Monte Carlo techniques.

939. Plane, Donald R., and Kochenberger, Gary A. *Operations Research for Managerial Decisions.* Homewood, IL: Richard D. Irwin, 1972. 321 p.
Textbook for a course in operations research. Topics include decision theory, classical optimization, linear programming and extensions, zero-one programming, analysis of waiting lines, and simulation with applications in queueing problems.

940. Plane, Donald R., and McMillan, Claude. *Discrete Optimization: Integer Programming and Network Analyses for Management Decisions.* Englewood Cliffs, NJ: Prentice-Hall, 1971. 251 p.
A text of integer programming for students of managerial analysis. Topics include management science and mathematical programming; problem formulation for zero-one programming; integer programming; integer linear programming; and network optimization.

941. Raiffa, Howard, and Schlaifer, Robert. *Applied Statistical Decision Theory.* Cambridge, MA: MIT Press, 1968. 356 p.
Textbook which discusses the concepts relating to statistical decision analysis. Includes topics such as regression analysis, distributions, and sampling.

942. Richmond, Samuel B. *Operations Research for Management Decisions.* New York: Ronald Press, 1968. 615 p.
Textbook for a course on operations research, which covers optimization models, probability theory and applications, allocation problems, stochastic models, and decision theory, including game theory and Bayes theorem.

943. Sadowski, Wieslaw. *The Theory of Decision-Making: An Introduction to Operations Research.* New York: Pergamon Press, 1965. 292 p.
The main topics in the book are linear and dynamic programming with applications and game theory.

944. Sasaki, K. *Statistics for Modern Business Decision Making.* Belmont, CA: Wadsworth, 1968. 562 p.
Textbook for a first course in quantitative decision-making techniques. Covers statistics, probability, sampling, linear programming, forecasting, Bayesian analysis, and regression techniques.

945. Sawaragi, Yoshikozu, et al. *Statistical Decision Theory in Adaptive Control Systems.* New York: Academic Press, 1967. 216 p.
Discusses control theory and statistical decision theory. Other topics included are sequential and nonsequential approached in adaptive control systems and applications of statistical decision theory to control processes.

946. Smith, David Eugene. *Quantitative Business Analysis.* Reprinted ed. New York: Wiley, 1982. 654 p.
Undergraduate text dealing with decision theory, mathematical programming, inventory and queueing theory, and simulation. Specific topics include linear programming, Monte Carlo methods, probability, project planning, scheduling, and PERT (project evaluation and review technique) and CPM (critical path method) network models.

947. Souder, William E. *Management Decision Methods: For Managers of Engineering and Research.* New York: Van Nostrand Reinhold, 1981. 317 p.
Introduction to quantitative techniques for managerial decision making. Includes topics such as statistics and probability, linear and integer programming, sampling, networking scheduling, Bayesian analysis, and regression techniques.

948. Srivastava, U. K. *Quantitative Techniques for Managerial Decision Making.* New York: Wiley, 1983. 923 p.
Basic undergraduate text dealing with topics such as statistics and probability, linear programming, queueing theory, Markov analysis, simulation, and forecasting.

949. Tawadros, M. A. *Basic Statistics and Probability for Business and Economic Decisions.* 2d ed. Dubuque, IA: Kendall/Hunt, 1979. 244 p.
Basic text which introduces the students to concepts such as graphic and descriptive statistics, probability, functions, expected value and variance of random variables, probability distributions, statistical inference, Bayesian decision theory, and statistical decision making.

950. Thierauf, Robert J., and Klekamp, Robert C. *Decision Making through Operations Research.* 2d ed. New York: Wiley, 1975. 650 p.
Operations research techniques have been advanced significantly in recent times in corporate decision-making processes. This book provides an introduction to analytical techniques such as linear programming, probability, and statistics, which are aids to decision making.

951. Thompson, Gerald E. *Management Science: An Introduction to Modern Quantitative Analysis and Decision Making.* New York: McGraw-Hill, 1976. 453 p.
Introductory work on modern quantitative approaches to decision making. Two topics are emphasized, namely, decision analysis, which is the widely applicable procedure for decision making under uncertainty, and linear programming, which is the main quantitative approach to decision making under conditions of certainty. Other topics include approaches to inventory decisions, Markov processes and decisions, project analysis through PERT (project evaluation and review technique) and CPM (critical path method), simulation as an approach to prediction queueing, interdependent decision making, and the game-model approach.

952. Thornton, Billy M., and Preston, Paul. *Introduction to Management Science: Quantitative Approaches to Managerial Decisions.* Columbus, OH: Charles E. Merrill Publishing Co., 1977. 476 p.
Text which deals with quantitative decision-making techniques under conditions of certainty and uncertainty. Areas analyzed include decision trees and present value analysis, linear programming, allocation problems, inventory models, network analysis, analysis of waiting lines or queueing, and simulation methodology.

953. Thrall, Robert McDowell; Coombs, C. H.; and Davis, R. L. *Decision Processes.* New York: Wiley, 1960. 332 p.
Discusses statistical decision techniques useful for corporate executives in the decision-making roles.

954. Trueman, Richard E. *An Introduction to Quantitative Methods for Decision Making.* New York: Holt, Rinehart & Winston, 1974. 624 p.
Deals with quantitative decision making, probability theory, decision making under certainty with emphasis on the Bayesian approach, and operations models including linear and dynamic programming networks.

955. Trueman, Richard E. *Quantitative Methods for Decision Making in Business.* Chicago: Dryden Press, 1981. 733 p.
Textbook covering quantitative concepts applicable to managerial decision making, including probability theory, linear programming, network modeling, dynamic programming, inventory models, queueing models, Markov analysis, and simulation.

956. Tummala, V. M. Rao. *Decision Analysis with Business Applications.* New York: Intext Educational Publishers, 1973. 578 p.
Undergraduate text which covers sets and functions, probability, random variables distributions, utility, single-stage and multistage decision analyses, sampling, estimation, hypothesis testing, and regression analysis.

957. Wagner, Harvey M. *Principles of Management Science, with Applications to Executive Decisions.* 2d ed. Englewood Cliffs, NJ: Prentice-Hall, 1975. 612 p.
Text which introduces quantitative concepts which have applications in managerial decision making. These include linear and dynamic optimization models, sensitivity testing, inventory scheduling, stochastic programming, computer simulation and integer programming, and combinatorial models.

958. Wagner, Harvey M. *Principles of Operations Research with Applications to Managerial Decisions.* Englewood Cliffs, NJ: Prentice-Hall, 1969. 937 p.
Aims at translating a verbal description of a decision problem into an equivalent mathematical model. Topics include linear, dynamic, integer, and nonlinear programming, using both deterministic and stochastic models, Markov chains inventories and waiting lines, network analysis, and simulation.

959. Wasson, Chester R., and Shreve, Richard R. *Interpreting and Using Quantitative Aids to Business Decision.* Austin, TX: Austin Press, 1976. 438 p.
Text dealing with the practical interpretive side of quantitative techniques and their use in managerial decision making. Topics covered include

numbers and mathematical symbols, measurement, sampling, graphic analysis, Bayesian techniques, matrix decision tools, game theory, linear programming, queueing, Markov theory, PERT (project evaluation and review technique) and critical path analysis, and computer simulation.

960. Weiss, Lionel. *Statistical Decision Theory.* New York: McGraw-Hill, 1961. 195 p.
Provides a complete discussion of decision theory at an intermediate mathematical level. Although the purpose of the text is to teach statistical decision theory, a substantial proportion of the text is devoted to a simple and relatively brief discussion of probability theory. Some of the other topics discussed include linear programming and making a sequence of nonsampling decisions over time.

961. White, D. J. *Fundamentals of Decision Theory.* Amsterdam, Holland: North-Holland, 1976. 387 p.
Book emphasizes the logical mathematical aspects of decision, with some consideration given to simple applications. Topics covered included values over n-dimensional Euclidean space, probability, decisions under uncertainty, game theory, group decision making, information value, and sequential value structures.

962. Williams, Douglas John. *Modern Mathematics for Business Decision Making.* 2d ed. Belmont, CA: Wadsworth, 1978. 548 p.
Textbook which deals with quantitative techniques such as probability statistics, linear programming, scheduling, queueing theory, forecasting, and simulation.

963. Williams, K., ed. *The Statistician and the Manager.* London: Knight, 1973. 115 p.
Introduces the manager to statistical decision-making concepts such as probability, sampling, linear programming, queueing theory, forecasting, and Monte Carlo methods.

964. Winkler, Robert L., and Hays, William L. *Statistics: Probability Inference, and Decision.* 2d ed. New York: Holt, Rinehart & Winston, 1975. 889 p.
Intended as an introduction to probability theory, statistical inference, and decision theory. The emphasis is on basic concepts and the theory underlying statistical methods rather than on a detailed exposition of all of the different methods. Topics covered include discrete and continuous random variables, Bayesian inference, sampling distribution, regression and correlation, including the theoretical regression curve, simple linear regression, least-squares curve fitting, curvilinear regression, and multiple regression.

Core Library Collection

This section contains a collection of basic reference materials designed to help a manager obtain appropriate information on different aspects of decision making. It includes some of the well-used abstracts, bibliographies, databases, dictionaries, handbooks, indexes, periodicals and books of general nature, as well as those devoted to mathematical tables and formulae.

ABSTRACTS

965. *International Abstracts in Operations Research.* Amsterdam, Holland: North-Holland, 1961–. (Quarterly)
Published for the International Federation of Operational Research Societies, this abstract covers worldwide journals devoted to, among other things, decision making. Specific topics are arranged by the following sections: application, technique, process and procedures, and professional. Includes a subject and an author index.

966. *Operations Research/Management Science.* Whippany, NJ: Executive Sciences Institute, 1961–. (Monthly)
Contains a classified digest of articles on decision making published in the major periodicals in the field. In addition to the summary of the content of the articles, each abstract includes the results of specific applications. Includes a subject index.

967. *Psychological Abstracts.* Washington, DC: American Psychological Association, 1927–. (Monthly)
This source is particularly useful for a literature search on the behavioral aspects of decision making, in terms of individual as well as group decision making.

BIBLIOGRAPHIES

968. Daniel, Wayne W. *Decision Trees for Management Decision Making: An Annotated Bibliography.* Public Administration Series: P-254. Monticello, IL: Vance Bibliographies, 1979. 11 p.

969. Goehlert, Robert. *Decision Making: Theories and Model.* Public Administration Series: P-781. Monticello, IL: Vance Bibliographies, 1981. 15 p.

970. Goehlert, Robert. *Economic Decision Making.* Public Administration Series: P-784. Monticello, IL: Vance Bibliographies, 1981. 13 p.

971. Goehlert, Robert. *Policy Studies on Decision Making: A Selected Bibliography.* Public Administration Series: P-1151. Monticello, IL: Vance Bibliographies, 1983. 9 p.

972. Hudson, Ivan. *A Bibliography on the Delphi Technique.* Exchange Bibliography: #652. Monticello, IL: Council of Planning Librarians, 1974. 17 p.

973. Manzoor, Suhati. *Systems Bibliography: A Thirty Years Literature Survey.* New Delhi, India: Metropolitan, 1982. 182 p.

974. Rand Corp. *A Bibliography of Rand Publications: Decision Making.* Santa Monica, CA, 1977.

975. Schneider, Karl. *Expert Systems and Computer Aids to Decision Making, 1970–85.* NAL Bibliography: QB 86–51. Beltsville, MD: National Agricultural Library, 1986. 13 p.

976. Thompson, Christine E. *Decision Support Systems: A Bibliography, 1980–84.* Public Administration Series: P-1745. Monticello, IL: Vance Bibliography, 1985. 7 p.

977. Wasserman, Paul. *Decision-Making: An Annotated Bibliography, Supplement, 1958–63.* Ithaca, NY: Graduate School of Business and Public Administration, Cornell University, 1964. 178 p.

978. Wasserman, Paul, and Silander, Fred S. *Decision-Making: An Annotated Bibliography.* McKinsey Foundation Annotated Bibliography. Ithaca, NY: Graduate School of Business and Public Administration, Cornell University, 1958. 111 p.

979. Worsham, John P. *Application of the Delphi Method: A Selected Bibliography.* Public Administration Series: P-432. Monticello, IL: Vance Bibliographies, 1980. 13 p.

DATABASES

980. ABI/INFORM. Louisville, KY: Data Courier, 1971–.
Covers nearly 600 general interest and core business and management journals containing articles on, among other things, decision making.

981. MANAGEMENT CONTENTS. Skokie, IL: Management Contents Inc., 1974–.
Covers over 700 English language periodicals, proceedings, and reports devoted to management literature including decision making.

982. PsycINFO. Washington, DC: American Psychological Association, 1967–.
This is the online counterpart of the printed index entitled *Psychological Abstracts.*

983. WILSONLINE. New York: H. W. Wilson, 1982–.
This is the online version of the printed index entitled *Business Periodicals Index.*

DICTIONARIES AND HANDBOOKS

984. Anderson, Barry F., et al. *Concepts in Judgment and Decision Research.* New York: Praeger, 1981. 310 p.
This is a dictionary containing definitions, sources, interrelations, and comments on the terminology relating to all aspects of decision making.

985. Bittel, Lester R., ed. *Encyclopedia of Professional Management.* New York: McGraw-Hill, 1978. 1304 p.
This is a very comprehensive encyclopedic dictionary containing contributions from over 200 experts. Coverage includes decision making in all its aspects.

986. Cornell, Alexander H. *The Decision Maker's Handbook.* Englewood Cliffs, NJ: Prentice-Hall, 1980. 262 p.
Deals with the processes and methods involved in managerial decision making.

987. Heyel, Carl, ed. *The Encyclopedia of Management.* 3d ed. New York: Van Nostrand Reinhold, 1982. 1,371 p.
Includes expert contributions from over 200 professionals. Contains definitions and explanations of terms and concepts relating to the field of decision making. Includes bibliographies.

988. Heyel, Carl, ed. *The VNR Concise Guide to Management Decision Making.* New York: Van Nostrand Reinhold, 1980. 213 p.
This paperback gives a general introduction to the basic concepts in decision making. Covers the conventional techniques of forecasting, statistical methods, and operations research as tools in decision making.

989. Hilker, Walter, and Gee, Erin Preston. *The MBA Toolkit.* Radner, PA: Chilton Book Co., 1985. 228 p.
Published in the Chilton's *Better Business Series,* this is a comprehensive manual on decision making as applied to industrial management.

GENERAL WORKS

990. Ackoff, Russell L. *The Art of Problem Solving: Accompanied by Ackoff's Fables.* New York: Wiley, 1978. 214 p.

991. Bass, Bernard M. *Organizational Decision Making.* Homewood, IL: Richard D. Irwin, 1983. 216 p.

992. Behn, Robert D., and Vaupel, James W. *Quick Analysis for Business Decision Makers.* New York: Basic Books, 1982. 403 p.

993. Braverman, Jerome D. *Management Decision Making: A Formal/ Intuitive Approach.* New York: AMACOM, 1980. 241 p.

994. Byrd, Jack, and Moore, Ted. *Decision Models for Management.* New York: McGraw-Hill, 1982. 407 p.

995. Elbing, Alvar Oliver. *Behavioral Decisions in Organizations.* 2d ed. Glenview, IL: Scott, Foresman & Co., 1978. 879 p.

996. Fabrycky, Walter J., and Thuesen, G. J. *Economic Decision Analysis.* 2d ed. Englewood Cliffs, NJ: Prentice-Hall, 1980. 431 p.

997. Gallagher, Charles A., and Watson, Hugh J. *Quantitative Methods for Business Decisions.* New York: McGraw-Hill, 1980. 604 p.

998. Gordon, Gilbert, and Pressman, Israel. *Quantitative Decision-Making for Business.* 2d ed. Englewood Cliffs, NJ: Prentice-Hall, 1983. 596 p.

999. Harrison, E. Frank. *The Managerial Decision-Making Process.* 2d ed. Boston: Houghton Mifflin, 1981. 391 p.

1000. Kepner, Charles H., and Tregoe, Benjamin B. *The Rational Manager: A Systematic Approach to Problem Solving and Decision Making.* 2d ed. Princeton, NJ: Kepner-Trego, Inc., 1976. 263 p.

1001. Morris, William Thomas. *Decision Analysis.* Columbus, OH: Grid, 1977. 290 p.

1002. Plunkett, Lorna C., and Hale, Guy A. *The Proactive Manager: The Complete Book of Problem Solving and Decision Making.* New York: Wiley, 1982. 221 p.

1003. Radford, K. J. *Modern Managerial Decision Making.* Reston, VA: Reston Publishing Co., 1981. 258 p.

1004. Raiffa, Howard. *Decision Analysis: Introductory Lectures on Choices under Uncertainty.* Reading, MA: Addison-Wesley, 1968. 309 p.

1005. Schlaifer, Robert. *Analysis of Decisions under Uncertainty.* New York: McGraw-Hill, 1969. 729 p.

1006. Stein, Judith K., and Holcolmbe, M. *Writing for Decision Makers.* Boston: CBI Publishing Co., 1980. 260 p.

1007. Wheeler, Daniel D., and Janis, Irving Lester. *A Practical Guide for Making Decisions.* New York: Free Press, 1980. 276 p.

INDEXES

1008. *Business Index.* Los Altos, CA: Information Access Co., 1981–. Microfilm. (Monthly)
Covers over 600 business periodicals and newspapers as well as business sections from nonbusiness periodicals. Also available as InFoTrac, which is in CD-ROM format. Coverage includes all aspects of decision making.

1009. *Business Periodicals Index.* New York: H. W. Wilson, 1954–. (Monthly with annual cumulation)
This is the most widely used index for literature search in the area of decision making, not only in the field of management but also accounting and finance, banking, economics, industrial relations and marketing. This is a printed counterpart of the online index entitled WILSONLINE.

PERIODICALS

While articles of interest to decision makers are frequently published in general management journals such as the *Harvard Business Review, Management Science, Management Review, Operations Research,* and the *Operational Research Society Journal,* the following journals are exclusively devoted to covering decision making.

1010. *Decision Support System.* Amsterdam: Elsevier Science Publishing Co/North-Holland, 1985–. (Quarterly)

1011. *MDE. Managerial and Decision Economics: The International Journal of Research and Progress in Management Economics.* Philadelphia, PA: Heyden & Son, 1980–. (Quarterly)

1012. *Management Decision.* Bradford, England: MCB, 1967–. (Frequency varies)

1013. *Organizational Behavior and Human Decision Processes.* San Diego, CA: Academic Press, 1985–. (Bimonthly)
Continues *Organizational Behavior and Human Performance.*

TABLES

Decision makers have to rely on various techniques to arrive at a solution to any given problem. For this purpose they rely on a number of books containing statistical tables and mathematical formulae. The following are some of the most-used publications in this area.

1014. Beyer, William H., ed. *CRC Standard Mathematical Tables.* 26th ed. Boca Raton, FL: CRC Press, 1981. 614 p.

1015. Bracken, Jerome, and Christenson, Charles J. *Tables for Use in Analyzing Business Decisions.* Homewood, IL: Richard D. Irwin, 1965. 289 p.

1016. Burington, Richard S. *Handbook of Mathematical Tables and Formulas.* 5th ed. New York: McGraw-Hill, 1973. 500 p.

1017. Burington, Richard S., and May, Donald C. *Handbook of Probability and Statistics with Tables.* 2d ed. New York: McGraw-Hill, 1970. 462 p.

1018. Vichas, Robert P. *Handbook of Financial Mathematics, Formulas and Tables*. Englewood Cliffs, NJ: Prentice-Hall, 1979. 870 p.

Other Sources of Information

The trade and professional associations listed below are likely sources of additional information.

American Institute for Decision Sciences. University Plaza, Atlanta, GA 30303 or (404) 658-4000.
Founded in 1969, has 5,500 members, with five regional groups. Conducts annual conventions and meetings for businesspersons and members of business school faculties. Bestows awards and maintains placement service. Publishes a bimonthly newsletter entitled *Decision Line*; a quarterly *Decision Sciences Journal* and also annual proceedings of its meetings.

American Management Association (AMA). 135 W. 50th St., New York, NY 10020 (212) 586-8100.
Founded in 1923, has 80,000 members with twelve divisional areas of interest. Conducts conferences, seminars, courses, briefings, and workshops on management topics. The association aims "to provide quality programs, products and services to the managerial process." Publications include *CompFlash*, monthly; *Management Review*, monthly; *Personnel*, monthly; *The President*, monthly; *Supervisory Sense*, monthly; *Supervisory Management*, monthly; *Compensation and Benefits Review*, bimonthly; *Organizational Dynamics*, quarterly; and management briefings and survey reports.

The Institute of Management Sciences. 290 Westminster St., Providence, RI 02903 (401) 274-2525.
Founded in 1953, has 6,500 members, with seven local groups. Aims to advance scientific knowledge and improve management practices; members contribute and/or learn about important findings in management technology, psychology, applied mathematics, economics, and other sciences. Conducts research programs. The institute's publications include *Management Science*, monthly; *Interfaces*, bimonthly; *OR/MS Today*, bimonthly newsletter; *Marketing Science*, quarterly; *Mathematics of Operations Research*, quarterly; *ORSA/TMS* membership directory, biennial; and also proceedings of symposia on planning and special issues.

Operations Research Society of America. Mount Royal and Guilford Aves., Baltimore, MD 21202 (301) 528-4146.
Founded in 1952, has 6,800 members, with eighteen regional groups. Members include scientists, educators, and practitioners engaged or interested in methodological subjects such as optimization probabilistic models, decision analysis, and game theory. Also involved in areas of public concern such as health, energy, urban issues and defense systems and

industrial applications including marketing, operations management, finance, and decision support systems. Society publications include *Interfaces*, bimonthly; *Operations Research*, bimonthly; *Operations Research Letters*, bimonthly; *OR/MS Today*, bimonthly newsletter; *Marketing Science*, quarterly; *Mathematics of Operations Research Quarterly; Transportation Science,* quarterly; ORSA/TIMS Bulletin (abstracts of papers), semiannual; and the *ORSA/TIMS Membership Directory,* biennial.

Author Index

Title Index

Numbers refer to citation numbers, not page numbers.

Subject Index

Numbers in italic refer to page numbers. All other numbers refer to citation numbers.